MW00443537

Proverbs

**Recent Titles in
Greenwood Folklore Handbooks**

Folk and Fairy Tales: A Handbook
D.L. Ashliman

Proverbs

A Handbook

Wolfgang Mieder

Greenwood Folklore Handbooks

GREENWOOD PRESS
Westport, Connecticut • London

Library of Congress Cataloging-in-Publication Data

Mieder, Wolfgang.
   Proverbs : a handbook / Wolfgang Mieder.
      p. cm.—(Greenwood folklore handbooks, ISSN 1549–733X)
   Includes bibliographical references and index.
   ISBN 0–313–32698–3
   1. Proverbs—History and criticism. I. Title. II. Series.
PN6401.M487   2004
398.9′09—dc22   2004007988

British Library Cataloguing in Publication Data is available.

Library of Congress Catalog Card Number: 2004007988
ISBN: 0–313–32698–3
ISSN: 1549–733X

First published in 2004

Greenwood Press, 88 Post Road West, Westport, CT 06881
An imprint of Greenwood Publishing Group, Inc.
www.greenwood.com

Printed in the United States of America

The paper used in this book complies with the
Permanent Paper Standard issued by the National
Information Standards Organization (Z39.48–1984).

10 9 8 7 6 5 4 3 2 1

Contents

Introduction

The wisdom of proverbs has guided people in their social interactions for thousands of years throughout the world. Proverbs contain everyday experiences and common observations in succinct and formulaic language, making them easy to remember and ready to be used instantly as effective rhetoric in oral or written communication. This has been the case during preliterate times, and there are no signs that proverbs have outlived their usefulness in modern technological societies either. Occasional claims persist that proverbs are on their way to extinction in highly developed cultures, but nothing could be further from the truth. While some proverbs have dropped out of use because their message or metaphor does not fit the times any longer, new proverbs that reflect the mores and situation of the present are constantly added to the proverbial repertoire. Thus the once well-known sixteenth-century proverb "Let the *cobbler* stick to his last" is basically dead today since the profession of the cobbler is disappearing. If shoes are repaired at all, people now take them to a shoe-repair shop, and they most likely would have no idea that a last is a wooden or metal model of the human foot on which a shoe is placed during repair. The proverb expressed the idea that one should stick to that work or field in which one is competent or skilled. As this text based on a specific profession is lost, the general proverb "Every *man* to his trade" might be employed, albeit at a clear loss in metaphorical expressiveness. On the other hand, obviously such proverbs as the mercantile "Another *day*, another dollar" or "*Garbage* in, garbage out" from the world of computers are of more recent vintage. In any case, proverbs are indeed alive and well, and as sapient nuggets they continue to play a significant role in the modern age.

There are literally thousands of proverbs in the multitude of cultures and languages of the world. They have been collected and studied for centuries as informative and useful linguistic signs of cultural values and thoughts. The earliest proverb collections stem from the third millennium B.C. and were inscribed on Sumerian cuneiform tablets as commonsensical codes of conduct and everyday observations of human nature. Since proverb collections usually list the texts of proverbs without their social contexts, they do not reveal their actual use and function that varies from one situation to another. Nevertheless, the long history of proverb collections from classical antiquity to the present is truly impressive, ranging from compilations of texts only to richly annotated scholarly compendia. For most languages there are major multivolume proverb collections available to readers interested in the origin, history, and distribution of their proverbs. In fact, the extant bibliographies of proverb collections have registered over 20,000 volumes with about 200 new publications each year. Many of these are small collections of several hundred texts for the general book market, but invaluable scholarly collections also continue to be produced with thousands of references. The numerous proverb collections make it possible to study proverbs on a comparative basis, establishing for example that the Latin proverb "One *hand* washes the other" and the biblical proverb "*Man* does not live by bread alone" (Deut. 8:3; Matt. 4:4) have been translated into dozens of languages in just that wording. On the other hand, the German proverb "*Morgenstunde* hat Gold im Munde" (The morning hour has gold in its mouth) finds its English equivalent in the entirely different metaphor of "The early *bird* catches the worm." With such a wealth of proverb collections it should not be surprising that proverb scholars consider paremiography (collection of proverbs) to be one side of the coin of proverb studies.

The other side is referred to as paremiology (study of proverbs). It too has a long history, dating back at least as far as Aristotle who had much to say about various aspects of proverbs. In contrast to paremiographers, who occupy themselves with the collecting and classifying of proverbs, the paremiologists address such questions as the definition, form, structure, style, content, function, meaning, and value of proverbs. They also differentiate among the proverbial subgenres that include proverbs as such, as well as proverbial expressions ("to bite the *dust*"), proverbial comparisons ("as *busy* as a bee"), proverbial interrogatives ("Does a *chicken* have lips?"), twin formulas ("*give* and take"), and wellerisms ("'Each to his *own*,' as the farmer said when he kissed his cow"). There are other related short and often formulaic verbal genres such as sententious remarks, literary quotations, maxims, slogans, and graffiti, but they usually lack the traditional currency of the proverbial genres, and, with the exception of graffiti, their authors are normally known. But since every proverb obviously originated from one person once upon a time, there is no reason why a quotation or a slogan should not become a generally accepted proverb, to wit Theodore Roosevelt's "*Speak softly and carry a big stick*" spoken on September 2, 1901, at the Minnesota State Fair. For some Americans this might be a political quotation or slogan, but for those speakers who are not aware of Roosevelt's coinage of the phrase, it is a proverb for sure.

The term "phrase" was used on purpose in the previous sentence as a rather general concept. Especially linguists have decided to refer to all formulaic phrases as phraseological units or phraseologisms. They have created a new subfield of study, which they have designated as phraseology (the study of phrases). That scholarly term serves as an umbrella for all phrasal collocations, including the entire area of paremiology. Linguists also occupy themselves with phraseography (collection and classification of phrases), once again incorporating paremiography as well. And yet, most linguists deal only tangentially with proverbs as such in their publications. When they do so, they usually employ the Greek term based on *paremia* (proverb), clearly indicating that proverbs are very special phraseological units. While phraseologists do and should include proverbs in their linguistic studies, paremiologists usually look at proverbs from a more inclusive point of view as they draw on such fields as anthropology, art, communication, culture, folklore, history, literature, philology, psychology, religion, and sociology.

As with paremiography, the paremiological scholarship has an impressive history and continues to be very active today. About 400 significant books, dissertations, and scholarly articles are published each year. The majority of these studies as well as the new or reprinted collections are listed in my annual bibliographies in *Proverbium: Yearbook of International Proverb Scholarship*. These lists include all the proverb publications that I have been able to add during any particular year to my international proverb archive at the University of Vermont. The archive contains close to 10,000 scholarly studies on proverbs and also about 4,000 proverb collections from many languages. About 9,000 slides of various iconographic representations of proverbs in art (woodcuts, misericords, emblems, oil paintings) and the mass media (caricatures, cartoons, headlines, advertisements) are also part of this archive that serves scholars and students worldwide.

For many cultures scholars have written a definitive book on the history of both the paremiographical publications and paremiological studies. Such books trace the development of various types of proverb collections and deal with the origin and dissemination of proverbs in the given language and culture, discuss definition problems of the various genres, analyze stylistic and structural aspects, investigate the function and use in different contexts (oral communication, literature, mass media), and attempt to give an inclusive picture of the meaning and significance of proverbs as verbal strategies. The English language is no exception in this regard. In the middle of the nineteenth century the philologist and theologian Richard Chenevix Trench (1807–1886) presented his slim volume *On the Lessons in Proverbs* (1853) that went through seven editions during his lifetime and several more later on, including a final edition in 1905 with the slightly changed title of *Proverbs and Their Lessons*. The book represents an important survey of the origin, nature, distribution, meaning, and significance of proverbs in the English-speaking world. Realizing that all scholars stand on the shoulders of their precursors, I prepared a reprint in 2003, about 150 years after the original publication, of this still invaluable and most readable study. Fifty years after Trench's book, F. Edward Hulme (1841–1909) published his volume on *Proverb Lore: Being a Historical Study of the Similarities, Contrasts, Topics, Meanings, and Other Facets of Proverbs, Truisms, and Pithy Sayings, as Explained by the Peoples of Many Lands and Times* (1902). Hulme's treatise basically replaced Trench's popular volume, and it was appropriate that it was reprinted in 1968 to honor the work of this folklore scholar.

But according to proverbial wisdom, "All good *things* come in threes," and thus there is also Archer Taylor's (1890–1973) magisterial volume on *The Proverb* (1931). As the world's leading paremiologist of the twentieth century, Taylor wrote the definitive book on the subject and pioneered a vigorous American interest in proverbs that included such renowned scholars as Alan Dundes, Wolfram Eberhard, Stuart A. Gallacher, Richard Jente, Wayland D. Hand, John G. Kunstmann, Charles Speroni, and Bartlett Jere Whiting. The book was reprinted in 1962 together with a previously published *An Index to "The Proverb"* (1934), and I had the distinct honor of reprinting *The Proverb and An Index to "The Proverb"* (1985) some 50 years after the original publication. Taylor's volume deals with definition problems, metaphorical proverbs, proverbial types, variants, proverbs in folk narratives and literature, loan translations, and the classical or biblical origin of many proverbs. Taylor also analyzes customs and superstitions reflected in proverbs, he looks at legal, medical, and weather proverbs, and he investigates their content and style. Proverbial stereotypes, proverbial expressions and comparisons, and wellerisms are also discussed in this comprehensive and comparative volume on European proverbs. Seventy-five years after its original publication, Archer Taylor's *The Proverb* is still considered to be *the* classic study on the proverb genre. Paremiologists around the globe have benefited from this unique volume, and there is no doubt that this book remains required reading for any-body interested in proverbs.

It is then a daunting task for me to present my own attempt of yet another treatise on proverbs. I have learned much from the three books by Trench, Hulme, and Taylor, but their volumes are 150, 100, and 75 years old, respec-tively. The time has clearly come to take a fresh look at proverbs that is based on the work of these three paremiological scholars but that is also informed by the new scholarship of the past seven decades, including to a considerable degree my own extensive work in this field. There will be considerable mate-rials and theoretical findings in my volume that were not available or known to my three precursors. In its approach, this new book will take a position be-tween the Trench and Hulme volumes on the one hand and Taylor's book on the other. The former were meant for a wide readership, while Taylor was ad-dressing a scholarly community that justified a comparative approach based on proverbs in various foreign languages. My book is intended for the edu-cated general reader with an emphasis on Anglo-American proverbs in En-glish-language contexts. It is also but one volume in the Greenwood Folklore Handbooks series, and as such it is by necessity and design confined to a pre-scribed outline and structure. Since the book is intended for English readers, almost all proverbs discussed will be from the Anglo-American corpus. When proverbs are cited from other languages, they will usually be rendered in En-glish translation only. This linguistic restriction is also evident in the short chapter bibliographies (often referring to journal articles or book chapters) and the extensive bibliography (including only book-length studies) at the end of the volume. The present book is thus not an inclusive international and comparative survey of paremiology, but it is an attempt to lay out the rich field of proverbs to general readers of English anywhere in the world. With English or the various "Englishes" gaining ever greater prominence as the global lingua franca, these linguistic limitations seem to be justified and to a considerable degree even desirable. What will be stated and explained by quoting from the Anglo-American stock of proverbs will for the most part be transferable to the proverbial wisdom of other cultures and languages. How could it be otherwise, since the human condition distilled in the world's proverbs proves to be more alike than different. The American proverb "Human *nature* is the same all over the world" quite literally hits the prover-bial nail on the head.

At the end of these introductory remarks I would like to thank George Butler, general editor of the Greenwood Folklore Handbooks series, for his help and guidance during my work on this book. I also extend many thanks to Audrey Klein and Karl F. Bridges for their help in obtaining various permissions. In addition I wish to express my sincere appreciation to my friend Alan Dundes (Berkeley) for his continued interest in and comments on my proverb studies. My colleagues and my students in the Department of German and Russian at the University of Vermont have also been most support-ive. The same is true for my wife, Barbara Mieder, who lets me be the proverbial fool obsessed with his research endeavors. And lasting thanks and appreciation are due my beloved father, Horst Mieder, whose death I grieved while working on this book. He instilled in me a solid work ethic and showed me by example that a good life includes helping and caring for others. As I aspire to live up to his commitment to high moral standards, I hope that I might do justice now and then to the proverb "Like father, like son" in its most positive sense.

Wolfgang Mieder

One

Definition and Classification

Of the various verbal folklore genres (i.e., fairy tales, legends, tall tales, jokes, and riddles), proverbs are the most concise but not necessarily the simplest form. The vast scholarship on proverbs is ample proof that they are anything but mundane matters in human communication. Proverbs fulfill the human need to summarize experiences and observations into nuggets of wisdom that provide ready-made comments on personal relationships and social affairs. There are proverbs for every imaginable context, and they are thus as contradictory as life itself. Proverb pairs like "*Absence* makes the heart grow fonder" and "Out of *sight,* out of mind" or "*Look* before you leap" and "He who *hesitates* is lost" make it abundantly clear that proverbs do not represent a logical philosophical system. But when the proper proverb is chosen for a particular situation, it is bound to fit perfectly and it becomes an effective formulaic strategy of communication. And contrary to some isolated opinions, proverbs have not lost their usefulness in modern society. They serve people well in oral speech and the written word, coming to mind almost automatically as prefabricated verbal units. While the frequency of their employment might well vary among people and contexts, proverbs are a significant rhetorical force in various modes of communication, from friendly chats, powerful political speeches, and religious sermons to lyrical poetry, best-seller novels, and the influential mass media. Proverbs are in fact everywhere, and it is exactly their ubiquity that has led scholars from many disciplines to study them from classical times to the modern age. There is no doubt that the playful alteration of the proverb "If the *shoe* fits, wear it" to "If the proverb fits, use it" says it all!

While the first part of this section deals with definition matters, the second part analyzes how proverbs have been classified in a multitude of different ways in thousands of proverb collections of differing quality and scope. This is not the place to review the status of internationally or nationally oriented paremiography (proverb collections) in great detail (see Mieder 1990). Suffice it to say that there exist many major proverb dictionaries that list equivalent proverbs from 2 to 15 different languages. Especially European paremiographers have worked on such synchronic comparative collections that at times include indices, frequency analyses, sources, geographical distribution, and so on. Collections of this type help to advance the structural, semantic, and semiotic studies of scholars like Grigorii L'vovich Permiakov and Matti Kuusi, who tried to develop an international type system of proverbs (see Permiakov 1970 [1979]; Kuusi 1972). By establishing lists of international proverb structures in combination with semantic and semiotic considerations, over 700 "universal" proverb types have now been found.

DEFINITION ATTEMPTS

The definition of a proverb has caused scholars from many disciplines much chagrin over the centuries. Many attempts at definition have been made from Aristotle to the present time (Kindstrand 1978; Russo 1983), ranging from philosophical considerations to cut-and-dry lexicographical definitions. The American paremiologist Bartlett Jere Whiting (1904–1995) reviewed many definitions in an important article on "The Nature of the Proverb" (1932), summarizing his findings in a lengthy conglomerate version of his own:

A proverb is an expression which, owing its birth to the people, testifies to its origin in form and phrase. It expresses what is apparently a fundamental truth—that is, a truism,—in homely language, often adorned, however, with alliteration and rhyme. It is usually short, but need not be; it is usually true, but need not be. Some proverbs have both a literal and figurative meaning, either of which makes perfect sense; but more often they have but one of the two. A proverb must be venerable; it must bear the sign of antiquity, and, since such signs may be counterfeited by a clever literary man, it should be attested in different places at different times. This last requirement we must often waive in dealing with very early literature, where the material at our disposal is incomplete. (Whiting 1932: 302; also in Whiting 1994: 80)

That certainly is a useful summation, albeit not a very precise statement. It represents a reaction to a tongue-in-cheek statement that Whiting's friend Archer Taylor had made a year earlier at the beginning of his classic study on

The Proverb (1931). Taylor begins his 223-page analysis of proverbs with the claim that a definitive definition of the genre is an impossibility. Of course, he then spends the next 200 pages explaining in much detail what proverbs are all about. His somewhat ironical introductory remark has become an often-quoted paragraph, and his claim that "an incommunicable quality tells us this sentence is proverbial and that is not" has gained "proverbial" status among paremiologists:

> The definition of a proverb is too difficult to repay the undertaking; and should we fortunately combine in a single definition all the essential elements and give each the proper emphasis, we should not even then have a touchstone. An incommunicable quality tells us this sentence is proverbial and that one is not. Hence no definition will enable us to identify positively a sentence as proverbial. Those who do not speak a language can never recognize all its proverbs, and similarly much that is truly proverbial escapes us in Elizabethan and older English. Let us be content with recognizing that a proverb is a saying current among the folk. At least so much of a definition is indisputable. (Taylor 1931 [1962, 1985]: 3)

In 1985 I put Taylor's supposition that people in general know what a proverb is to the test and simply asked a cross section of 55 Vermont citizens how they would define a proverb. After all, the general folk use proverbs all the time, and one would think that they too know intuitively what a proverb represents. A frequency study of the words contained in the over 50 definition attempts made it possible to formulate the following general description:

> A proverb is a short, generally known sentence of the folk which contains wisdom, truth, morals, and traditional views in a metaphorical, fixed and memorizable form and which is handed down from generation to generation. (Mieder 1985: 119; also in Mieder 1993: 24)

This summary definition mirrors that of Whiting, while the short conglomerate version "A proverb is a short sentence of wisdom" based on the words most often used in the 50-odd definitions resembles Taylor's statement. In any case, people in general, not bothered by academic concerns and intricacies, have a good idea of what a proverb encompasses. This is also born out by a number of proverbs about proverbs, representing folk definitions as it were: "*Proverbs* are the children of experience," "*Proverbs* are the wisdom of the streets," and "*Proverbs* are true words." Proverbs obviously contain a lot of common sense, experience, wisdom, and truth, and as such they represent ready-made traditional strategies in oral speech acts and writings from high literature to the mass media (see Hasan-Rokem 1990).

But proverb scholars have, of course, not been satisfied with the vagaries of this type of definition. Again and again they have tried to approximate *the* definition, but there is no space or necessity to comment on all of them here. Suffice it to cite two more general work-definitions starting with Stuart A. Gallacher's short statement from 1959, which as his student has served me well in my proverbial endeavors: "A proverb is a concise statement of an apparent truth which has [had, or will have] currency among the people" (Gallacher 1959: 47). The parenthetical modifications have been added by me to indicate that while some proverbs have been in use for hundreds of years, some have passed out of circulation and new ones will certainly be coined. In a number of encyclopedia articles I have had to deal with the vexing problem of defining proverbs precisely as well. My attempt in *American Folklore: An Encyclopedia* (1996) shows my indebtedness to my teacher Stuart A. Gallacher:

> Proverbs [are] concise traditional statements of apparent truths with currency among the folk. More elaborately stated, proverbs are short, generally known sentences of the folk that contain wisdom, truths, morals, and traditional views in a metaphorical, fixed, and memorizable form and that are handed down from generation to generation. (Mieder 1996a: 597)

Certainly these short and general definitions do not pay proper attention to numerous fascinating aspects of proverbs as formulaic and metaphorical texts and as regards their use, function, and meaning in varied contexts. No wonder then that paremiologists have expanded on basic definitions by being more inclusive and descriptive and by exemplifying various proverbial characteristics by means of examples.

PROVERB MARKERS AND MEANINGS

One of the major concerns of paremiologists is to get to the bottom of that "incommunicable quality" of what may be called proverbiality. It is my contention that not even the most complex definition will be able to identify all proverbs. The crux of the matter lies in the concept of traditionality that includes both aspects of age and currency. In other words, a particular sentence might sound like a proverb, as for example "Where there are stars, there are scandals," and yet not be one. The invented sentence is based on the common proverb pattern "Where there are Xs, there are Ys," and it appears to contain some perceived generalizations about the behavior of movie stars. But that does not attest to its alleged proverbiality. This piece of created wisdom would have to be taken over by others and be used over a period of time to be considered a bona fide proverb. As it stands here on this page, it is nothing more than a "proverb-like" statement. Proverb definitions often include the term "traditional," but proving that a given text has gained traditionality is quite another matter. This makes it so very difficult to decide what new statements have in fact gained proverbial status. Such modern American texts as "Been *there,* done that," "The *camera* doesn't lie," "No *guts,* no glory," and "You can't beat (fight) *city hall*" have made it (see Doyle 1996). Why is this so? Simply stated, they have been registered numerous times over time. The last example also shows the formation of variants. And it is exactly the requirement of all folklore, including proverbs, that various references and possibly also variants are found that attest to oral currency.

Stephen D. Winick, in an erudite essay on "Intertextuality and Innovation in a Definition of the Proverb Genre" (2003), has tried valiantly to break with the requirement of traditionality for new proverbs, arguing that a text becomes a proverb upon its creation (see also Honeck and Welge 1997). That would make the sentence "Where there are stars, there are scandals" a proverb! As a folklorist and paremiologist I disagree with this assessment. The fact that the sentence is "proverb-like" does not make it a folk proverb, putting in question Winick's convoluted definition:

> Proverbs are brief (sentence-length) entextualized utterances which derive a sense of wisdom, wit and authority from explicit and intentional intertextual reference to a tradition of previous similar wisdom utterances. This intertextual reference may take many forms, including replication (i.e., repetition of the text from previous contexts), imitation (i.e., modeling a new utterance after a previous utterance), or use of features (rhyme, alliteration, meter, ascription to the elders, etc.) associated with previous wisdom sayings. Finally, proverbs address recurrent social situations in a strategic way. (Winick 2003: 595)

While Winick goes too far in claiming proverbiality for "proverb-like" utterances (i.e., "explicit and intentional intertextual reference to a tradition of previous similar wisdom utterances"), he includes other valid and important criteria of proverbiality that summarize the findings of important theoretical work in paremiology.

Winick speaks of "features" of proverbiality, while other scholars have talked of "markers" that help to identify texts as proverbs in addition to the requirement of traditionality. The anthropologist George Milner observed that many proverbs are characterized by a quadripartite structure. This is the case with such proverbs as "Who pays the *piper,* calls the tune" and "What the *eye* doesn't see, the heart doesn't grieve over." These texts can be divided into four parts with either positive or negative values to each of the four elements. There are thus sixteen possible structural patterns that characterize this type of proverb (see Milner 1971). However, "Who buys the beer, determines the party" also exhibits a quadripartite structure and is most certainly not a proverb. Folklorist Alan Dundes runs into a similar problem with his definition of a proverb being a propositional statement consisting of at least a topic and a comment, as for example in "*Money* talks." This also means that a proverb must at least consist of two words. For longer proverbs Dundes is able to show that they are based on an oppositional or non-oppositional structure, as "*Man* proposes but God disposes" or "Where there's a *will,* there's a way." Yet the statement "Politicians decide but soldiers fight" is certainly not a proverb, even though it follows an oppositional structure. Dundes knew of this problem with his structural approach to proverbs, and he did well in adding the aspect of traditionality to his otherwise useful definition:

> The proverb appears to be a traditional propositional statement consisting of at least one descriptive element, a descriptive element consisting of a topic and a comment. This means that proverbs must have at least two words. Proverbs which contain a single descriptive element are non-oppositional. Proverbs with two or more descriptive elements may be either oppositional or non-oppositional. (Dundes 1975: 970; also in Mieder and Dundes 1981 [1994]: 60)

As can be seen, the structural approach to the conundrum of a proverb definition does not seem to solve the problem either. The necessary ingredient of traditionality keeps rearing its ugly head.

But speaking of structural matters, it is also important to mention that the thousands of proverbs of any language can be reduced to certain structures or patterns (see Peukes 1977). How else could there be so many proverbial texts based on a few words? Some of the more common patterns, and by no means only in the English language, are "Better X than Y," "Like X, like Y," "No X without Y," "One X doesn't make a Y," "If X, then Y," calling to mind such well-known proverbs as "Better *poor* with honor than rich with shame," "Like *father,* like son," "No *work,* no pay," "One *robin* doesn't make a spring," and

"If at first you don't *succeed,* then try, try again." These common structures frequently also serve as the basis of modern proverbs, as "Better *Red* than dead" and its reverse "Better *dead* than Red" from the time of the Cold War with its anticommunism propaganda (see Barrick 1979).

While structural paradigms might at least help in identifying traditional proverbs, there are several other markers available to the scholar. Shortness is certainly one of them, with the average length of a proverb consisting of about seven words. But there are, of course, also much longer proverbs that break the conciseness feature, as for example the paradoxical Bible proverb "It is easier for a *camel* to go through the eye of a needle, than for a rich man to enter into the kingdom of God" (Matt. 19:24). Furthermore, proverbs are often shortened to mere allusions owing to their general recognizability. Such truncated proverbs appear in oral speech as well as in literature or the mass media. Why should a journalist cite the entire proverb "A *bird* in the hand is worth two in the bush" in a large-print headline when the remnant "A bird in the hand..." will bring the entire proverb to mind automatically, at least in the case of native speakers of English. Earlier scholars have overstated the fixity of proverbs. In actual use, especially in the case of intentional speech play, proverbs are quite often manipulated. Neal Norrick in his valuable study on *How Proverbs Mean* (1985) has concluded that "for well known proverbs, mention of one crucial recognizable phrase [i.e., part] serves to call forth the entire proverb," speaking of "this minimal recognizable unit as the *kernel* of the proverb" (Norrick 1985: 45). Proverbs are definitely fixed only in the proverb collections; otherwise they can be used rather freely, even though the predominant way of citing them is in their unaltered entirety.

Many proverbs also exhibit certain stylistic features that help a statement to gain and maintain proverbial status (see Blehr 1973). Paremiologists have long identified numerous poetic devices, but Shirley Arora summarized them well in her seminal article on "The Perception of Proverbiality" (1984). Such stylistic markers include alliteration: "*Practice* makes perfect," "*Forgive* and forget," and "Every *law* has a loophole"; parallelism: "Ill *got*, ill spent," "Nothing *ventured*, nothing gained," and "Easy *come*, easy go"; rhyme: "A little *pot* is soon hot," "There's many a *slip* between the cup and the lip," and "When the *cat's* away, the mice will play"; and ellipsis: "More *haste,* less speed," "Once *bitten,* twice shy," and "*Deeds,* not words." Besides these external markers there are also internal features that add to the rhetorical effectiveness of proverbs, among them hyperbole: "All is *fair* in love and war," "Faint *heart* never won fair lady"; paradox: "The longest *way* around is the shortest way home," "The nearer the *church,* the farther from God"; and personification: "*Love* will find a way," "*Hunger* is the best cook." Not all but most proverbs contain a metaphor, among them such common texts as "A watched *pot* never boils," "The squeaky *wheel* gets the grease," and "*Birds* of a feather flock together." But some non-metaphorical proverbs have reached equal popularity, for example "*Knowledge* is power," "*Honesty* is the best policy," and "*Virtue* is its own reward."

The preference for metaphorical proverbs lies in the fact that they can be employed in a figurative or indirect way. Verbal folklore in general is based on indirection, and much can indeed be said or implied by the opportune use of such proverbs as "Don't look a *gift horse* in the mouth," "Don't count your *chickens* before they are hatched," "Every *cloud* has a silver lining," "You cannot teach an old *dog* new tricks," or "All that glitters is not *gold*." By associating an actual situation with a metaphorical proverb, the particular matter is generalized into a common occurrence of life. Instead of scolding someone directly for not behaving according to the cultural customs of a different social or cultural setting, one might indirectly comment that "When in *Rome*, do as the Romans do." If someone must be warned to be more careful with health issues, the proverb "An ounce of *prevention* is worth a pound of cure" might well serve the purpose to add some commonly accepted wisdom to the argument. Or instead of explaining at great length that the time for action has come, the proverb "Strike while the *iron* is hot" expresses the matter in metaphorical but strong language that contains much traditional wisdom. Kenneth Burke has provided the following explanation of this effective use of metaphorical proverbs: "Proverbs are strategies for dealing with situations. In so far as situations are typical and recurrent in a given social structure, people develop names for them and strategies for handling them. Another name for strategies might be attitudes" (Burke 1941: 256). Proverbs in actual use refer to social situations, and it is this social context that in turn gives them meaning (see Seitel 1969). They act as signs for human behavior and social contexts and as such must be studied both from the structural and semiotic point of view (see Grzybek 1987; Zholkovskii 1978).

The meaning of proverbs is thus very much dependent on the contexts in which they appear. Barbara Kirshenblatt-Gimblett has shown how a number of common proverbs have in fact multiple meanings that come to light only in particular situations. For example, she asked about 80 students in Texas to explain the meaning of the proverb "A *friend* in need is a friend indeed." Here are the different explanations with comments on the different sources of the multiple meanings:

1. Someone who feels close enough to you to be able to ask you for help when he is in need is really your friend.—Syntactic ambiguity (is your friend in need or are you in need).

2. Someone who helps you when you are in need is really your friend.—Lexical ambiguity (indeed or in deed).

3. Someone who helps you by means of his actions (deeds) when you need him is a real friend as opposed to someone who just makes promises.—Key meaning.

4. Someone who is only your friend when he needs you is not a true friend.—Does "a friend indeed" mean "a true friend" or "not a true friend"? (Kirshenblatt-Gimblett 1973: 822; also in Mieder and Dundes 1981 [1994]: 113–114).

Clearly only a specific context will reveal what the proverb does in fact want to say. The Estonian paremiologist Arvo Krikmann has spoken in this regard of the "semantic indefiniteness" of proverbs that results from their hetero-situativity, poly-functionality, and poly-semanticity (see Krikmann 1974a and 1974b). The meaning of any proverb must therefore be analyzed in its unique context, be it social, literary, rhetorical, journalistic, or whatever.

ORIGIN AND DISSEMINATION OF PROVERBS

Proverbs, like riddles, jokes, or fairy tales, do not fall out of the sky and neither are they products of a mythical soul of the folk. Instead they are always coined by an individual either intentionally or unintentionally, as expressed in Lord John Russell's well-known one-line proverb definition that has taken on a proverbial status of sorts: "A proverb is the wit of one, and the wisdom of many" (ca. 1850). If the statement contains an element of truth or wisdom, and if it exhibits one or more proverbial markers, it might "catch on" and be used first in a small family circle, and subsequently in a village, a city, a region, a country, a continent, and eventually the world. The global spread of proverbs is not a pipe dream, since certain ancient proverbs have in fact spread to many parts of the world. Today, with the incredible power of the mass media, a newly formulated proverb-like statement might become a bona fide proverb relatively quickly by way of the radio, television, and print media. As with verbal folklore in general, the original statement might well be varied a bit as it gets picked up and becomes ever more an anonymous proverb whose wording, structure, style, and metaphor are such that it is memorable. Older literary sources show very clearly that proverbs existed in such variants until one dominant wording eventually became the standard, to wit the following three historical variants of a proverb of prudence: "It is good to be *wise* before the mischief" (1584), "After the business is over, every one is *wise*" (1666), and "It is easy to be *wise* after the event" (1900), with the latter version having become today's standard form (Smith 1935 [1970]: 898).

It is usually quite difficult to trace the origin and history of a proverb in a particular language. Such studies very quickly take on major proportions, and they get very involved if the proverb under investigation proves to go back to medieval times or even further to classical antiquity. Any bilingual speaker or translator will have noticed that there exist two types of proverbs. On the one hand, there are those proverbs that have the same meaning but different structures, vocabulary, and metaphors, and they consequently have different origins in their respective languages. Thus English speakers since Shakespeare say "*Brevity* is the soul of wit," while the Germans utter "In der *Kürze* liegt die Würze" (In brevity there is [lies] spice). Whoever needs to translate one of these texts would have to know the quite different equivalent in the target language or find it in a dictionary. Regional proverbs become especially difficult translation problems, since possible equivalents are often missing from dictionaries that tend to include only the more common proverbs. On the other hand, many proverbs are identical not only in German and English but in most Germanic, Romance, and Slavic languages of Europe, and these do not present any particular translation problem. In other words, there exist general European proverbs, that is proverbs that have been disseminated through precise loan translations throughout Europe. That is why Emanuel Strauss could publish his three-volume *Dictionary of European Proverbs* (1994) and why Gyula Paczolay could follow suit with his invaluable collection of *European Proverbs in 55 Languages* (1997), to name but two of the many polyglot proverb collections. But how can all of this be explained? Since when do these common European proverbs exist, of which many also made it to North America with the waves of immigrants?

Four sources for the distribution of European proverbs can be identified (similar issues have occurred in the dissemination of proverbs in Asian, African, and other linguistic and cultural groups). There is first of all Greek and Roman antiquity, whose proverbial wisdom found a broad geographical dissemination primarily through the Latin language. The scholarly study of proverbs begins with Aristotle, and many Greek proverbs have been found in the works of Plato, Sophocles, Homer, Aristophanes, Aeschylus, Euripides, and so on. Many of them reappeared in Latin translation in Plautus, Terence, Cicero, Horace, and other Roman writers (see Mieder and Bryan 1996). Ancient writers also added new Latin proverbs, and many of these classical texts became part of a rich medieval Latin proverb tradition. More importantly, however, these common Latin texts were then translated into the many developing European languages. Erasmus of Rotterdam played a major role in spreading this classical and medieval wisdom throughout Europe by means of the many editions of his *Adagia* (1500ff.) that contains over four thousand explanatory notes and essays on classical proverbs and proverbial expressions (see Phillips 1964). His works were read and translated, and he himself had also shown interest in early Dutch regional proverbs. The same is true for Martin Luther in Germany, who was a masterful translator of classical proverbs but who also employed indigenous German proverbs in his writings (see Cornette 1942 [1997]). Latin proverbs were used in school translation exercises, and many of them entered the various languages through oral channels, thus spreading classical wisdom through the written and spoken word all over Europe. By way of English they traveled on to Australia, Canada, the United States, and the rest of the world where English is used as a second language. Some of these proverbs have truly taken on an international and global currency, showing once again that they contain universal human experiences and insights.

There is then no doubt that a considerable corpus of common European proverbs can be traced back to classical times. Since they were loan translated from the same sources, they exist in the many languages of Europe in identical forms. Little wonder then that Gyula Paczolay was able to find exact equivalents of the classical proverb "Where there is *smoke,* there is fire" in 54 European languages. A few other very popular proverbs from classical times that are still very much in use today in Europe and elsewhere are: "Barking *dogs* do not bite" (51 European languages), "One *swallow* does not make a summer" (49), "*Walls* have ears" (46), "One *hand* washes the other" (46), "Make *haste* slowly" (43), "*Children* and fools tell the truth" (41), "Still *waters* run deep" (38), "*Love* is blind" (37), and "*Fish* always begin to stink at the head" (33). Their general use in present-day Europe and beyond indicates a strong intellectual, ethical, and human bond among people. All of these texts express general human wisdom without any specific national or ethnic references. And since they are basically identical in all languages, they are and will continue to be effective modes of metaphorical communication among Europeans, North Americans, and other peoples.

A second source of proverbs for the entire European continent and beyond is the Bible, whose proverbs date back to classical antiquity and early wisdom literature. As a widely translated book, the Bible had a major influence on the distribution of common proverbs since the various translators were dealing with the same texts. Several dozen biblical proverbs are thus current in identical wordings in many European languages, even though speakers might not remember that they are employing proverbs from the Bible. A few obvious examples are "As you *sow,* so you reap" (Paczolay lists 52 European references; see Gal. 6:7), "He who digs a *pit* for others, falls in himself" (48; Prov. 26:27), "He that will not *work,* shall not eat" (43; 2 Thess. 3:10), "*Do* as you would be done by" (Matt. 7:12), "A *prophet* is not without honor save in his own country" (39; Matt. 13:57), "An *eye* for an eye, a tooth for a tooth" (38; Exod. 21:24), and "There is nothing new under the *sun*" (29; Eccles. 1:9). It is important to mention, however, that the number of biblical proverbs in various European languages is not identical. Much depended on the linguistic skills of the translators. In the case of Martin Luther, quite a few of his German formulations have actually become proverbial without having been proverbs in the original text.

The third source for common European proverbs is medieval Latin. It must not be forgotten that the Latin language of the Middle Ages had the status of a lingua franca, and as such it developed new proverbs that cannot be traced back to classical times. Hans Walther and Paul Gerhard Schmidt have put together thousands of medieval proverbs in their massive 9-volume collection of *Lateinische Sprichwörter und Sentenzen des Mittelalters* (1963–1986), and the 13-volume *Lexikon der Sprichwörter des romanisch-germanischen Mittelalters* (1995–2002) by Samuel Singer and Ricarda Liver shows the relationship of many of these Latin proverbs to those of the vulgate languages. Many medieval Latin proverbs in their exact translations have spread to European languages, and they certainly belong to some of the most popular proverbs today. A few well-known examples are: "*Crows* will not pick out crows' eyes" (Paczolay lists 48 European references), "Strike while the *iron* is hot" (48), "New *brooms* sweep clean" (47), "All that glitters is not *gold*" (47), "When the *cat* is away, the mice will play" (46), "The *pitcher* goes so long to the well until it breaks at last" (40), "No *rose* without thorns" (39), "At night all *cats* are grey" (38), and "*Clothes* do not make the man" (37). Of special interest is the Middle Latin proverb "Mille *via* ducunt hominem per secula ad Romam" from the twelfth century, for which Gyula Paczolay cites 33 European equivalents. In all these languages the direct loan translation of "All *roads* lead to Rome" exists. However, there are also variants that replace "Rome" with another city. In an Estonian proverb the city is St. Petersburg, a Finnish proverb refers to the old capital Turku, a Russian proverb mentions Moscow, and a Turkish proverb names Mecca. But these are variants that one might well have expected in Europe, and perhaps one day the American version "All roads lead to Washington" will also appear in a proverb collection. It probably exists, but has simply not been recorded yet. As for one speaker, I know that I have used this variant from time to time when discussing national politics.

The fourth source for common European proverbs reverses the historical move of proverbs from Europe to the United States. They are modern texts that have been disseminated since the middle of the twentieth century throughout Europe by means of the mass media. A few American proverbs that are already spreading across the European continent either in the new lingua franca of English or in new loan translations are "A *picture* is worth a thousand words," "It takes two to *tango*," and "*Garbage* in, garbage out" (from the world of computers). Of special interest is also the "Europeaniza-tion" of the well-known American proverb "What's *good* for General Motors is good for America," which the president of General Motors Charles Erwin Wilson coined on January 15, 1953, during a Senate hearing. Willy Brandt, the renowned European politician, changed this proverb in a loan translation to fit the European context. Calling for European solidarity in a speech on November 18, 1971, he exclaimed: "Im übrigen könnte man jedoch in Ab-wandlung eines alten amerikanischen Sprichwortes sagen: Was gut ist für Eu-ropa, ist gut für die Vereinigten Staaten. Die Zeit des Feiertags-Europäertums ist vorbei, Europa ist unser Alltag" (All around one could say by changing an old American proverb: What is good for Europe, is good for the United States. The time of holiday-Europeanness is over, Europe is our normal work-day). One is inclined to change the sixteenth-century proverb "*Handsome* is as handsome does" to the new proverbial slogan "Europe is as Europe does" to fit the new European consciousness as the move towards unity continues (Mieder 2000). In any case, the United States and its English language are not only spreading new words throughout Europe and the rest of the world, they are also disseminating new proverbs from popular culture (music, film, etc.) and the mass media (advertisements, cartoons, etc.) as bits of wisdom that fit the twenty-first century.

TRADITIONAL FORMS RELATED TO THE PROVERB

Although this book is concerned primarily with proverbs as such, it is of interest to take at least a cursory glance at some of the other proverbial genres (see Barley 1974). While proverbs are complete thoughts that can stand by themselves, there are such subgenres as proverbial expressions, proverbial comparisons, proverbial exaggerations, and twin (binary) formulas, which are fragmentary and for the most part metaphorical phrases that must be inte-grated into a sentence. Proverbial expressions are usually verbal phrases, as for example "to throw the *book* at someone," "to cry over spilled *milk*," "to blow one's own *horn*," "to be a *tempest* in a teacup," "to look for a *needle* in a haystack," "to be a stumbling *block*," "to be between a *rock* and a hard place," and "to carry *coals* to Newcastle." Proverbial comparisons can conveniently be divided into two structural groups. The first follows the pattern of "as X as Y," as indicated by such common comparisons as "as *black* as night," "as *busy* as a bee," "as *clear* as daylight," "as *drunk* as a fish," "as *mad* as a hatter," "as *soft* as putty," and "as *swift* as the wind." The second group is based on a verbal comparison with "like": "to *work* like a dog," "to *look* like a million dollars," "to *watch* like a hawk," "to *sleep* like a lamb," "to *spend* money like a drunken sailor," "to *squeal* like a pig," and "to *vanish* like snow." As can be seen from just these examples, such texts add much metaphorical expressiveness both to oral and written communication. Nevertheless, English teachers tend to discourage their students from using what they call "clichés" in their various writing assignments. They might be partially correct in these admonitions, especially when their students overuse them. But an occasional proverbial statement at the right place and time is quite appropriate for emphasis and colorful imagery. One need only to look at the writings of such Nobel prize winners for literature as Thomas Mann, Eugene O'Neill, or Winston S. Churchill to see that they made repeated and effective use of proverbial language (see Bryan and Mieder 1995; Mieder and Bryan 1995).

Proverbial exaggerations can also take on important stylistic functions, especially if one wants to ridicule a person or situation. Such exaggerations usually describe the extraordinary degree to which someone or something possesses a certain characteristic. Many of these formulaic phrases are based on the structural pattern "so...(that)," as is the case in the following examples: "He's so *angry* he can't spit straight," "She is so *stupid* that she is unable to boil water without burning it," "It *rained* so hard that the water stood 10 feet out of the well," "He is so *miserly* that he crawls under the door to save the hinges," "She moves so *slowly* that you can watch the snails whiz by," and "You are so *stingy* you would take candy from a child." There is a great deal of folk humor in these exaggerations, but depending on how and in what context they are uttered, they can take on a very satirical tone. But still, these phrases are certainly more entertaining and creative than some of the standard curses based on scatological expletives.

So-called twin (binary) formulas are traditional word pairs that are linked together by alliteration and/or rhyme, as for example "*short* and sweet," "*tit* for tat," "*spick* and span," "*rags* and riches," "*live* and learn," "*sink* or swim," and "*men* and mice." None of these proverbial phrases or phraseological units (phraseologisms), as the linguists prefer to refer to them, contain any complete thought or wisdom. But they are proverbial in that they are traditional and metaphorical, being employed even more frequently than actual proverbs. While they supply colorful elements of folk speech to oral and written communication, they cannot take on an existence by themselves. Employing a metaphor from the building trade, one might say that proverbs are the bricks, while proverbial phrases are the mortar.

But proverbs can at times hit people like a hard brick with their continuous claim of moral authority and didactic intent. While the folk has usually accepted proverbs at face value, eagerly handing them on from generation to generation, there have obviously also been moments where people have been fed up with all of this straightforward wisdom. Some comic relief was desired, and just as tall tales provide an outlet for folk humor in the realm of folk narratives, so-called wellerisms are replete with humor, irony, and satire. Wellerisms consist of a triadic structure: (1) a statement (often a proverb), (2) an identification of a speaker (a person or animal), and (3) a phrase that places the statement into an unexpected situation. In the case where proverbs make up the first part, their claim to truth or wisdom is questioned by the resulting pun. The term "wellerism" is a scholarly designation and has made its way into only a few dictionaries. It is based on the character of Sam Weller in Charles Dickens's novel *The Pickwick Papers* (1837), because Weller delighted in using these triadic structures (see Baer 1983; Bryan and Mieder 1997). Following the success of the novel in the nineteenth century, there was quite a craze of publishing made-up wellerisms in the British and American press. Some of them were reprinted again and again and took on a life of their own as traditional wellerisms. But the genre was well established long before Dickens, and wellerisms have been recorded for centuries in many languages. Here then are a few traditional texts that employ a proverb in their first part:

"*Business* before pleasure," as the man said when he kissed his wife before he went out to make love to his neighbor's.

"Much *cry* and sm' wool," as the barber said when he sheared the sow.

"All *flesh* is grass," as the horse said when he bit a piece out of a man's arm.

"Every *evil* is followed by some good," as the man said when his wife died the day after he became bankrupt.

"Every *little* bit helps," as the old lady said when she pissed in the ocean to help drown her husband.

"*Silence* gives consent," as the man said when he kissed the dumb [mute] woman.

"Where there's a *will*, there's a way," as the hog said when he rooted the back gate off its hinges to come at the kitchen swill barrel.

"Everyone to his own *taste,*" as the farmer said when he kissed the cow.

"*Tit* for tat," quoth the wife when she farted at the thunder.

"One good *turn* deserves another," said the customer, as he padded the chorus girls' tights.

But enough already. As can be seen from these examples and from many more in Wolfgang Mieder's and Stewart A. Kingsbury's *A Dictionary of Wellerisms* (1994), the traditional humor of wellerisms quite easily enters the sexual and scatological spheres. Wellerisms are thus clear indications that solid proverbs could serve as the start of some very basic humor. All of this is not to say that there are no folk proverbs that contain imagery from the vulgar tongue. New proverbs are still created along this line, as for example "If you got them by the *balls,* their hearts and minds will follow," "*Opinions* are like assholes— everybody's got one," and "It's better to be *pissed* off than pissed on." And, of course, there is also the American proverb "*Shit* happens" that started to appear on bumper stickers during the 1980s (see Doyle 1996). It is a succinct text, it consists of a topic and a comment, it expresses a truth in metaphorical language, and it has definitely gained currency among my students. But it can also be heard among the older generation, leaving no doubt that it has become a bona fide proverb. It will be interesting to see whether paremiographers of the future will include the text in their proverb collections. Their earlier colleagues have left most proverbs of this type out of their compilations, an unfortunate example of censorship in light of the fact that folk proverbs do indeed contain elements of *all* aspects of life.

THE INTERNATIONAL TYPE SYSTEM OF PROVERBS

The organization of thousands of proverbs into a meaningful order presents major lexicographical challenges. Fortunately Matti Kuusi (1914–1998) and subsequently his daughter Outi Lauhakangas have created an international classification system of proverbs that starts out with 13 main themes, which for the most part represent basic aspects of human life:

A. Practical knowledge of nature

B. Faith and basic attitudes

C. Basic observations and socio-logic

D. The world and human life

E. Sense of proportion

F. Concepts of morality

G. Social life

H. Social interaction

J. Communication

K.   Social position

L.   Agreements and norms

M.   Coping and learning

T.   Time and sense of time

Under the 13 main themes there are 52 main classes (from A1 to T4). The main theme of "G Social life," having 8 main classes, may serve as an example here:

G. Social life

   G1   kinship

   G2   development—a person's background

   G3   child : parents / upbringing

   G4   man : woman / ranking and position of both sexes

   G5   marriage

   G6   youth : old age

   G7   health : illness

   G8   death / the dead

The 52 main classes are once again subdivided into 325 subgroups with different numbers of subgroups for each main class. Some subgroups register 7 or fewer proverb types, but there are also those subgroups that list 50 or more types. Thus subgroup "G8g life from death" contains merely 6 proverb types, while subgroup "G5e woman and man—the right moment of offer of marriage, norms, criteria of choosing (mostly by men)" offers 73 proverb types! An example from subgroup G8g is the Japanese text "A *candle,* by consuming itself, gives light to others," and another example from subgroup G5e is the English proverb "Never seemed a *prison* fair or a mistress foul."

This obviously is a very complex classification system with the intent of establishing universals or archetypes of human thinking. Basing his studies on a large comparative database of proverbs from basically every corner of the world, Kuusi's idea of a universal "proverb type" in the broadest sense of that word "encompasses similar proverb types from different nations, presenting them as a global type having a common idea. That is why we can speak of universal proverb types if we wish to compare them to our local proverb titles or proverb types in the narrowest sense of the word. [...] There are no standard models or patterns for a proverb type. In the Matti Kuusi type system the concept of type is not very strict and it moves between a relatively abstract proverb title [...] to a cluster of proverbs using different images but having the same idea" (Lauhakangas 2001: 62–63; see Mieder 2001).

Since the death of Matti Kuusi in 1998, his daughter Outi Lauhakangas has continued his fascinating and extremely important work, presenting a list of over 700 "universal [proverb] types and their criteria" (Lauhakangas 2001: 125–158), which are in most cases more like clusters of proverb types, having variants from four main cultural areas: European, African, Islamic, and Asiatic cultures. With the new classification system now finished, and with its inclusion of universal proverb types, international studies of an individual proverb type can be carried out synchronically *and* diachronically as well as contextually, semantically, functionally, and so on.

Let me give at least one example of the universal proverb types that can be found under the main theme "C" (Basic observations and socio-logic) and its main class "C6" (appearance : internal values). The subgroup "C6c" (everything is not as it appears; the deceptiveness of identifying marks [- -]) includes the following universal types:

All that glitters is not *gold.*

All are not *hunters* that blow the horn.

There are more *maids* than Maukin and more men than Michael.

A *wolf* in sheep's clothing.

All are good *maids,* but whence come the bad wives?

The classification system includes elaborate notations with incredible information and, above all, also cross-references to other proverb types. This takes care of the problem of the at times somewhat subjective assignment of proverbs to a certain position in the classification system.. And, to be sure, the computerized database does (thank God!) permit a precise search by key words (usually nouns) that will help to locate each and every proverb in the system if one is not certain under what main theme, main class, and subgroup it might have been registered by Matti Kuusi and Outi Lauhakangas.

Lauhakangas makes a number of honest and critical comments regarding her father's and her classification system, basically admitting to its somewhat subjective nature:

It is obvious that the viewpoint or the aim of the interpreter has an effect on defining proverb texts as a proverb type. [...] The Matti Kuusi international type system of proverbs represents only one solution to the classification of proverbs—and not necessarily the best. It has primarily been an attempt to find a practical way to arrange a large collection of literature [i.e., proverbs found in collections] references. [...] We can and we should say that the Matti Kuusi index is permanently "under construction." Consequently also the file of universal proverb types is unfinished. (Lauhakangas 2001: 76)

This is the way it should be! Yes, the classification system might not be the very best solution, but there is no better index at this time. And perhaps there will never be another research team as that of Matti Kuusi and Outi Lauhakangas who would be willing to even attempt to work out a practical and international type system. It should gladly, enthusiastically, and thankfully be accepted and worked with by international scholars.

It is indeed an open system that will permanently be under construction, and much work lies ahead for Outi Lauhakangas. Her father did indeed cast his net very widely regarding the hundreds of proverb collections used in establishing the classification system. And yet, there are many older and above all newer major proverb collections waiting to be included in the database. A few comparative collections that must be integrated are: Jens Aage Stabell Bilgrav, *20,000 Proverbs and Their Equivalents in German, French, Swedish, Danish* (1985), Henryk L. Cox, *Spreekwoordenboek: Nederlands, Fries, Afrikaans, Engels, Duits, Frans, Spaans, Latijn* (2000), Harold V. Cordry, *The Multicultural Dictionary of Proverbs* (1997), Luis Iscla, *English Proverbs and Their Near Equivalents in Spanish, French, Italian and Latin* (1995), and Emanuel Strauss, *Dictionary of European Proverbs* (1994). Of utmost importance, especially for diachronic purposes, are the 13 volumes of Samuel Singer's and Ricarda Liver's *Thesaurus proverbiorum medii aevi. Lexikon der Sprichwörter des romanisch-germanischen Mittelalters* (1995–2002). The numerous proverbs of important bilingual and single-language collections that also need to be incorporated are among others those by John Lazarus, *A Dictionary of Tamil Proverbs* (1894 [1991]), Peter Mertvago, *The Comparative Russian-English Dictionary of Russian Proverbs and Sayings* (1995), Wolfgang Mieder, Stewart A. Kingsbury, and Kelsie B. Harder, *A Dictionary of American Proverbs* (1992), Ryszard Pachocinski, *Proverbs of Africa* (1996), Albert Scheven, *Swahili Proverbs* (1981), Bartlett Jere Whiting, *Modern Proverbs and Proverbial Sayings* (1989), and Metin Yurtbasi, *A Dictionary of Turkish Proverbs* (1993).

There is much work to be done, as Matti Kuusi knew and Outi Lauhakangas is only too aware of at this time. In the best of all worlds, Lauhakangas should now continue with the "work in progress" of this truly unique international type system of proverbs. She knows its structure and intricacies the best, and she can go on to expand the system in the most consistent way possible, both according to the ideas of her father as well as her own. This relates not only to older proverbs but also to such new texts as for example "*Hurry* up and wait," "One man's *trash* is another man's treasure," and "It's the *thought* that counts." After all, the creation of new proverbs is not over, and it behooves scholars to integrate them into the international classification system to see how such innovative texts fit into the universal type system.

Even if the work on this international type system of proverbs were to stop completely at this time, paremiologists have a fantastic and beneficial research tool at their disposal for serious comparative proverb scholarship. The work must go on, but doubtlessly the *International Type System of Proverbs* with its computer database will reign as *the* standard work in comparative paremiography and paremiology. Generations of scholars will benefit from this classification system as they continue to look for universal bits of human wisdom in the form of proverbs.

TYPES OF INTERNATIONAL PROVERB COLLECTIONS

The *International Type System of Proverbs* just described is intended for serious comparative work by experts. But for most proverb research there are numerous extremely useful multilingual proverb collections available that simply list proverb equivalents. The preferred setup is to list the proverbs alphabetically by key word in the language of the compiler with the various foreign language equivalents registered underneath. The value of such collections is clearly enhanced if they also contain key-word indices of the proverbs in the target languages, making them accessible reference works especially for translators. While some collections do include sources and other scholarly references (see for example Kuusi et al. 1985; Paczolay 1997), most of these volumes on the market cite texts alone. They are dictionaries and don't claim to be more than that. A typical example is the entry for "*Love* is blind" in Jerzy Gluski's *Proverbs: A Comparative Book of English, French, German, Italian, Spanish and Russian Proverbs with a Latin Appendix* (1971):

En	Love is blind.*
Fr	L'amour est aveugle.
De	Die Liebe ist blind.
It	L'amore è ceco.
El	El amor es ciego
Ru	Liubov' clepa.

(Gluski 1971: 159)

The asterisk after the English text indicates that a Latin version is listed in the appendix as "Amor caecus." As can be seen from the linguistically identical foreign language texts, the Latin proverb was loan translated in its precise wording. Since the proverb goes back to classical antiquity, it actually entered many more languages that are included in those international proverb dictionaries that list additional foreign languages.

There is a second group of international proverb collections that has quite another purpose. Their compilers simply want to indicate what proverbs exist in other cultures about a certain theme. The proverbs are all cited in translation and the individual texts are not necessarily equivalents of each other. Harold V. Cordry's *The Multicultural Dictionary of Proverbs* (1997) offers a good example for proverbs from different cultures about "possession":

Possession

Better hold by a *hair* than draw by a tether. *Scottish*
Better to *have* than to wish. *English*
Blessed are those who *possess*. *Latin*
Everything goes to him who has *nothing*. *French*
Father's *having* and mother's having is not like having oneself. *Chinese*
Great *possessions* are great cares. *American*
So much as you *have,* so much are you sure of. *Spanish*
To each his *own*. *Latin*
Who has the *hilt* has the blade. *Welsh*
You can't *take* it with you. *American*

(Cordry 1997: 204–205)

These examples represent only about a fourth of the proverbs listed under the theme of "possession," but it suffices to show that this type of classification makes it possible to find various types of proverbs that express wisdom along these lines without necessarily being equivalents of each other.

A third group of international dictionaries again registers hundreds of proverbs from around the world in but one language, but this time each text contains the same key word and the individual proverbs are arranged alphabetically. My own *Encyclopedia of World Proverbs* (1986) follows this particular classification system, as can be seen from this selection of examples under the noun "life":

Life

A good *life* defers wrinkles. *Spanish*
An ill *life* makes an ill end. *Scottish*
All of *life* is a struggle. *Yiddish*

Human *life* is like a candle. *Albanian*
Life is more fragile than the morning dew. *Japanese*
Living *life* is not like crossing a field. *Russian*
Long *life* has misery. *English*
The *life* of man is as spotted as a woodpecker's coat. *Latvian*
There is *life* and death in the quiver. *African (Ovambo)*
When *life* is exhausted, death comes. *Vietnamese*

(Mieder 1986: 276–277)

And finally, there is a fourth group of international proverb collections that just lists proverbs from different languages in groups of their own. Gerd de Ley has arranged his *International Dictionary of Proverbs* (1998) in this fashion. He lists proverbs from 300 different nations and languages in English translation, ranging from just a few proverbs to several pages of them per language. For Iraq he offers the following selection:

Iraq

A beautiful *bride* needs no dowry.
Tell me who your *friends* are, and I'll tell you who you are.
One night of *anarchy* does more harm than a hundred years of tyranny.
Whoever writes a *book,* should be ready to accept criticism.
Stealing leads to poverty.
Sometimes you have to sacrifice your *beard* in order to save your head.
The *poor* are the silent of the land.
The *day* will wipe out all the promises of the night.

(Ley 1998: 192–193)

Unless a collection of this type has at least a comprehensive key-word index of the proverbs, it is extremely difficult to find proverbs dealing with a particular subject among the various languages.

The many bilingual collections follow similar classification systems. The proverbs are arranged either by key words or by general themes. The smaller popular volumes do not contain indices, but the larger dictionaries provide them so that proverbs in both languages can be located with ease. There are, of course, literally hundreds of bilingual collections, once again being of particular use to translators and people acquiring a foreign language.

MAJOR ANGLO-AMERICAN PROVERB COLLECTIONS

Single-language proverb collections also follow two basic classification systems, arranging the texts either by key words or by themes. There are thousands of collections for the many languages of the world. To be sure, hundreds of collections exist also for the English language, of which many are intended for the popular market. This is especially the case for regional or dialect collections, although they too can adhere to rigid scholarly standards by providing detailed linguistic and historical annotations (see bibliography).

Regarding the major scholarly English-language proverb collections, it can be said with justifiable pride that the work by Anglo-American paremiographers has served as the model for serious historical proverb dictionaries in other countries. As early as the 1920s, G.L. Apperson published his impressive *English Proverbs and Proverbial Phrases: A Historical Dictionary* (1929 [1969, 1993]), which was followed by William George Smith's *The Oxford Dictionary of English Proverbs* (1935 [1970, 3rd edition by F.P. Wilson]). There is also Morris Palmer Tilley's monumental *A Dictionary of the Proverbs in England in the Sixteenth and Seventeenth Centuries* (1950), and when Bartlett Jere Whiting published his equally invaluable dictionary of *Proverbs, Sentences, and Proverbial Phrases from English Writings Mainly Before 1500* (1968), paremiographers had assembled historical references for English proverbs ranging from the Middle Ages to the mid-twentieth century. In the 1950s the two friends Archer Taylor and Bartlett Jere Whiting decided to add an American component to this historical survey by jointly assembling *A Dictionary of American Proverbs and Proverbial Phrases, 1820–1880* (1958). And then, while Taylor busied himself with other paremiological and folkloristic projects, the avid reader Bartlett Jere Whiting came out with his important volume of *Early American Proverbs and Proverbial Phrases* (1977). A dozen years later Whiting completed the survey of American references for English-language proverbs with his large collection of *Modern Proverbs and Proverbial Sayings* (1989). Three years later my co-editors Stewart A. Kingsbury and Kelsie B. Harder and I added *A Dictionary of American Proverbs* (1992) to these volumes. Our dictionary is based on thousands of proverbs and their variants collected during 1945 to 1985 in the United States and parts of Canada, thus giving a picture of the proverbs that were in fact in oral use. Where possible, we provided historical references from the earlier volumes mentioned here. But there are certainly many proverbs in this volume that had not been registered before, taking Anglo-American paremiography a few steps further as well. And finally, Gregory Titelman's *Dictionary of Popular Proverbs & Sayings* (1996) needs to be added to this list, since he includes many historical references from the mass media of the twentieth century. It should also be noted that these valuable dictionaries, with the exception of *A Dictionary of American Proverbs,* also include proverbial expressions, proverbial comparisons, twin formulas, and at least some wellerisms.

Scholars or students seriously interested in the origin and history of an English-language proverb have thus incredible and unmatched resources at their disposal. Assuming as an example that they wish to know the origin and dissemination of the proverb "A burnt *child* dreads the fire" in English (it was loan translated into English and other languages from medieval Latin; see Singer and Liver 1995–2002: II,93), they will find a truly impressive number of historical references, albeit with some duplications:

Apperson 1929 (1969, 1993): 73: 7 references from the years 1300, 1400, 1580, 1616, 1725, 1760, 1820.

Smith 1935: no references, but in the 2nd edition of 1948: 70: 12 references from the years 1300 (twice), 1350, 1400, 1450, 1470, 1546, 1553, 1580, 1592, 1670, 1837 (no change in the 3rd edition of 1970: 92).

Tilley 1950: 96: 17 references from the years 1515, 1536, 1540, 1552, 1566, 1578, 1598, 1614, 1616 (twice), 1639, 1659, 1666, 1668, 1670, 1721, 1732.

Whiting 1968: 81: 16 references from the years 1250, 1325, 1340, 1395, 1400 (twice), 1406, 1410, 1412, 1450 (twice), 1470 (twice), 1484, 1515, 1546.

Taylor and Whiting 1958: 68: 3 references from the years 1817, 1818, 1855.

Whiting 1977: 69–70: 13 references from the years 1755, 1775 (thrice), 1777, 1781, 1787 (twice), 1815 (twice), 1816, 1817, 1844.

Whiting 1989: 110–111: 9 references from the years 1913, 1919, 1922, 1935 (twice), 1950, 1957, 1968, 1975.

Mieder, Kingsbury, and Harder 1992: 95: 6 references of variants recorded in the United States between 1945 and 1985.

Titelman 1996: 35: 5 references from the years 1250, 1546, 1755, 1913, 1984.

This is an imposing historical record of 88 references counting a few duplicates. The following citations represent some highlights, with names of authors in whose works they were located in parentheses:

1250:	Brend child fuir fordredeth. (Hendyng)
1395:	O! fy, for shame! they that han been brent, Allas! kan they nat flee the fires heete? (Chaucer)
1410:	For brent child dredith fyer. (Lydgate)
1484:	Brent chylde fyre dredeth. (Caxton)
1515:	For children brent still after drede the fire. (Barclay)
1546:	And burnt childe fyre dredth. (Heywood)
1580:	A burnt childe dreadeth the fire. (Lyly)

1614:	Burnt child fire dreades. (Camden)
1670:	The burnt child dreads the fire. (Ray)
1787:	I hope and pray our own country may have wisdom sufficient to keep herself out of the fire. I am sure she has been a sufficiently burnt child. (John Adams)
1855:	It's only the child that burns its fingers that dreads the fire. (Haliburton)
1913:	As a burnt child would recoil from fire. (Dreiser)
1935:	He's a burnt child who dreads the fire. (Gardner)
1975:	A burnt child dreads the fire. (Russell)

Just these few examples suffice to show that as with all folklore, there are variants also of folk proverbs. In this case the wording "A burnt child dreads the fire" has become the standard form. The main point is that the consulted nine proverb dictionaries supplied this information in just the time it took to find the proverb under discussion in them. And, to be sure, there are a number of other helpful Anglo-American proverb collections to round out the results (see Dent 1981 and 1984, Flavell 1993, Hazlitt 1869 [1969], Lean 1902–1904 [1969, 2000], Simpson 1982 [1998], etc.).

VARIOUS SPECIALIZED PROVERB COLLECTIONS

While the major proverb collections register as many proverbs as possible, there exist also specialized proverb dictionaries for various subject matters, as for example collections of regional proverbs, medical proverbs, weather proverbs, anti-proverbs, and so on. They too are set up according to key words or themes, and many of them are of a more popular nature. There is no need to list titles here (see "Regional and Thematic Proverb Collections" in the bibliography), but a few comments regarding their content and purpose are warranted.

It should be noted that it is extremely difficult to ascertain which proverbs might belong to a particular region of the United States (see above all Hendrickson 1992–2000). The problem is even more vexing when scholars have put forth proverb collections of particular states. Thus, when I published my small popular book *Talk Less and Say More: Vermont Proverbs* (1986), I added the following statement at the end of the introduction:

Some proverbs in this small collection like "*Vermont* has only two seasons—winter and the Fourth of July" or "It's time to plant *corn* when the icicles fall off the ledge on Snake Mountain" are obviously truly Vermont proverbs, but how about such proverbs as "*Sap* runs best after a sharp frost," "The *world* is your cow, but you have to do the milking," or "Every cider *apple* has a worm?" They sound like they originated in Vermont, but why not in New Hampshire or New York? Only through painstaking research of each individual proverb might the actual origin come to light, but for many such texts the proof of a Vermont source would be impossible. What is of importance is that many of the proverbs in the present collection probably originated among Vermonters and that the rest are without doubt current in the state of Vermont. Heeding these points, we can legitimately call the present collection "Vermont Proverbs." (Mieder 1986: 9)

What I was trying to say in this paragraph was that collections that indicate in their title that they contain texts from a particular region or state always imply the more general claim that they are known and used there, but that they did not necessarily originate at that location. It follows that regional or state collections are of considerably higher value if the proverbs were in fact collected from oral sources.

Weather proverbs also present a problem since many of them are not really bona fide proverbs in the scholarly interpretation of the proverb genre. While normal folk proverbs can be used in multiple contexts, many weather proverbs are prognostic signs and do not exhibit any metaphorical character (see Arora 1991; Dundes 1984). Their major function is to predict the weather. They are based on long observations of natural phenomena by people who couched their findings into proverbial form. Since weather proverbs usually contain prognostic statements, they have also been called predictive sayings, weather rules, and weather signs. Their intent is to establish a causal or logical relationship between two natural events that will predict the weather of the next hour, day, week, month, or even year. Little wonder that many predictive sayings follow the basic structure of "If (When) A then B," as for example in "If it *rains* before seven, it will clear by eleven," "When the *cat* in February lies in the sun, she will again creep behind the stove in March," and "If the *spring* is cold and wet, then the autumn will be hot and dry." Some of these "proverbs" are in fact superstitions, as illustrated by "When it *rains* and the sun shines, the devil is beating his grandmother." Matti Kuusi wrote a 420-page book on *Regen bei Sonnenschein* (1957) about the many variants that exist around the world of this superstition couched in proverbial language, to wit the following examples:

When it rains and the sun shines,

...foxes are on a marriage parade. (Japanese)

...the devil is getting married. (Bulgarian)

...the devil is beating his wife. (Hungarian)

...witches are doing their wash. (Polish)

...the gypsies are washing their children. (Finnish)

...a tailor is going to hell. (Danish)

...mushrooms are growing. (Russian)

...good weather is coming. (German)

...husband and wife are quarreling. (Vietnamese)

But there are also such proverbs as "Make *hay* while the sun shines," "Every *cloud* has a silver lining," "*Lightning* never strikes twice in the same place," and "*April* showers bring May flowers" that can be used figuratively even though they relate to some weather matters. In any case, not all of these weather signs can be reduced to superstitions, and modern meteorologists have gone to great lengths to prove some of the proverbial weather signs as scientifically valid (see Brunt 1946; Mieder 1996b), including the well-known predictive saying "Red *sky* at night, sailor's delight; red sky in the morning, sailor take warning." In any case, the folk and the collectors usually look at various weather expressions as proverbs (see Dunwoody 1883; Freier 1992; Garriott 1903 [1971]; Inwards 1898 [1994]; Lee 1976). Cognizant of the problems with the so-called genre of "weather proverbs," my co-editors Stewart A. and Mildred E. Kingsbury and I chose the title *Weather Wisdom: Proverbs, Superstitions, and Signs* (1996) for our annotated collection of over four thousand such sayings that were recorded in North America during the second half of the twentieth century.

While there are a number of major collections registering legal and medical proverbs in German, there are only some minor treatises of them with a few examples in English (see Bond 1936; Elmquist 1934–1935; Mieder 1991). Already Jacob Grimm had shown much interest in rules of law couched in proverbs, with the study of folk law being part of the curriculum of folklore studies at German universities. It would certainly be desirable if someone were to put together an English-language collection of such legal proverbs as "*Possession* is nine (eleven) points of the law" (see Geise 1999), "*Finders,* keepers," "*Ignorance* of the law is no excuse," "A man's *home* is his castle," and "First *come,* first served." The same holds true for medical proverbs, as for example, "Stuff a *cold* and starve a fever" (see Gallacher 1942), "One hour's *sleep* before midnight is worth three after," "Never rub your *eye* but with your elbow," "An *apple* a day keeps the doctor away," and the more recent "When you hear *hoofbeats,* think horses, not zebras" (Dundes, Streiff, and Dundes 1999). The last proverb is a medical diagnostic proverb, telling especially young physicians to look for the obvious first when trying to determine the illness of a patient. Helmut Seidl has put together at least a German-English comparative collection of medical proverbs with many annotations with the title of *Medizinische Sprichwörter im Englischen und Deutschen* (1982). There are also E.U.C. Ezejideaku's paper on "Disability and the Disabled in Igbo Proverbs" (2003) and Yisa Kehinde Yusuf's and Joyce T. Methangwane's study on "Proverbs and HIV/AIDS" (2003) that show how proverbs are used to describe and combat illnesses. Of course, many other specialized collections could follow on other subjects. There are plenty of small collections of proverbs on love, animals, plants, the sea, and so on. There are also two major treatises with hundreds of proverbs about women (see Kerschen 1998; Rittersbacher 2002), many of them unfortunately of a misogynist nature, to wit "A woman's *tongue* wags like a lamb's tail" from the sixteenth century or "*Diamonds* are a girl's best friend" of newer twentieth-century vintage. Little wonder that feminists created the slogan turned proverb "A *woman* without a man is like a fish without a bicycle" during the 1970s to combat such gender stereotyping.

Of late, paremiographers have also delighted in putting together collections of so-called anti-proverbs, that is, parodied, twisted, or fractured proverbs that reveal humorous or satirical speech play with traditional proverbial wisdom (see Mieder and Litovkina 1999; Mieder 2003). For example, the proverb "A *fool* and his money are soon parted" has resulted in such anti-proverbs as "A fool and his father's money are soon parted," "A fool and his money are soon popular," "A fool and his money stabilize the economy," "A fool and his wife are soon parted," "A married man and his money are soon parted," "A widow and her money are soon courted," "If a fool and his money are soon parted, why are there so many rich fools?," and "There was a time when a fool and his money were soon parted, but now it happens to everybody" (Mieder 2003: 33). As can be seen, anti-proverbs often follow the structure of the original proverb while changing some of the individual words. At other times the wisdom of the proverb is put into question by adding a contradictory phrase beginning with the conjunction "but." Of course, it is the juxtaposition of the traditional proverb with the innovative anti-proverb that makes these puns so effective. The anti-proverbs also indicate clearly that the structure and wording of proverbs are by no means sacrosanct. The fixity of proverbs is not as rigid as it once was believed to be. Unintentional variants have always existed in as much as proverbs are part of folklore, but intentional variations have also been part of the use and function of proverbs, both oral and written. And yet, more often than not proverbs are cited in their standard traditional form to add some common sense to human communication.

SELECTED BIBLIOGRAPHY

Collections and book-length studies are listed in the major bibliography at the end of this book. Cross-references at the ends of entries correspond to collections listed in the bibliography.

Arora, Shirley L. 1984. "The Perception of Proverbiality." *Proverbium* 1: 1–38; also in Mieder 1994: 3–29.

———. 1991. "Weather Proverbs: Some 'Folk' Views." *Proverbium* 8: 1–17.

Baer, Florence E. 1983. "Wellerisms in *The Pickwick Papers.*" *Folklore* (London) 94: 173–183.

Barley, Nigel. 1974. "'The Proverb' and Related Problems of Genre-Definition." *Proverbium,* no. 23: 880–884.

Barrick, Mac E. 1979. "'Better Red than Dead.'" *American Notes & Queries* 17: 143–44.

Blehr, Otto. 1973. "What is a Proverb?" *Fabula* 14: 243–246.

Bond, Donald F. 1936. "English Legal Proverbs." *Publications of the Modern Language Association* 51: 921–935.

Brunt, D. 1946. "Meteorology and Weather Lore." *Folklore* (London) 57: 66–74.

Burke, Kenneth. 1941. "Literature [i.e., proverbs] as Equipment for Living." In *The Philosophy of Literary Form: Studies in Symbolic Action,* by K. Burke, 253–262. Baton Rouge: Louisiana State University Press.

Doyle, Charles Clay. 1996. "On 'New' Proverbs and the Conservativeness of Proverb Dictionaries." *Proverbium* 13: 69–84; also in Mieder 2003: 85–98.

Dundes, Alan. 1975. "On the Structure of the Proverb." *Proverbium,* no. 25: 961–973; also in Mieder and Dundes 1981 [1984]: 43–64.

———. 1984 (1989). "On Whether Weather 'Proverbs' are Proverbs." *Proverbium* 1: 39–46; also in A. Dundes. *Folklore Matters,* 92–97. Knoxville: University of Tennessee Press.

Dundes, Lauren, Michael D. Streiff, and Alan Dundes. 1999. "'When You Hear Hoofbeats, Think Horses, not Zebras': A Folk Medical Diagnostic Proverb." *Proverbium* 16: 95–103; also in Mieder 2003: 99–107.

Elmquist, Russell A. 1934–1935. "English Medical Proverbs." *Modern Philology* 32: 75–84.

Ezejideaku, E.U.C. 2003. "Disability and the Disabled in Igbo Proverbs." *Proverbium* 20: 159–169.

Gallacher, Stuart A. 1942. "'Stuff a Cold and Starve a Fever.'" *Bulletin of the History of Medicine* 11: 576–581; also in Mieder and Dundes 1981 (1994): 211–217.

———. 1959. "Frauenlob's Bits of Wisdom: Fruits of His Environment." In *Middle Ages, Reformation, Volkskunde. Festschrift for John G. Kunstmann,* no editor given, 45–58. Chapel Hill: University of North Carolina Press.

Geise, Nancy Magnuson. 1999. "'Possession is Nine-Tenths of the Law': History and Meaning of a Legal Proverb." *Proverbium* 16: 105–124.

Grzybek, Peter. 1987. "Foundations of Semiotic Proverb Study." *Proverbium* 4: 39–85.

Hasan-Rokem, Galit. 1990. "The Aesthetics of the Proverb: Dialogue of Discourses from Genesis to Glasnost." *Proverbium* 7: 105–116.

Honeck, Richard P., and Jeffrey Welge. 1997. "Creation of Proverbial Wisdom in the Laboratory." *Journal of Psycholinguistic Research* 26: 605–629; also in Mieder 2003: 205–230.

Kindstrand, Jan Fredrik. 1978. "The Greek Concept of Proverbs." *Eranos* 76: 71–85; also in Carnes 1988: 233–253.

Kirshenblatt-Gimblett, Barbara. 1973. "Toward a Theory of Proverb Meaning." *Proverbium,* no. 22: 821–827; also in Mieder and Dundes 1981 [1994]: 111–121.

Krikmann, Arvo. 1974a (1984). *On Denotative Indefiniteness of Proverbs.* Tallinn, Estonia: Academy of Sciences of the Estonian SST, Institute of Language and Literature; also in *Proverbium* 1: 47–91.

———. 1974b (1985). *Some Additional Aspects of Semantic Indefiniteness of Proverbs.* Tallinn, Estonia: Academy of Sciences of the Estonian SST, Institute of Language and Literature; also in *Proverbium* 2: 58–85.

Mieder, Wolfgang. 1985. "Popular Views of the Proverb." *Proverbium* 2: 109–143; also in Mieder 1993: 18–40.

———. 1990. "Prolegomena to Prospective Paremiography." *Proverbium* 7: 133–144.

———. 1991. "'An Apple a Day Keeps the Doctor Away': Traditional and Modern Aspects of Medical Proverbs." *Proverbium* 8: 77–106; also in Mieder 1993: 152–172.

———. 1996a. "Proverbs." In *American Folklore: An Encyclopedia,* ed. by Jan Harold Brunvand, 597–601. New York: Garland Publishing.

———. 1996b. "Proverbs." In *Encyclopedia of Climate and Weather,* ed. by Stephen H. Schneider, II, 617–621. New York: Oxford University Press.

———. 2000. "The History and Future of Common Proverbs in Europe." In *Folklore in 2000. Voces amicorum Guilhelmo Voigt sexagenario,* ed. by Ilona Nagy and Kincso Verebélyi, 300–314. Budapest: Universitas Scientiarum de Rolando Eötvös.

———. 2001 (2002). "'Like Father, Like Daughter'—A Joint Paremiological Accomplishment." *FF [Folklore Fellows] Network* 22: 16–21; also in *Proverbium* 19: 427–438.

Milner, George. 1971. "The Quartered Shield: Outline of a Semantic Taxonomy [of Proverbs]." In *Social Anthropology and Language,* ed. by Edwin Ardener, 243–269. London: Tavistock.

Russo, Joseph. 1983. "The Poetics of the Ancient Greek Proverb." *Journal of Folklore Research* 20: 121–130.

Seitel, Peter. 1969. "Proverbs: A Social Use of Metaphor." *Genre* 2: 143–161; also in Mieder and Dundes 1981 [1994]: 122–139.

Whiting, Bartlett Jere. 1932. "The Nature of the Proverb." *Harvard Studies and Notes in Philology and Literature* 14: 273–307; also in Whiting 1994: 51–85.

Winick, Stephen D. 2003. "Intertextuality and Innovation in a Definition of the Proverb Genre." In *Cognition, Comprehension, and Communication: A Decade of North American Proverb Studies (1990–2000),* ed. by Wolfgang Mieder, 571–601. Baltmannsweiler, Germany: Schneider Verlag Hohengehren.

Yusuf, Yisa Kehinde, and Joyce T. Methangwane. 2003. "Proverbs and HIV/AIDS." *Proverbium* 20: 407–422.

Zholkovskii, Alexandr K. 1978. "At the Intersection of Linguistics, Paremiology and Poetics: On the Literary Structure of Proverbs." *Poetics* 7: 309–322.

Two
Examples and Texts

This section is once again divided into two major parts. The first consists of six case studies to illustrate the ways of investigating the origin, history, meaning, and function of individual proverbs. The first case study looks at the classical proverb "Big *fish* eat little fish," which exists in many languages and continues to be very much used in English as well. The second study analyzes the medieval legal proverb "First *come*, first served," which had its origin in the world of millers and farmers. Some additional proverbs and proverbial expressions are looked at as well to show how the miller profession gave rise to them. The third study traces the path of the sixteenth-century German proverb "Der *Apfel* fällt nicht weit vom Stamm" (The *apple* doesn't fall far from the tree) from Europe to the United States. The fourth study looks at the American stereotypical proverb "The only good *Indian* is a dead Indian," also indicating that its basic structure has been used to create invectives against other ethnic groups. The fifth study investigates the inherent ambiguity of the nineteenth-century American proverb "Good *fences* make good neighbors," showing its importance both on the personal and international level. And finally, the sixth study brings to light how the twentieth-century American proverb "A *picture* is worth a thousand words" is a clear expression of the modern visually oriented age.

As the attached selected bibliography indicates, I have published major studies on these six proverbs in previous years. They are up to 50 printed pages in length and contain many more historical references as well as dozens of notes and bibliographical details that cannot possibly be included here. I am simply presenting significantly shortened versions without any references. They are meant to tell intriguing stories, leaving the many pages of annotations to my previous publications where they can easily be found.

The second part of this section presents a small florilegium of foreign, American, regional, and ethnic proverbs. While it is not possible to include large selections of proverbs in this book, several representative lists have been assembled from various standard collections to let readers get a feeling for the different metaphorical expressions of wisdom from various cultures and languages of the world. They are cited in English translation only, but it is no problem to find them in their original languages in many of the bilingual proverb collections listed in the bibliography at the end of this book. A small collection of English-language proverbs that have been coined in the United States is also provided. Two samples of proverbs in regional use in Vermont and Texas (together with some Mexican American proverbs) are included as well, and so are two sets of Native American and African American proverbs to illustrate the unique proverb lore of these minorities. It was difficult to decide which linguistic groups should be represented. After much thought, I decided on African, Arabic, Chinese, German, Indian, Irish (Gaelic), Italian, Japanese, Russian, Spanish (Mexican), and Yiddish proverbs because large immigrant waves brought native speakers of these languages to the United States over the years. Regarding various minorities, it seems appropriate to cite examples from the meager number of recorded proverbs of the Native Americans and from the rich proverb tradition of African Americans. There is one caveat to keep in mind when reading through these lists. Again and again attempts have been made to delineate a particular worldview or even national character from lists of proverbs. This is a dangerous undertaking, since such generalizations are often based on just a small number of texts (see Robinson 1945; Nicolaisen 1994). The examples listed here are not intended to say anything in particular about the nationalities or minorities under consideration. The proverbs are simply cited to indicate the wealth of different metaphorical proverbs in the world. When the proverbial push comes to shove, the wisdom expressed in proverbs is actually quite similar from culture to culture. That is why so many proverbs have found a wide distribution beyond national borders and why there are so many equivalent proverbs that might have different images and structures, but that mean the same thing!

"BIG FISH EAT LITTLE FISH": A CLASSICAL PROVERB ABOUT HUMAN NATURE

The proverb "Big fish eat little fish" is one of the oldest international proverbs, whose origin can be traced back to the earliest written documents of antiquity. The first recorded allusion to the proverb appears in the didactic poem *Works and Days* by the Greek writer Hesiod of the eighth century B.C.:

"Fish and beasts of the wild and birds that fly in the air eat one another, since justice has no dwelling among them." What differentiates humans from this unruly animal world is justice or a sound government, for without it anarchy would rule supreme as one learns from the Sanskrit epic *Mahabharata:* "Men, in days of old, in consequence of anarchy, met with destruction, devouring one another like stronger fishes devouring the weaker ones in the water." Without the control of government the stronger or rich will prey on the weaker or poor, and this fish-like behavior of the survival of the fittest will prevail. The same thought is also expressed by the Hebrew prophet Habakkuk in the Old Testament when he asks God "why dost thou look on faithless men, and art silent when the wicked swallow up the man more righteous than he? For thou makest men like the fish of the sea, like crawling things that have no ruler" (Hab. 1:13–14). The Babylonian Talmud from about 450 B.C. includes the following explanation of this passage in the *Abodah Zarah* tractate: "Just as among fish of the sea, the greater swallow up the smaller ones, so with men, were it not for fear of the government, men would swallow each other alive."

From these early textual references it becomes obvious that this fish metaphor is part of a common tradition of the Indo-European people. The step from a vivid metaphor about human nature to a precise metaphorical proverb must have taken place once people wanted to express its basic meaning in a concise and repeatable way. By the time of Aristotle in the fourth century B.C. the actual proverb was well established, as can be seen from his simple statement: "There is war between the larger and the lesser fishes: for the big fishes prey on the little ones." Once solidly established in the Greek language, it was loan translated into Latin as well. The Roman scholar and writer Varro, for example, employed the proverb in its social meaning with an underlying moralistic tone in the first century B.C.: "Qui pote, plus urget, piscis ut saepe minutas magna comest" (He who is strongest, oppresses, as the great fish often eats the lesser). Eventually the common Latin text became "Piscem vorat maior minorem" (The larger fish eats the smaller fish), and it survived in this standard form until the Latin of the Middle Ages.

In addition to the appearance of Greek and Latin references of the proverb in secular literature and medieval Latin proverb collections, there was also a considerable influence that the early church fathers had on the dissemination of the proverb. St. Basil shows in his writings during the fourth century A.D. that men act like fish primarily out of avarice or greed coupled with the lust for power: "The greater number of the fishes devour one another and the smaller among them is the food of the greater. And if it ever happens that one which has overcome a lesser becomes the prey of a still greater, then both go into the belly of the last one." And a few decades later, St. Augustine echoes these sentiments as well: "The sea is said to be the world, bitter with salt, tossed by tempests, where men through their perverse and evil lusts become like the fishes devouring each other [...] and when one bigger fish has devoured a lesser, he is also devoured by a bigger still."

Of importance for the appearance of the classical proverb in so many modern European languages is also the allusion to it in the Latin pseudo-scientific bestiary *Physiologus* from around A.D. 200 that was translated into all major European languages. In the tale concerning the whale it is pointed out that "when he grows hungry he opens his mouth very wide and many a good fragrance comes out of his mouth. Tiny little fish, catching the scent, follow it and gather together in the mouth of that huge whale, who closes his mouth when it is full and swallows all those tiny fish." In added religious comments the whale is seen to be evil (the devil himself), and he tricks the smaller fish (the sinners) by his sweet breath (cunning) into his mouth (damnation or death). Thus the fish appear to be swimming voluntarily into the beast's mouth since they are attracted by the sweet-smelling monster. Two splendid illustrations from a *Physiologus* manuscript of the twelfth century show this most clearly. In later illustrations right up to modern cartoons one can see small fish entering the big fish's mouth headfirst, which might be interpreted as a sign of deception or "stupidity." Other small fish will definitely be pursued by the big fish, symbolizing an involuntary capture by an aggressive and stronger rival.

Realizing that this fish metaphor was known to people of the Middle Ages through secular, patristic, and biblical literature as well as through the extremely popular *Physiologus,* it is not surprising that the Latin proverb "Piscem vorat maior mionorem" could catch on quickly in the vernacular languages once it was used for translation purposes in the monastery schools. The first English appearance of the proverb is in an old English homily on St. Andrew from the twelfth century that first quotes the Latin text and then adds the loan translation to it: "In mari piscem maiores deuorant minores. Est—sone the more fishes in the se eten the lasse." The religious writer of this text also interprets the meaning of the proverb with a particular emphasis on the dichotomy of rich and poor: "The greater fishes in the sea eat the smaller and live on them. So in this world do the rich who are lords, destroy the poor men who are underlings, and moreover live on them and obtain from their labors all that they possess." Two centuries later John Wycliffe repeats that "as the greet fishes eeten the smale, so mighti riche men of this world deuouren the pore." John Lydgate cites the proverb repeatedly in his writings of the first half of the fifteenth century, commenting explicitly on the oppression that occurs among animals as well as humankind in *A Disputation between a Horse, a Sheepe and a Goose for Superioritie* (1440):

> Man, best, & fowle & fisshis been opressid
> In ther natur bi female or bi male;
> Of grettest fissh devourid been the smale.

Sixty years later Alexander Barclay addresses the conflict between rich and poor in the chapter "Of ryches vnprofytable" in his *Ship of Fools* (1509), comparing the greed of the rich with the way the wolf eats sheep. This unfair behavior also brings to mind the "fish" proverb:

> He that nought hathe, shall so alway byde pore
> But he that ouer moche hath, yet shall haue more
> The wolfe etis the shepe, the great fysshe the small.

And by 1578 the proverb appears as "The great fishe eateth the little" in John Florio's proverb collection *Firste Fruites: which yeelde familiar speech, merie Prouerbes, wittie Sentences, and golden sayings.*

Having presented a somewhat superficial literary history of the proverb well into the sixteenth century, it must also be mentioned that there exists a parallel iconographic history of the proverb attesting to its currency and popularity. Two English misericords of the fifteenth century show a big fish (whale) that swallows a smaller fish headfirst, bringing to mind the *Physiologus* tale and its illustrations. Later in the fifteenth century Hieronymus Bosch illustrated the "Big fish eat little fish" motif repeatedly in small scenes of three of his grotesque pictures. In the center panel of *The Garden of Earthly Delights* (1500) he too has a large fish (whale) swallowing up a smaller one headfirst. In context of the whole picture this scene signifies that the Epicurean small fish (the sinner searching for earthly pleasures) will be damned and go to the hell of the devil represented by the whale. At least as grotesque is another fish scene that Bosch included in the left panel of his famous painting *The Temptation of Saint Anthony* (1500). Here the giant fish has grasshopper legs, a church seems to ride on its back, and it even has a wheel in the form of a shield (war) for propulsion. Since the beast is also swallowing a fish, this scene might be referring to the devilish greed of the world, which includes the rapacity of the church and which will clearly lead to war, devastation, and anarchy. But a third scene in the right panel of Bosch's *The Hay Wain* (1485) is even more direct in its social satire. The entire picture illustrates the biblical proverb "All *flesh* is grass" (Isa. 40:6; 1 Pet. 1:24), thereby showing the transitory nature of life. Once again there is a fish-like monster, but this time it has human legs and a man is being devoured headfirst.

The artist who continued Bosch's satirical view of the world in the sixteenth century was Pieter Bruegel the Elder who included a simple realistic scene of a big fish eating a little fish headfirst in his celebrated oil painting *Netherlandish Proverbs* from 1559. An illustration of a stranded whale with a fish in its mouth appears as a detail in Bruegel's *The Triumph of Death* (c. 1562). Here death is the final winner as can be seen in some of the early English literary texts as well. But there is also a much more important and influential drawing by Pieter Bruegel executed in pen and gray ink in 1556 and reproduced in 1557 as a mirror image copperplate engraving by Pieter van der Heyden with the addition of Latin and Dutch captions: "Grandibvs exigvi svnt pisces piscibvs esca. Siet sone dit hebbe ick zeer langhe ghiweten dat die groote bissen de clejne" (The small fish are eaten by the big fish. See son, this I have known for a very long time, that the great [fish] bite the small). The picture shows the world upside-down as can be seen immediately from the soldier-like figure in the center, which is sawing open the large stranded fish by holding the grotesque saw upside-down. Devouring of smaller fish is

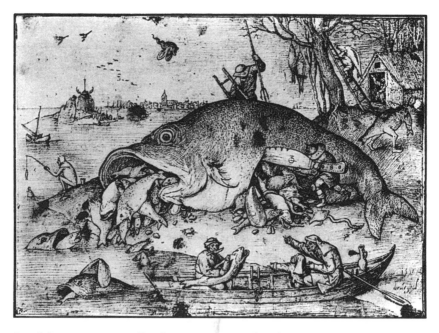

Cited from Max J. Friedländer, *Pieter Bruegel.* Berlin: Propyläen Verlag, 1921, plate 32.

going on everywhere, indicating that the world knows no law and order and that anarchy rules supreme. The absolute chaos is also shown by the fact that the fish are being swallowed with their heads first, sideways (an impossibility), and tail first. It is a world of violence, threat, doom, and death. Everybody wants to live, prosper, and exert power over the other, including even a fantastic fish-like monster flying through the skies with a gaping mouth. The oppressor who victimizes the small, weak, and poor becomes the victim, and this unceasing chain reaction is splendidly illustrated in a small scene of the right bottom corner, where a big fish has a smaller one by its tail which in turn has clasped its jaws around a smaller fish yet.

The engraving from 1557 with its many reproductions was part of a popular satirical and didactic print media during the sixteenth and seventeenth centuries, and it is well possible that William Shakespeare might have had one of them in front of him when he wrote the following lines in *Pericles* (1608):

Third Fisherman: Master, I marvel how the fishes live in the sea?
First Fisherman: Why, as men do a-land,—the great ones eat up the little ones: I can compare our rich misers to nothing so fitly as to a whale; he plays and tumbles, driving the poor fry before him, and at last devours them all at a mouthful: such whales have I heard all over the land, who never leave gaping till they've swallowed the whole parish, church, steeple, bells and all.
Pericles: [aside] How from the finny subject of the sea
These fishers tell th' infirmities of men;
And from their watery empire recollect
All that may men approve or men detect!
(*Pericles,* act 2, scene 1)

But one need not look far to find literature and art joining forces in the emblematic publications of the early seventeenth century. The German Joachim Camerarius presents a round emblem in 1604 showing a singular fish eating a smaller one of its own kind. Another German emblem by Peter Isselburg from 1617 again shows a sea monster devouring a fish headfirst, and there is also an emblem from 1660 by the Spaniard Sebastián de Covarrubias Orozco that depicts a giant fish once again swallowing up a smaller one headfirst. It is little wonder that this motif gained such popularity in the seventeenth century. War, might, and oppression were rampant in Europe, and one is justified to look at these emblems as sociopolitical statements. They are satirical caricatures of sorts without attacking any person in particular. The proverb and its emblematic illustration permitted the artists to express their interpretations of the human condition in an indirect but still comprehensible fashion. Such indirect criticism of the politics of the day couched in the language of natural phenomena most certainly was an effective way to vent frustrations and to moralize and teach at the same time. This can be seen from an Italian drawing from 1678 by Giuseppe Maria Mitelli, who illustrated the Italian variant of the proverb "Il pesce grosso mangia il minuto" (The big fish eats the little). Just as in the Bruegel drawing, an old man is teaching a young boy about the nature of things. But while the fish in the emblems show the inevitability of their fate by swimming towards the monster, in this picture the smaller fish try to swim away, that is, they try to flee from the stronger who is temporarily hampered in its cruel ways by having caught a fish sideways. Too much greed does have its trouble too, and even the big fish is not always absolutely successful in its evil schemes.

But the seventeenth century also provides the first American references of the proverb. Roger Williams, the founder of Rhode Island, in his treatise on *The Blovdy Tenent, of Persecution, for Cause of Conscience, discussed in A Conference betweene Trvth and Peace* (1644) presents an interpretation of the proverb that goes right back to the prophet Habakkuk. He has "Truth" exclaim how good it would be if everybody were free from the persecutions of the fish, who clearly represent a chaotic political situation:

> *Habacucks* Fishes keep their constant bloody game of *Persecutions* in the Worlds mighty *Ocean;* the greater taking, plundring, swallowing up the lesser: O happy he whose portion is the *God* of *Iacob!* who hath nothing to lose under the *Sun,* but hath a *State,* a *House,* an *Inheritance,* a *Name,* a *Crowne,* a *Life,* past all the *Plunderers, Ravishers, Murtherers* reach and furie!

Such political considerations are echoed some 50 years later in William Penn's *Essay Towards the Present and Future Peace of Europe* (1693), in which he outlines a sort of confederation among the national entities that might finally bring an end to their strifes and wars: "The sovereignties are as they were, for none of them have now any sovereignty over one another; and if this be called a lessening of their power, it must be only because the great fish can no longer eat up the little ones and that each sovereignty is equally defended from injuries and disabled from committing them."

Almost a hundred years later, John Adams wrote in a letter of December 12, 1785, that he was distressed by avarice in the loan of money, somewhat reminding readers today of the modern term "loan shark": "While such Interest can be obtained, much Property will be diverted from Trade. But this must have an End. The great Fish will have eaten all the little ones, and then they must look out for other Prey." His wife Abigail Adams, one of the brightest women of revolutionary times in America, had already written to her husband on November 27, 1775, in a more general sense that the nature of humankind has barely evolved from that of the fish world:

> I am more and more convinced that Man is a dangerous creature, and that power whether vested in many or a few is ever grasping, and like the grave cries give, give. The great fish swallow up the small, and he who is most strenuous for the Rights of the people, when vested with power, is as eager after the prerogatives of Government. You tell me of degrees of perfection to which Humane Nature is capable of arriving, and I believe it, but at the same time lament that our admiration should arise from the scarcity of the instances.

This somewhat fatalistic view that the logic of the fish will always be here continued into the nineteenth century and beyond. In a Thanksgiving Day sermon preached in Boston on November 28, 1850, by the abolitionist Theodore Parker, the proverb appears in an argument for morality, solid work ethics, and a fair and just government to prevent the young American nation from falling prey to stronger fish in the ocean of civilization: "Do you know how empires find their end? Yes, the great States eat up the little. As with fish, so with nations. Aye, but how do the great States come to an end? By their own injustice, and no other cause. They would make unrighteousness their law, and God wills not that it be so. Thus they fall; thus they die."

It is exactly this nagging question of why life has to be like this that characterizes the many occurrences of the proverb in modern times. For the most part its written or pictorial uses continue the fatalistic tradition that the bigger and stronger will always take advantage of the smaller and weaker. In an alienating satirical text entitled *If the Sharks Were Humans* (1930) Bertolt Brecht shows this by indirectly writing about Germany's move toward National Socialism. He clearly states that sharks as humans would be much worse than normal sharks since they would go about their destructive business of annihilating others in an ordered and carefully planned way: welfare, education, politics, culture, and religion would all be structured so as to be in absolute control of a few big fish. The entire society would consist of a carefully orchestrated process of creating small and meek fish that could easily be controlled or devoured if they were to step out of line. Brecht wrote his apocalyptic text in the subjunctive, but history showed that Germany under Nazi rule lived by the logic of the fish, and the proverb, which is never directly stated by Brecht, fits precisely a description of a dictatorship of fear, oppression, cruelty, and murder:

> [...] If the sharks were humans, they would teach little fish how to swim into the jaws of the sharks. [...] If the sharks were humans, they would of course carry on wars with one another. [...] The theaters on the ocean's floor would show how courageous little fish would swim enthusiastically into the jaws of the sharks, and the music would be so wonderful that the little fish would rush dreamily into the jaws of the sharks. There would also be a religion, if the sharks were humans. It would teach that the little fish would only begin to live properly in the bellies of the sharks. Moreover, there would also be an end to equality of all the little fish if the sharks were humans. Some of them would receive offices and would be placed above others. Those who were a bit larger would even be allowed to devour the smaller ones. That would of course be pleasant for the sharks since they themselves would then get larger pieces to devour.

And how are things in the socio-political situation of the world today? Has Brecht's prophetic vision become obsolete? Judging by the appearance of literally dozens of illustrations of various interpretations of the proverb in caricatures, cartoons, and advertisements of the mass media, one certainly gets the feeling that it is still very much a world of "Big fish eat little fish."

References of such reinterpretations of the classical "fish" proverb can be found in newspapers and magazines throughout the world. Some are extremely satirical and cynical, others are full of irony or even humor, but such are the reactions of modern people who so much would like to break out of this endless chain reaction of rapacity of all kinds. The pictorial representations of the proverb in the mass media can basically be divided into five groups:

1. One large fish randomly pursuing several smaller ones who are trying to flee, that is, the aggressor preys on the weaker. Involuntary takeovers (merger mania) in the business world is a frequent motif.

2. A big fish planning to devour one small fish, making the aggressive nature of the beast even more drastic. Again, the business world is depicted in this way, when one large company swallows up a smaller one. The metaphor also fits political situations when a large country overpowers a smaller one.

3. A sequence of three or more fish trying to swallow each other, indicating through this chain of successive incorporations the strategy of the survival of

the fittest. Spiraling inflation, the relationship of wages and prices, the class struggle, and minority issues have been depicted by such fish chains.

4. A vicious circle of fish of the same size trying to devour each other, showing perhaps the futility of this constant rapacity. Multiple takeover attempts by equally strong companies have been illustrated by such circular fish groups.

5. The attempt of little fish ganging up on the larger fish, showing the importance of solidarity and illustrating perhaps yet another classical proverb: "In union is strength." A number of cartoons show such "solidarity" fish, and there is also the children's book *Swimmy* (1963) by Leo Lionni, showing children that working together might overcome any powerful opponent. The problem is that the "collective" fish turns into a large fish and dominates others once again.

In conclusion it can be stated that the fatalistic proverb "Big fish eat little fish" contains wisdom that has been recognized in the world for many centuries and that still holds true today. Even the symbolic inversion of this proverbial law in some texts and illustrations seems only momentarily able to liberate humankind from its basic and unfortunate truth about human nature. Everyone might wish that the proverb "Big fish eat little fish" would be rendered obsolete, but that would assume that humankind has become more humane at last. Judging by the recorded history of this proverb, which spans almost three thousand years, nothing really has changed at all. Rapacity is as rampant as ever, and although the large perpetrators might take on ever new shapes, the metaphorical proverb "Big fish eat little fish" will always be a most fitting description of this unfortunate situation.

"FIRST COME, FIRST SERVED": A MEDIEVAL LEGAL PROVERB FROM THE MILLERS

Proverbs from all nations contain much wisdom based on trades and occupations, and the venerable profession of milling is no exception. Mills driven by water were in use during classical antiquity, and windmills have been recorded since the very early Middle Ages. They clearly occupied a central role in mercantile life for centuries, and because of their common appearance in villages and cities, the folk began to generalize their observations and experiences relating to millers and their mills into colorful metaphors. There exist literally dozens of such proverbs, proverbial expressions, and proverbial comparisons based on the milling trade in many languages and cultures. Although some of them date back to ancient times and even though the traditional life of millers and mills has basically been replaced by modern machines, some of the proverbial wisdom remains in common use today. People use this old formulaic language without necessarily understanding the precise meaning of the metaphors dealing with the vanished water- or wind-driven mills and their traditional millers. The old phrases have become linguistic relics of sorts, and while many have indeed gone out of use, there are those that hang on and that people of the modern age would not want to miss.

This certainly is the case with that ever present elliptic proverb "First come, first served," which belongs to one of the most popular proverbs today. But this somewhat colorless piece of folk wisdom actually had its origin in the world of milling, as can be seen from Geoffrey Chaucer's longer version in his *The Wife of Bath's Prologue* (c. 1386): "Whoso that first to *mille* comth, first grynt" (389). About one hundred years later the *Paston Letters* (c. 1475) contain the reference "For who comyth fyrst to the *mylle,* fyrst must grynd." But another hundred years later Henry Porter in his *Two Angry Women of Abington* (1599) already cites the truncated version "So, first come, first seru'd." For the next three centuries the longer version referring to grinding at the mill continued to compete with the shorter more general rule. From 1616 stems the variant "He that first putteth his *corne* into the mill-hopper, is first served"; from 1659 the three variants "The first that brings in *grist,* let him grind," "Who is first at the *mill* let him grind," and "First come to the *mill* first grinde"; and from 1666 "Who first goes to the *mill,* first grindes." Both the longer variants and the shortened proverb "First come, first served" expressed the legal concept that whoever arrived first has the right to be taken care of first. But with mills disappearing from the landscape, the longer proverb variants have by now vanished from general parlance, and hardly anybody is aware anymore that the proverb "First come, first served" is in fact a legal proverb based on the customary law of grinding that person's grain first who is first in line at the mill.

And it should be noted that this mill law is common throughout the European languages. It goes back to medieval Latin records, where the proverb appears in various wordings. The following three medieval Latin variants clearly indicate the legal nature of the old proverb by using such words as right and rightfully (law and lawfully):

Qui capit ane molam, merito molit ante farinam. (Whoever arrives first at the mill, rightfully grinds his flour first)

Ante de iure molit, molam qui prius adivit. (He by right grinds first, who first came to the mill)

Iure, molendinum qui tardus adit, molet imum. (Rightfully he grinds last, who came late to the mill)

But notice in two additional medieval Latin references how the legal implications of the proverb are not expressed as explicitly any longer:

> Qui ad molendinum prior venit, prius molit. (Whoever comes to the mill first, grinds first)
> Qui cicius venerit, cicius molit. (Whoever comes earlier, grinds earlier)

When Erasmus of Rotterdam cited the proverb in Latin as "Qui primus venerit, primus molet" (Whoever has come first, will grind first) in his *Adagia* (1500ff.), he also dropped the direct legal associations and any allusion to a mill, thus making the proverb a more general behavioral rule. The many translations of his *Adagia* proverb collection helped to spread this fascinating proverb from language to language through the process of loan translations.

Interestingly enough, however, many European languages have maintained the proverb's association with milling that has been lost in the truncated English version of "First come, first served." For example:

French:	Qui premier vient au moulin, premier doit mouldre. (Whoever comes first to the mill, should grind first)
Italian:	Chi prima giógne, prima macini. (Who arrives first, should grind first)
Spanish:	Quien primero viene, primero muele. (Who comes first, grinds first)
Dutch:	Die eerst ter molen comt sal eerst malen. (Who comes to the mill first, shall grind first)

The Swedish scholar Sven Ek has even written an entire monograph on *Den som kommer först till kvarns—ett ordsprak och dess bakgrund* (1964), treating many variants of the Swedish proverb "Den som kommer först till kvarnen far först mala" (Who comes first to the mill grinds first) and showing how the proverb fits into the historical and cultural setting of grain mills.

The German dialect proverbs also very explicitly state "Wer zuerst auf der Mühle ist, der kriegt auch zuerst gemahlen" (He who gets to the mill first, gets his grain ground first). But while such texts from rural areas maintain the mill metaphor as part of traditional life, the standard German version is less explicit: "Wer zuerst kommt, mahlt zuerst" (He who comes first, grinds first). Many young Germans have no idea what is meant by "first grinding," since they do not think of mills and grain. It is conceivable therefore that this German text might in time be changed to "Wer zuerst kommt, kommt zuerst dran" (He who comes first, gets served first), thereby following the pattern of the English history of this medieval legal proverb based on the miller profes-

Cited from Betty Fraser, *First Things First. An Illustrated Collection of Sayings Useful and Familiar for Children.* New York: Harper & Row, 1990, no page numbers.

sion. In any case, examples of the longer mill proverb can be found in many Germanic and Romance languages today, but in English it has been lost and has become a very general and barely metaphorical rule of conduct.

But while the proverb "First come, first served" is very much in use today, there is a second early English proverb to be found in the prologue of Chaucer's *Canterbury Tales* (c. 1386) that has disappeared and is incomprehensible without any historical and cultural explanation: "Wel coude he stelen corn and tollen thries, / And yet he hadde a thombe of gold." The "tollen thries" refers to the miller who takes his toll three times, and the "thombe of gold" is an old jibe directed against a merchant keeping his thumb on the scales when weighing something. The actual proverb is the ironic "An honest *miller* has a thumb of gold," meaning that millers always cheat. Here is the way Chaucer describes such a stereotypical miller in the "Prologue" to the *Canterbury Tales* around 1386:

The Miller

The miller was a stout churl, be it known,
Hardy and big of brawn and big of bone;
Which was well proved, for when he went on lam
At wrestling, never failed he of the ram [prize].
He was a chunky fellow, broad of build;
He'd heave a door from hinges if he willed,
Or break it through, by running, with his head.
His beard, as any sow or fox, was red,
And broad it was as if it were a spade.
Upon the coping of his nose he had
A wart, and thereon stood a tuft of hairs,
Red as the bristles in an old sow's ears;
His nostrils they were black and very wide.
A sword and buckler bore he by his side.
His mouth was like a furnace door for size.
He was a jester and could poetize,
But mostly all of sin and ribaldries.
He could steal corn and full thrice charge his fees;
And yet he had a thumb of gold, begad.
A white coat and blue hood he wore, this lad.
A bagpipe he could blow well, be it known,
And with that same he brought us out of town.

(Prologue, 545–566)

This description reduces the miller to a Judas-like deceiver with his red beard, black nostrils, furnace-like mouth and chunky as well as broad body frame. And one might well ask why the miller and his honorable profession deserve such a prejudicial characterization? For the most part it must have been a psychological reaction by customers who felt very much dependent on the miller. They needed him to get their grain ground, and they wanted the most meal and as quickly as possible from their grain. This placed them in the controlling hands of the miller. In fact, they were actually at his mercy, and they projected their fears and anxieties of being controlled and perhaps cheated upon this tradesman. The proverb "An honest miller has a thumb of gold" is thus a bit of folkloric and behavioral indirection by farmers upon the millers, but doubtlessly there were millers who did in fact cheat their customers as best they could. Thus the proverb relates to problems of deception and mistrust among members of two very basic professions.

A short poem by Nicholas Breton from the year 1614 shows all of this quite clearly, indicating one more time how the folk saw the role of the miller whose broad thumb influenced the weight scales to his own advantage and to the detriment of his customers:

> I would I were a Myller and could grind
> A hundred thousand bushels in an hour,
> And ere my Master and my Dame had dinde
> Be closely filching of a bag of flour. [...]
> And yet I would not; least my Thumbes should be
> Held all too great upon my towling-dish,
> And such as did my secret cunning see,
> Might curse and wish me many a bitter wish,
> And say when they before the Mill-dore stand
> The Miller's thumbs as broade as half a hand.

That is a wonderfully satirical verse about human greed at the expense of the miller profession. The final line includes the telling proverb that "The *miller* has thumbs as broad as half a hand." The implication is, of course, that he is in fact quite a skillful manipulator of weight scales.

Perhaps the seventeenth-century proverb "The *miller* never got better moulter [toll] than he took with his own hands" with the meaning of knowing how to help oneself is a bit more positive, but it seems to allude at taking advantage of a situation as well. That certainly is the case with the proverb "The *meal* came home short from the miller" as an expression of disappointed expectations. Whether the expectations were justified or not, many a farmer will have felt cheated by the miller when confronted by the small amount of ground flour from the large quantity of grain originally supplied.

Such stereotypical expressions exist about other professions as well, notably against lawyers, physicians, and priests. But the invectives against millers are quite numerous, perhaps because farmers who brought their grain to the gristmill simply felt at the mercy of the miller's (dis)honesty in providing them with the meal due them. Such proverbs as "Put a *miller*, a weaver, and a tailor in a bag and shake them, the first that comes out will be a thief," "A *miller* is a thief," "Many a *miller*, many a thief," "Every *miller* draws water to his own mill," "*Millers* are the last to die of famine," "A *miller* is never dry" (is often intoxicated), and "The miller's *pigs* are fat, but God knows whose meal they ate" all reflect the questionable character of the miller in the eyes of those who are dependent on him.

But then there is also the sixteenth-century proverb that states that "Much *water* goes by the mill that the miller knows not of" which William Shakespeare cited as "More water glideth by the mill / Than wots the miller of" (*Titus Andronicus,* II,1,85). This is not necessarily directed negatively against the miller. The proverb simply states that one cannot pay attention or be aware of everything, using the metaphor of the mill and its miller to describe this fact through known facts. This is exactly the way Shakespeare employs this metaphorical proverb. In the literary context of its appearance in *Titus Andronicus,* it has absolutely nothing to do with a mill or a miller. Instead it is Demetrius who uses the proverb to advise his brother Chiron, both sons of the Queen of the Goths Tamora, that he can woo Lavinia, daughter of the Roman general Titus Andronicus, even though there will be much upset about his love among the feuding Goths and Romans:

Why mak'st thou it so strange?
She is a woman, therefore may be woo'd;
She is a woman, therefore may be won;
She is Lavinia, therefore must be lov'd.
What, man! more water glideth by the mill
Than wots the miller of; and easy it is
Of a cut loaf to steal a shive, we know.

Here the proverb functions simply as a bit of rationalization and positive persuasion to encourage the brother to pursue his amorous desires. Of course, there is also a bit of misogyny in those sentences preceding the proverb with its metaphorical message that Chiron should be able to win Lavinia in a clandestine fashion. After all, just as the miller does not know everything about the water flowing by his mill, so the Romans don't know everything that is happening between the Goth Chiron and their own Lavinia. Shakespeare's use of the proverb in this context is a fine example of how proverbs express messages in a metaphorical way without any reference to their actual and realistic wording.

Clearly the proverb "The *miller* grinds more men's corn than one" is a positive statement that comments on his involvement and experience with many parties, stressing that any particular person is not the only one to be considered. And the somewhat odd but still heard proverbial expressions "To put out the *miller's eye*" or "To drown the *miller*" are also not vicious attempts to harm a dishonest miller. They are nothing but innocuous metaphorical phrases referring to someone having added too much water to a recipe, especially one thickened with flour. A plausible explanation of the origin of the first expression states that the "miller's eye" refers to lumps of flour not fully mixed into the batter or dough. In certain recipes such lumps are desirable, but adding too much water can eliminate them, that is putting the miller's eyes out. The second expression with the same meaning simply alludes to the fact that millers using water-wheels for power had little need for more water.

And proverbs about the mill itself? The proverb "The *mill* cannot grind with the water that is past" with its earliest citation from 1616 is still well known today and refers to missed opportunities. But the fifteenth-century proverb "A *mill* that grinds not is worth as much as an oven that bakes not" is not known anymore. Yet texts like "Enter the *mill* and you come out floury" and its longer variant "If you don't want *flour* on your happern [happin], you should keep out of the mill" as well as "*Mills* won't grind if you give them no water," "Still *waters* turn no mills," "Too much *water* drowned the miller," and "No *mill*, no meal" have all been recorded in use during the twentieth century in the United States. Somewhat related to the last text are the proverbs "The *mill* gets (gains) by going" and "The *mill* stands that wants [lacks] water," meaning only an operating mill will get things done. These proverbs seem almost simplistic in their wisdom. The same is true for the proverb "A little *stream* drives a light mill" if one takes it only literally. In its metaphorical meaning the proverb alludes to the general truth that small causes will have small effects.

There is also the ever popular proverb "The *mill*(s) of God grind(s) slowly," which in its Greek and Latin form was "The *mills* of the gods grind slowly, but they grind small." The proverb has been traced back to the Greek philosopher Sextus Empiricus (c. A.D. 190), who is, however, quoting an earlier unknown poet. As is the case with hundreds of proverbs, this proverb found its way into the vernacular languages. By 1640 it is registered in George Herbert's proverb collection *Outlandish Proverbs (Jacula Prudentum)* as "God's Mill grinds slow, but sure." Here it is, of course, the singular God of the monotheistic Christian religion. But the message is the same: justice is often a slow process, but it is inevitable. There is also a small poem by the German poet Friedrich von Logau called "Retribution" (1654), which Henry Wadsworth Longfellow in 1870 rendered into English as follows:

Though the mills of God grind slowly,
yet they grind exceeding small;
Though with patience He stands
waiting, with exactness grinds he all.

Thus retribution may be delayed, but it is certain to overtake the wicked sinners. Here we have God (or the ancient gods) as the ultimate miller metaphorically grinding up his imperfect children, that is, punishing them for their sins. This interpretation can also be seen in a passage in A. White's *Modern Jew* (1899): "The capture and destruction of the Spanish fleet [...] satisfied them that though the mills of God grind slowly the ruin of Spain was an equitable adjustment of her debt to the Jews." But the religious basis of this punitive proverb has been lost to a large degree in modern times. In fact, often "God" is simply replaced by the secularized notion of "justice" or such banal terms as bureaucracy, administration, government, and so on. This can be seen quite well from two references out of letters by George Bernard Shaw. In 1896 he wrote: "How long the mills of the gods must grind you before they grind exceeding small enough to become indeed 'der Reine Thor' [the Pure Fool], I don't know"; and in 1937 he returned to the proverb by changing it to: "You will find yourself in the grip of the Public trustee, whose mill grinds quickly and grinds exceeding large." But Shaw had also used the proverb quite traditionally in his play *Captain Brassbound's Conversion* from 1900. Here Sir Howard states: "'The mills of the gods grind slowly,' Mr. Rankin; 'but they grind exceeding small'." Such varied uses of proverbs cited in their traditional wording or altered in innovative ways show clearly the adaptability of old proverbs to ever new contexts and situations.

There is also the proverbial expression "To be (bring) *grist* to one's mill" which has maintained its currency since the sixteenth century. Thus Winston S. Churchill wrote in 1902 "all is grist that comes to my mill" and "It is all grist to the Labour mill." And in 1958 that masterful employer of proverbs and proverbial expressions Harry S. Truman used the phrase effectively to deliver a Cold War slam at the Soviet Union:

> The Soviet Union has hitherto refused to cooperate with the free nations on real disarmament or control of arms and has used every conference or international discussion on disarmament merely to further her own design for conquest. In the face of past failures and even realizing the Russians still are seeking only further grist for their peace propaganda mills, while they arm for imperialistic purposes, we ought to put the burden of proof on the Russians by answering them with a concrete counter-proposal.

That is quite a jump from the mill of the miller to Russian peace propaganda mills, but the message of directing the grist or the benefits to one's own advantage comes through very clearly. The Truman reference is a splendid example of how rhetorically apt politicians can in fact add metaphorical expressiveness to their speeches and writings, thus communicating effectively and convincingly with the people who know the expressions in their traditional sense and who understand their innovative manipulations.

And then there is, of course, the well-known proverbial expression "To lay a *millstone* on someone's neck" and its variants "To be (carry) a *millstone* around one's neck" to refer to an especially heavy burden. The metaphor is based on a biblical passage in which Jesus warns those who would dare to corrupt children: "But whoso shall offend one of these little ones which believe in me, it were better for him that a millstone were hanged about his neck, and that he were drowned in the depth of the sea" (Matt. 18:6).

One is reminded of a modern interpretation of this phrase in D.H. Lawrence's essay on "Democracy" (1917, published 1936): "Every individual is born with a millstone of ideals around his neck, and, whether he knows it or not, either spends his time trying to get his neck free or else he spends his days decorating his millstone." This is reminiscent of the proverbial comparison "To be like *corn* under a millstone" that refers metaphorically to life's often grievous oppression. And for individuals between millstone or with millstones around their neck, it is only natural that the wish would appear that their lives could at least at times be "As *calm* (placid, smooth, still) as a millpond" without the noise of the ever turning waterwheel of that gristmill of life.

What are the chances of survival of the proverbial language cited as examples in this short survey of metaphorical wisdom relating to millers and mills? Some of them have already dropped out of general use, and their old and antiquated metaphors are in need of historical and cultural explanation in order to be understood at all. But there are also those more common expressions that will definitely continue to be effective images for a modern life that is becoming ever more devoid of traditional mills. The stereotypical expressions relating to the miller are well to have disappeared, but people certainly will continue to struggle with millstones around their necks, and they will insist that the millers of the future will heed the old mill proverb "First come, first served." Nobody would want to miss that basic wisdom of fair social behavior.

"THE APPLE DOESN'T FALL FAR FROM THE TREE": A PROVERB'S WAY FROM GERMANY TO AMERICA

The earliest reference of the German proverb "Der *Apfel* fällt nicht weit vom Baum" (The apple doesn't fall far from the tree) is included in a 1554 sermon by the preacher Johann Mathesius. There are no earlier classical or medieval Latin variants to be found, but the proverb itself is actually quite well known throughout Europe, especially in countries neighboring Germany. None of these references from other languages predate the German text, and it can be safely assumed that they are in fact later loan translations from the German original, the Dutch equivalent "De *appel* valt niet verre van den boom" having been recorded no earlier than 1788. With such an international dissemination of the proverb it should not be surprising that it also made its way to the distant United States, but let me mention here as an aside that it never really made it across the English Channel. For while the proverb today competes successfully with such old English equivalents as "A *chip* of(f) the old block" and "Like *father* (*mother*), like son (daughter)" in North America, it appears only rarely in British oral or written communication.

Turning first to English language references that have been found through traditional historical research, it is interesting to note that it was Ralph Waldo Emerson who included it in a small section listing nine "Proverbs" in one of his *Notebooks* around 1830. While he cites it only in English translation, he does attach the statement that it is a German proverb: "The apple does not fall far from the stem. German." It will probably never be known exactly when and where Emerson came across this German proverb, but it must have stuck in his mind, for in a letter of December 22, 1839, to his aunt Mary Moody Emerson, he quotes it again in a slightly varied form together with an introductory formula identifying it as a common saying: "[...], and as men say the apple never falls far from the stem." But even though Emerson does not identify the proverb as being German any longer, this citation can hardly be taken as proof that it had become generally accepted in nineteenth-century American speech.

Americans most likely learned the German proverb from immigrants who carried it with them to their new homeland. It should surprise no one that W.J. Hoffman in his early article on the "Folk-Lore of the Pennsylvania Germans" (1889) recorded the proverb in dialect form with the following explanations: "*Der apb'l falt net wait fum shtam.* The apple does not fall far from the trunk.—Equivalent to 'a chip of the old block,' when speaking of a child taking after its father." By the way Hoffman feels compelled to explain the proverb to the readers of the *Journal of American Folklore,* it becomes evident that the proverb was only in use among ethnic groups of German immigrants in the nineteenth century. Edwin Fogel includes it again in German in his superb collection of *Proverbs of the Pennsylvania Germans* (1929), but in the subsequent decades it was registered in English translation in regional collections from North Carolina, New York, Illinois, and Washington. By 1945 the proverb must have been quite current throughout the United States as an English loan proverb from the German, for it was recorded numerous times by field researchers from the mid-1940s to 1985. The *Dictionary of American Proverbs* (1992) that is based on this major collecting exercise from oral sources ascribes a general United States currency to it.

Checking through 18 German-English dictionaries dating from 1792 to 1990, it becomes clear that English and American lexicographers have struggled for many years to find the appropriate equivalent to the German proverb, when at least by the 1950s if not earlier they could have cited the loan translation that had become quite established in the United States at least. But lexicography appears to be a rather conservative endeavor, and it would behoove lexicographers to pay more attention to the impressive comparative research that phraseologists and paremiologists have been conducting for quite some time. As it is, it took until 1981 for the translated proverb to appear in a foreign-language dictionary. The most common equivalent is the English proverb "Like *father,* like son," which dates back to at least the early sixteenth century. It is interesting to note that none of the lexicographers ever cite the parallel proverb "Like *mother,* like daughter," which has been current in the English language as long as its male equivalent. The German proverb, of course, has no particular gender implication as such, but Alan Dundes is probably correct in stating that the word "'apple' appears to have somewhat of a male association in such a proverb as 'Der Apfel fällt nicht weit vom Baum' [The apple doesn't fall far from the tree] implying that the son looks like or acts like the father, roughly equivalent to American idioms such as a 'chip off the old block' or 'the spitten image'." In any case, the "bookish" references from published proverb collections and language dictionaries have not exactly established a convincing currency of the German proverb as a loan translation in the Anglo-American language.

Alan Dundes was able to make available to me an impressive 73 references of this proverb that were collected by his students at the University of California at Berkeley between 1964 and 1991. Since the student collectors also include informants' comments as to when, where, and from whom they learned the proverb, these archival materials establish that the proverb was already known around the turn of the twentieth century. They also make clear that immigrants like the Pennsylvania Germans brought the proverb with them to America. In fact, 35 of the 73 references state that this is a *German* proverb. But there are 12 informants who consider the proverb of Yiddish origin, two informants each claim that it is Swedish or Russian, and one informant thinks it to be Irish. This should not be surprising since, as has been shown, the proverb is well known throughout most of Europe. But much more important and truly exciting is that the remaining 21 informants con-

sider this proverb to be American! The German proverb in English translation has become Americanized in the folk's mind, and these invaluable
archival records help to establish this fact. What follows are some quotations
from these records to illustrate the importance and value of folklore archives
for the historical and geographical study of proverbs.

A reference that cites the proverb in the German language was collected
by a student on January 26, 1969, from Frieda Barkley, a retired German-
American teacher from Benicia, California. One learns from the student collector that "Mrs. Barkley was born in North Dakota of German parents, both
of whom had emigrated from Leipzig to North Dakota c. 1880. The proverb
would be used to mean that, no matter how different a child thinks he is from
his parents, in reality he isn't much different." At the time of interviewing
Mrs. Barkley in 1969, she was 82 years old. Surely she had heard and learned
the proverb from her parents before the turn of the century, and this reference
is an indication of how immigrants maintain their proverbs within the family
setting where the native language continues to be spoken.

Another older German immigrant placed the proverb into an alarming
context in 1979 that, unfortunately, applies also to the present-day situation
in the reunified Germany. Being asked by the student collector to elaborate
on the meaning of the proverb, Gutrune Falckon said "that today there are
many young Nazis in Germany because their parents were Nazis and the
children were raised that way. In this way if something shows a great resem-
blance to its creator or predecessor one might say 'The apple doesn't fall far
from the tree.' Just as the seeds from the apple will create another tree, the
children will become adults like their parents."

The Folklore Archive at Berkeley does, however, also contain twelve citations of the proverb either in German or in English by Jewish immigrants,
who most likely also knew it in Yiddish, as can be seen from the following
comments by a student collector: "My informant learned the proverb 'The
apple doesn't fall far from the tree' as she was growing up in Omaha, Nebraska. She believes she learned it from her mother, Sarah Beber, between the
ages of 10 or 15, circa 1929. This proverb is a Yiddish saying that was used by
everyone. Sarah Beber moved to the United States from Germany, and this
proverb was one of those that she had learned when she had been little."
Many of the Jewish informants remember learning the proverb in Germany
before immigrating to the United States during the Nazi period. Just as other
German immigrants, they continued citing it in Yiddish or German in this
country, eventually also translating it into English when communicating with
people who knew only that language. There is no doubt that the Jewish population in America did play its part in spreading this proverb. It was well

established in Yiddish among the European Jews, as can be seen from its inclusion in Ignaz Bernstein's famous collection *Jüdische Sprichwörter und Redensarten* (1908) as "Das epele gerut nuch dem schtam, das kind gerut nuch der am" (The apple takes after the stem, and the child after the nurse) and "Das epele falt nit weit fün'm bejmele" (The apple doesn't fall far from the tree).

Even though the Folklore Archive at Berkeley contains no references by Dutch immigrants, it must be mentioned here that they also brought the proverb with them to the United States. This is made abundantly clear in a letter to the editor of *U.S. News & World Report* (1987): "At last, we're again discussing what has long been folk wisdom! Though well into my 70s, I can still hear my elders speaking their native Dutch about the accomplishments and peccadilloes of neighbors and family: *Ya, de appel valt niet ver van de boom*—Yes, the apple falls not far from the tree." And there is also the reference in Peter De Vries's novel *Sauce for the Goose* (1981): "He smiled fondly at her again. 'You know the old expression about heredity. The apple doesn't fall far from the tree.' She knew it quite well, even its Old World version. 'De appel valt niet ver van de boom'." The name of the author already tells of his Dutch background, but it is also a fact that Peter De Vries was born in 1910 in Chicago as the son of Dutch immigrants who cited the proverb while he was growing up in America.

The 21 informants who think of the proverb as being of American origin prefer by far the standard variant "The apple doesn't fall far from the tree." These references also show that by about 1950 the proverb had become quite Americanized. But such invaluable archive materials don't do anybody any good if they are not being used or put together into valuable research tools. Modern scholars might belittle the positivistic folklore collections of earlier times, but they still need accessible texts, hopefully with contexts, to do serious historical and geographical work. It behooves folklorists from time to time to publish new collections in order to show the modern use of proverbs and other verbal folklore genres. The folklore archives contain not only texts in contexts, they often also include invaluable interpretive comments by both the informants and collectors. These are treasures that should be used, published, and interpreted, if folklore as a scholarly discipline wants to maintain its credibility.

In the meantime, the modern computer offers diachronic research possibilities that can only be called the dream of any historically minded folklorist let alone paremiologist. Computerized textual databases are constantly expanding, and one of the most useful on-line databases is LEXIS/NEXIS, offering full-text coverage for hundreds of legal [lexis] documents and also extensive news [nexis] and business information resources. Included are dozens of newspapers, magazines, wire services, newsletters, journals, reports, broadcast transcripts, and so on. While the database goes back only to the end of the 1970s, it is now constantly being expanded to become more and more inclusive. Doing a "giant" search for a particular proverb is relatively simple. In this case all that was necessary was to code the proverb "The apple doesn't fall far from the tree" into something like "*apple* /within 3 words of / *fall* /within 3 words of/ *tree*." The rest is a proverbial "piece of cake." Within seconds the computer screen informs the scholar that the database contains 232 (!) references, and every one of them can be called onto the screen, displaying in each case precise bibliographical information and a few lines with the proverb in context. This short contextualized reference can then be printed out at once, but one can also decide to print out the entire (wonder upon wonders!) publication in which the proverb appears.

Obviously the miraculous world of computer searches of databases has its problems and snags at times, but none of them negate their positive value. In the case of the 232 references that were found for the triad of "apple/fall/tree," a total of 123 citations were useless. The most common "error" referred to statements that dealt with Sir Isaac Newton discovering gravity by observing an apple falling from a tree. Others were duplications of good references, but 109 references, or about 50 percent of the total, hit the proverbial "bull's eye." The over 100 references from 1981 to 1992 have never before been registered by proverb scholars, and they most certainly establish the modern American currency of this proverb. Furthermore, there is not a single Anglo-American proverb collection that would even come close to listing over a hundred references for any proverb. In fact, not even *all* such collections could together come up with that number of citations for a single proverb. Database searching for particular proverbs is truly revolutionizing paremiography as it has been known thus far.

Taking now a closer look at this wealth of materials, it should be of interest that 14 of the 109 proverb references are identified by so-called introductory formulas, at times being even referred to as "old" and as a traditional piece of "Yankee wisdom." How more American can anything possibly be?

Mention has already been made that the proverb appears to exhibit somewhat of a male association. This fact is certainly born out by the 45 contextualized references that clearly refer to a father and son relationship. A typical use of the proverb in this meaning is the following excerpt from an article on Pennsylvania politics:

The state is well into its second generation of moderate-to-leftish Republican leaders. Its gubernatorial candidate, Lt. Gov. William W. Scranton III, 39, is the son of former governor William Scranton, a man who symbolized the species in the 1960s. This summer, the younger Scranton is showing that in Pennsylvania, the apple does not fall far from the tree.

The proverb is rarely used to refer to the relationship of mother and son, probably because the physiognomic and physical similarities between them might not be as striking as between two males. But the proverb does, of course, also refer to character traits, and let me at least cite former President Bill Clinton's relationship with his mother as *People* magazine explained it proverbially: "They say the apple doesn't fall far from the tree, and in the case of America's President-elect and his mother, the proverb holds. If you want to know where Clinton first learned to use his head—not to mention where he got his indomitable, take-a-licking-and-keep-on-ticking spirit—look no further than Virginia Clinton Kelley."

As would be expected, references to mothers and daughters are more frequent, but the nine texts are a mere 20 percent of the 45 citations that deal with fathers and sons. No immediate reason for this discrepancy comes to mind, save that the proverb is in fact of a predominantly male orientation. A rather negative reference can be found in Shirley Faessler's short narrative *The Apple Doesn't Fall Far from the Tree* (1983): "She knows what she was doing. Let's talk straight. The apple doesn't fall far from the tree. The mother was a *kurveh* [whore] and so is the daughter." Another quite nasty use of the proverb appeared in connection with the relationship of Prince Charles and Camilla Parker Bowles, an affair that has occupied tabloids throughout the world: "The apple never falls far from the tree: Camilla's great-grandmother was the mistress of King Edward VII." At least there is Goldie Hawn who described her daughter Kate as having her "strong personality—the apple doesn't fall far from the tree." And there is also that somewhat bittersweet love song "Apples Don't Fall Far from the Tree" (1973) written by John Durrell and performed by Cher. Here the proverb takes on the role of a leitmotif, clearly indicating the hereditary "truth" of this proverb for three related women:

When I was five
I'd put on mama's high-heeled shoes and paint my face
And dance across the living room at Ruby's place
Where the music was always playing,
Girls would laugh while the men were saying

Apples don't fall far from the tree
Hey, Honey come sit on my knee

Apples don't fall far from the tree
And I remember mama's tears when they said in
a few years I'd be something to see

At seventeen,
I had me a diamond and a string of pearls
The men said they preferred me to the other girls
They took me to the best of places,
But I could read it on their faces

Apples don't fall far from the tree
Hey, Honey come sit on my knee
Apples don't fall far from the tree
And I remember mama's tears when they said in
a few years I'd be something to see

Then my mama died
I made up my mind
To get on a Greyhound, get out of this town
And leave it all behind

But life goes on
A child of three smiles up at me, while she plays
The man I love has never heard of Ruby's place
When he holds her with affection,
And he uses that old expression

Apples don't fall far from the tree
Hey, Honey come sit on my knee
Apples don't fall far from the tree
And I remember mama's tears when they said in
a few years I'd be something to see

There are also seven references that cite the proverb as reflecting on the relationship of children with both their mother and father. After all, children are usually a product of the traits and attitudes of both parents. No wonder that Charles Gallagher published his small "pastoral and matrimonial" booklet on *Sexuality Is Heredity* (1990) with the proverbial subtitle *The Apple Doesn't Fall Far from the Tree*. But it must also be said that this proverb does not always refer to family relations either. This can be seen in an interesting article in

Sports Illustrated from 1991 on the basketball superstar Michael Jordan. The headline and subtitle read quite similarly "The Unlikeliest Homeboy: For all his fame and fortune, Jordan is, at heart, just a Carolina kid called Mike." And the article itself starts with the statement: "Because the apple doesn't fall far from the tree, isn't it possible that Michael Jordan is not some sort of glorious phenomenon but rather a simple, shining fragment of nature, grounded in family and friends and roots from which he has never strayed? In a word, yes. If the term *homeboy* wasn't invented for him, surely it should have been." Thus the proverb identifies a great basketball player as having solid roots in his social environment, something that neither national nor international fame can ever take away.

And who will be surprised to see this proverb being used to refer to the Apple Computer company and its steady stream of products, or should I say its impressive "*Apples*" born on the parental tree? The LEXIS/NEXIS computer search yielded three headlines in magazines that employed the proverb with the fruit being replaced by the company's identical name. The proverb is changed to state that the apples fall *far* from the tree, a shrewd advertising trick or pun to indicate that new models of Apple computers are reaching ever expanding markets.

There was a time when the doyen of proverb studies, Archer Taylor, stated in the old *Proverbium* journal that one must not leave any stone unturned when investigating the origin, history, and dissemination of a particular proverb (see Taylor 1971). Taylor accomplished his numerous historical studies of individual proverbs by searching through proverb collections and literary works for references and variants. But just imagine if he had had such folklore archives as the one at Berkeley at his disposal. Or even further, what would Archer Taylor have thought of such databases as LEXIS/NEXIS? The conclusion that all historical proverb dictionaries are sorely out of date is certainly justified. Much updating work is needed to register older as well as newer references for at least the more important proverbs. The investigation of individual proverbs has indeed become revolutionized by the electronic age. Leaving no stone unturned in proverb searches now means even more consultation of printed texts, the careful scrutiny of folklore archives based on field research, and many fruitful hours scanning vast computerized databases.

"THE ONLY GOOD INDIAN IS A DEAD INDIAN": A SLANDEROUS PROVERBIAL STEREOTYPE

Although much is known about proverbial stereotypes among different nationalities and regions, and although numerous studies have been undertaken to study verbal slurs against Jews and African Americans, especially in the United States, there has been a definite dearth of interest in the proverbial invectives that have been hurled against the Native Americans ever since Christopher Columbus and later explorers, settlers, and immigrants set foot on the American continent. As people look at these slurs, it is becoming ever more obvious that the native population suffered terribly in the name of expansion and progress. Native Americans were deprived of their homeland, killed mercilessly or placed on reservations, where many continue their marginalized existence to the present day. The early concepts of the "good Indian" or "noble savage" quickly were replaced by reducing the native inhabitants to "wild savages" who were standing in the way of expansionism under the motto of "manifest destiny." Anybody resisting this policy was "bad," and once the popular white attitude was geared towards the demonization of the Native Americans, the stage was set for killing thousands of them or driving the survivors onto inhuman reservations. The unpublished and little known dissertation by Priscilla Shames with the title *The Long Hope: A Study of American Indian Stereotypes in American Popular Fiction* (1969) shows how this cruel treatment of the native population is described in literature, while Dee Brown's best-selling book *Bury My Heart at Wounded Knee: An Indian History of the American West* (1970) gives a more factual account. This latter book contains a telling chapter with the gruesome proverbial title "The Only Good Indian Is a Dead Indian," the word "dead" meaning both literal death, and for those who survived the mass killings, a figurative death, that is, a restricted life on the reservation with little freedom to continue the traditional lifestyle.

It is alarming that this invective against Native Americans that became current on the frontier around 1850 is still in use today, astonishingly enough both by the general population and the Native Americans themselves. Witness for example the book title *The Only Good Indian: Essays by Canadian Indians* (1970) that was chosen for a collection of short prose and poetic texts in which these native inhabitants from Canada express their frustration with their marginalized life in modern society. How bad must their plight be if the editor, Waubageshig, decided to choose this invective against his own people as a title! The explanation is given in the introduction as follows:

Police brutality, incompetent bureaucrats, legal incongruities, destructive education systems, racial discrimination, ignorant politicians who are abetted by a country largely ignorant of its native population, are conditions which Indians face daily. Yes, the only good Indian is still a dead one. Not dead physically, but dead spiritually, mentally, economically and socially.

Yes, this is Canada, but the same picture emerges for the United States in the dissertation by folklorist Rayna Green. Herself a Native American, she chose the title *The Only Good Indian: The Image of the Indian in American Vernacular Culture* (1973) for her voluminous and enlightening study. The proverbial title sets the tone—here is a meticulous account of the "popular" view of Native Americans as expressed by the American population of all age groups, all social classes, and all regions. The result is a shocking stereotypical image that permeates all modes of expression, of which linguistic examples are only a small part. There can be no doubt about the sad fact that Native Americans were declared proverbially dead by the middle of the nineteenth century, especially after the end of the American Civil War, when United States soldiers joined bigoted frontier settlers in a mercilessly carried out campaign to kill off the native population of this giant land.

Such willfully planned and ruthlessly executed destruction of the Native Americans needed its battle slogan, a ready-made catchphrase that could help the perpetrators to justify the inhuman treatment of their victims. The proverb that gained currency at that time and that can still be heard today is the mindless and absurd American proverb "The only good Indian is a dead Indian." It was indeed a devilish stroke of genius that created this dangerous slur. Its poly-semanticity is grotesque to say the least. On the one hand, it is a proverbial slogan that justifies the actual mass slaughter of Indians by the soldiers. But it also states on a more figurative level that Indians can only be "good" persons if they become Christians and take on the civilized ways of their white oppressors. Then they might be "good," but as far as their native Indian culture is concerned they would in fact be dead. Be it by physical or spiritual death, Native Americans were doomed victims of perpetrators who acted with manifest destiny on their side while so-called innocent bystanders did nothing to prevent the holocaust of the Native Americans.

The time was ripe for this all-encompassing and all-telling proverb, but whence did it come? Who coined the invective "The only good Indian is a dead Indian," which, unfortunately, fit the stereotypical worldview of three-quarters of the population of the United States in the late nineteenth century? Although most lexicographers attribute it to a remark allegedly made by General Philip Sheridan in 1869, the terminus a quo for this slur can be found in *The Congressional Globe: Containing the Debates and Proceedings of the Second Session [of the] Fortieth Congress* (1868). During a debate on an "Indian Appropriation Bill" that took place on May 28, 1868, in the House of Representatives, James Michael Cavanaugh from Montana uttered the following despicable words:

I will say that I like an Indian better dead than living. I have never in my life seen a good Indian (and I have seen thousands) except when I have seen a dead Indian. I believe in the policy that exterminates the Indians, drives them outside the boundaries of civilization, because you cannot civilize them.

The sentence "I have never in my life seen a good Indian except when I have seen a dead Indian" is, of course, a mere prose utterance that lacks many of the poetic and formal markers of traditional proverbs save for its parallel structure. Yet it is easily noticeable that this subjective sentence contains the clear possibility of becoming shortened into the much more proverbial formula "A good Indian is a dead Indian."

Indians and death were tragically connected in the frontier worldview, and it should not be surprising that United States soldiers and their officers shared this negative view. Major William Shepherd described the general stereotype in his book *Prairie Experiences* (1884) as follows: "On the frontier a good Indian means a 'dead Indian.' The Indian must go, is going, and will soon be gone. It is his luck."

While the early variants cited thus far do *not* associate any particular person with having coined them, such an ascription was in fact started by Edward Ellis in his book *The History of Our Country: From the Discovery of America to the Present Time* (1895). Entitling a short paragraph with "Sheridan's Bon Mot," Ellis relates the following event from an eyewitness account of Captain Charles Nordstrom:

It was in January, 1869, in camp at old Fort Cobb, Indian Territory, now Oklahoma, shortly after Custer's fight with Black-Kettle's band of Cheyennes. Old Toch-a-way (Turtle Dove), a chief of the Comanches, on being presented to Philip Sheridan, desired to impress the General in his favor, and striking himself a resounding blow on the breast, he managed to say: "Me, Toch-a-way; me good Injun." A quizzical smile lit up the General's face as he set those standing by in a roar by saying: "The only good Indians I ever saw were dead."

This anecdotal paragraph with its author's obvious delight in telling the gruesomely "humorous" event appears of questionable authenticity at first. It is, of course, understandable that General Philip Sheridan (1831–1888) repeatedly denied having made such a statement, but there is no doubt that Sheridan was known as a bigot and Indian hater, as the historian Paul Andrew Hutton has shown in a chapter of his book on *Phil Sheridan and His Army* (1985) so appropriately called "Forming Military Indian Policy: 'The Only Good Indian Is a Dead Indian'." It is of interest, however, that Hutton does not quote Sheridan's statement "The only good Indians I ever saw were dead" but rather its more generalized and more powerful proverbial form "The only good Indian is a dead Indian," which became synonymous with the Indian policy of Sheridan and most other generals and soldiers. As Stephen Ambrose puts it so clearly in his account of the parallel lives of the two American warriors *Crazy Horse and Custer* (1975): "Frontier posts reverberated with tough talk about what would be done to the Indians, once caught, and it became an article of faith among the Army officers that 'you could not trust an Indian.' Sheridan's famous remark, 'The only good Indian I ever saw was dead,' was often and gleefully quoted." Naturally Sheridan has had his defenders who have tried to disclaim his having coined this proverb, and they are technically correct, for it will probably never be known whether the proverb developed from Sheridan's statement or whether his ill-conceived utterance was a subjective reformulation of the proverb already in currency. It must be remembered that James Michael Cavanaugh from Montana had expressed a quite similar sentence already in 1868 in the United States House of Representatives, and nobody is claiming that he originated this frontier proverb.

If it was not General Philip Sheridan who coined the proverb in its present form, it was certainly also not an even more famous, or rather infamous, Indian fighter who made the following incredible remarks during a speech in January of 1886 in New York:

I suppose I should be ashamed to say that I take the Western view of the Indian. I don't go so far as to think that the only good Indians are dead Indians, but I believe nine out of every ten are, and I shouldn't like to inquire too closely into the case of the tenth. The most vicious cowboy has more moral principle than the average Indian. Reckless, revengeful, fiendishly cruel, they rob and murder, not the cowboys, who can take care of themselves, but the defenseless, lone settlers on the plains.

The person who spoke this incredulous passage was that "rough rider" who published his racist and expansionist views and an account of his exploits on the American frontier in his acclaimed book *The Winning of the West* (1889)—no one less than Theodore Roosevelt himself, who became President of the United States five years after delivering these hateful comments!

Just as this proverb persists in oral communication, so it also permeates written sources from scholarly books to novels, from magazines to newspapers, and even on to cartoons. In Mary Rinehart's detective novel *The Circu-*

lar Staircase (1908), for example, one finds the grotesque double statement: "Just as the only good Indian is a dead Indian, so the only safe defaulter is a dead defaulter." While the proverb actually serves only to introduce a characterization of a male person obsessed with money, it nevertheless is used to describe this man's dishonesty by comparing him to the stereotypical devious Indian. This early reference also shows already what is to become a pattern in more modern uses of the proverb. Often it is not even cited, but rather it is reduced to the formula "The only good X is a dead X," giving its speaker or author a ready-made proverbial slogan with all the negative and prejudicial connotations of its original proverbial form.

It is interesting to see how this proverbial formula has been utilized as a slogan against the German enemy in particular during the two world wars, as indicated by the following references in various novels: "No good Fritzes but dead 'uns'" (1929), "The only good Germans were dead Germans" (1930), and "There's only one good Boche, and that's a dead one" (1930). Such variants show, of course, also the regrettable internationalization of the slanderous proverb and its underlying proverbial formula.

Besides the German enemy there were, of course, also the Japanese soldiers to contend with. It will surprise no one to learn that the proverb was adapted to fit this menace as well, as Richard Butler documents in his novel *A Blood-Red Sun at Noon* (1980): "'Ye believe all the propaganda our side have stuffed into your head—things like bishops blessing the flag and telling you God's on our side, not theirs. Generals telling you that the only good Jap is a dead Jap'." In the late 1960s there also circulated the anti-Vietnamese variant "The only good gook is a dead gook." Yet another "national" variant of the proverb appears in a book on early Spanish conquests in South America, stating that the native population doubtlessly thought of many of the intruders in terms of "The only good Spaniard was a dead Spaniard." And there was also the statement from 1992 in a German newspaper: "How was that in America? The only good Indian is a dead Indian. How is that in the former Yugoslavia? The only good Bosnian, Moslem, Christian, Croatian is . . ." There is clearly no end to applying this powerful slogan against any enemy as a propagandistic tool. Its adaptability as a national stereotype is clearly without limit.

The same is true for some of the following trivializations of the original proverbial invective. Some of them might even seem "humorous" in their absurdity, but it must not be forgotten that the actual proverb of "The only good Indian is a dead Indian" is subconsciously juxtaposed to these seemingly harmless variations, thus continuing the slur against Native Americans in a camouflaged manner. In the following list it will be noticed that the texts are usually built on the structure "The only good X is a dead X":

1933:	The only good poacher is a dead poacher.
1942:	The only good teacher is a dead teacher.
1957:	The only good mouse is a dead mouse.
1964:	The only good raccoon was a dead one.
1968:	The only good cop (pig) is a dead cop (pig).
1970:	The only good snake was a dead snake.
1980:	The only good cow's a dead cow.
1991:	The only good priest [is a dead priest].
1998:	A good vacuum is a dead vacuum.

As can be readily seen from these variants, they express to a large degree anxieties of people about such things as murders (in detective novels) or animals such as raccoons, snakes, and mice. It might be worthwhile to cite at least the "mouse" variant in its literary context. Paul Gallico in his novel *Thomasina* (1957) describes in many pages the art of "mousehole watching" that is being practiced by one of his characters for whom this is "a full-time job":

> It isn't catching mice, mind you, that is the most necessary. Anyone can catch a mouse; it is no trick at all; it is putting them off and keeping them down [by locating the mousehole(s)] that is important. You will hear sayings like—"The only good mouse is a dead mouse," but that is only half of it. The only good mouse is the mouse that isn't there at all. What you must do if you are at all principled about your work, is to conduct a war of nerves on the creatures. This calls for both time, energy and a good deal of cleverness which I wouldn't begrudge if I wasn't expected to do so many other things besides.

Sure, this is a bit of humor perhaps, especially if one continues to read another two pages of this seemingly futile exercise, but the careful reader might

Cited from *The Burlington Free Press* (August 16, 1998), comic section.

have a rude awakening when the "mouse" variant of the traditional proverb brings to mind the fate of the Native Americans being hunted down by superior weapons and strength just like a defenseless little mouse. Behind the animalistic trivialization of the slanderous proverb hovers inescapably the historical truth of human extermination.

The step from a mouse to scorning another racial minority besides Native Americans is far too quickly taken, as is documented in Joseph Carr's novel *The Man with Bated Breath* (1934). There a prejudiced white man from the southern United States makes the following comment about an African American servant named Jesse: "'That is one of the houseboys. Honest enough if you discount the saying in these parts that the only honest nigger is a dead nigger.'" That this proverb about Native Americans has, in fact, been easily transferred to African Americans is documented in George Bernard Shaw's compelling introduction to his drama *On the Rocks* (1934). With Nazi Germany on the rise, he prophetically writes about Germany's plans of racial purity and Jewish extirpation in a section entitled "Present Exterminations":

> The extermination of what the exterminators call inferior races is as old as history. "Stone dead hath no fellow" said Cromwell when he tried to exterminate the Irish. "The only good nigger is a dead nigger" say the Americans of the Ku-Klux temperament. "Hates any man the thing he would not kill?" said Shylock naively. But we white men, as we absurdly call ourselves in spite of the testimony of our looking glasses, regard all differently colored folk as inferior species.

Shaw in 1934 even draws attention already to the fact that racial fanatics refer to undesirable people as "vermin," thus robbing them of their basic human dignity. The Nazis did exactly that as time went on, degrading in particular the Jewish population with verbal and proverbial invectives to "vermin." In light of what happened in Germany and Europe under National Socialism in the many concentration camps, and in consideration of the harm done to Native Americans and African Americans or any other minority, any variant of the proverb "The only good Indian is a dead Indian" seems unacceptable.

In the meantime the proverb as a direct slur against the Native Americans continues to be in use, an ever ready invective to be cited to keep the painful stereotype alive. In John Buchan's frontier novel *Salute to Adventures* (1915) a young man is willing to give the native population the benefit of the doubt by exclaiming: "'But they tell me the Indians are changed nowadays. They say they've settled down to peaceful ways like any Christian'." But to this a more knowledgeable old-timer answers grimly and without any feeling of reconciliation or understanding about the plight of the original inhabitants of this land: "'Put your head into a catamount's mouth, if you please, but never trust an Indian. The only good kind is the dead kind. I tell you we're living on the edge of hell. It may come this year or next year or five years hence, but come it will'." Fear and hate combine to a point of accepting such blind judgments and beliefs.

There is no end in sight as far as eradicating this proverb from common parlance. Maxwell Bodenheim's comment in his book on *My Life and Loves in Greenwich Village* (1954) appears to be saying something like that: "There is no good Indian but a dead Indian, we are told by the grandsons of men who have been scalped," that is, the image of the Indian savages will always remain among us. The *New Yorker* magazine in 1957 even published a disgusting cartoon showing two frontiersmen and a Native American around a campfire with one of them observing: "I say the only good Indian is a dead Indian. Present company excepted, of course." Is that so-called eastern intellectual sophistication or rather a sign that even the crème de la crème of this society is not free of prejudice? Who then can be surprised to hear common people making such generalizations as "That only went to show that the only good Indian was a dead Indian" or "'They're the Indians—and the only good Injun is a dead one, you can take that from me'." And is it conceivable that people actually compose jokes around this most hurtful slander against Native Americans, just as terribly sick minds have come up with Auschwitz jokes? The cartoon in the *New Yorker* just mentioned is a small example of this type of sick humor, but even more upsetting is a short story by Mack Reynolds with the suspect title *Good Indian* (1964). In its mere nine pages the author describes three Indians coming to sign a treaty. The director of the Department of Indian Affairs gets them intoxicated and cheats them out of their land. Gleefully he tells his secretary the next morning:

"Miss Fullbright haven't you ever heard the old proverb *The only good Indian is a dead* —"

Millie's hand went to her mouth. "Mr. *Dowling,* you mean...you put the slug on all three of those poor Seminoles? But...but how about the remaining fifty-five of them. You can't possibly kill them all!"

"Let me finish," Dowling growled. "I was about to say, *The only good Indian is a dead drunk Indian.* If you think I'm hanging over, you should see Charlie Horse and his pals. Those redskins couldn't handle firewater back in the old days when the Dutch did them out of Manhattan with a handful of beads and a gallon of applejack and they *still* can't."

The joke centers around the proverb "The only good Indian is a dead Indian," but the author does not only base his short story on this terrible stereotype, he also alludes, of course, to the other proverbial invective of being "*drunker* than an Indian." This is a tasteless, despicable, and racially motivated joke at the expense of Native Americans, and it shows the tenacity of proverbial stereotypes in today's United States of America.

Far too long has this proverb given justification to the literal and spiritual killing of Native Americans. In its poetic brevity is expressed the national shame of a people whose majority succumbed to the worldview that Native Americans had to give up their identity or be killed. The fact that this tiny piece of folk wisdom is still current today is a very sad comment on this society and its behavior towards Native Americans. As long as there remain prejudices and stereotypes about this minority population, the proverb will not cease to exist. Wherever it will be uttered or written, it will expose blatant inhumanity towards the Native Americans. The conscious attempt to refrain from using the proverb "The only good Indian is a dead Indian" might at least help to bring about some changes towards a better life for Native Americans, one of pride and dignity as is befitting for the indigenous people of this great country—better the proverb die a long overdue death than any Native American get hurt by it anymore.

"GOOD FENCES MAKE GOOD NEIGHBORS": AN AMBIGUOUS PROVERB OF RELATIONSHIPS

There is an inherent ambiguity in the proverb "Good fences make good neighbors" that stems from the fact that its metaphor contains both the phenomenon of fencing someone or something in while at the same time fencing the person or thing out. This being the case, it is only natural to ask such questions as: When and why do good fences make good neighbors?, When and why should we build a fence or wall in the first place?, and When and why should we tear such a structure down? In other words, the proverb contains within itself the tension between boundary and openness, between demarcation and common space, between individuality and collectivity, and between many other conflicting attitudes that separate people from each other, be it as neighbors in a village or city or as nations on the international scene. Much is at stake when it comes to erecting a fence or a wall, no matter whether the structure is meant for protection or separation from the other, to wit the Great Wall of China, the Berlin Wall, the walls that separate Americans from Mexicans or Israelis from Palestinians, and one individual neighbor from another. What for heaven's sake is the folk wisdom of the proverb

"Good fences make good neighbors"? Should it not be the goal of humankind to tear down fences and walls everywhere? How can anybody justify the erection or maintenance of barriers between people and neighbors?

People everywhere and at all times have seen the pros and cons of a fence marking property lines and keeping people from infringing on each other's personal space. They have expressed their insights in various proverbs that are actually quite similar to the basic idea of the proverb "Good fences make good neighbors" that advocates some distance between neighbors: "There must be a *fence* between good neighbors" (Norwegian), "Between neighbors' gardens a *fence* is good" (German), "Build a *fence* even between intimate friends" (Japanese), "Love your *neighbor,* but do not throw down the dividing wall" (Indian [Hindi]), and "Love your *neighbor,* but put up a fence" (Russian). There are also two English proverbs that express the principal idea of "Good fences make good neighbors," albeit in different images and structures, namely "Love your *neighbor,* but don't pull down your hedge" (1640) and "A *hedge* between keeps friendship green" (1707). Folk wisdom states again and again that some distance between neighbors might be a good idea for the sake of privacy, as can also be seen in the late medieval Latin proverb "Bonum est erigere dumos cum vicinis" (It is good to erect hedges with the neighbors). While the two "hedge" proverbs express similar ideas as the "fence" proverb, they certainly don't have the same linguistic structure upon which "Good fences make good neighbors" might have been constructed. Such proverbs do exist, however, in the English language, to wit "Good *beginning* maketh [makes a] good ending," "A good *husband* makes a good wife," "A good *Jack* makes a good Jill," "Good *masters* make good servants," and "A good *wife* makes a good husband." Any of these texts might well have provided the structure and pattern for the "fence" proverb.

The origin of the American proverb might well be found in a passage of a letter that the Reverend Ezekiel Rogers of a settlement at Rowley, Massachusetts, wrote to Governor John Winthrop on June 30, 1640: "Touching the businesse of the Bounds, which we haue now in agitation; I haue thought, that a good fence helpeth to keepe peace betweene neighbors; but let vs take heede that we make not a high stone wall, to keepe vs from meeting." Certainly this text connects fences and neighbors, but it is still a far cry from the "fence" proverb under discussion. In fact, the next reference that comes at least close in commenting on fences and neighbors and that might have a proverbial ring to it appeared in a farmer's almanac over 160 years later in 1804: "Look to your fences; and if your neighbor neglects to repair and keep in order his half, do it yourself; you will get your pay." More to the proverbial point is the following statement in Hugh Henry Brackenridge's volume on *Modern Chivalry* (1815) that satirizes various aspects of social and political life in America. Reflecting on Thomas Jefferson as President, he states: "I was always with him in his apprehensions of John Bull [England]. Good fences restrain fencebreaking beasts, and *preserve good neighborhoods*." This formulation from 1815 contains the twofold use of the adjective "good" and approaches to a considerable degree the wording of the "fence" proverb. The passage also already mirrors the political interpretation of the proverb that has become quite prevalent in the modern mass media.

A fascinating variant, stressing the negative results of not keeping up one's fences, appeared 15 years later in *The Vermont Anti-Masonic Almanac for 1831:* "Poor fences make lean cattle and ill-natured neighbors." This text is cited as a piece of farm wisdom, and there is no reason to doubt its proverbiality, even though a few more references would be welcome. It basically is the other side of the coin of the "fence" proverb, especially if one were to simply state "Poor fences make poor neighbors."

It took another 20 years until the proverb "Good fences make good neighbors" finally appeared in print in that precise wording, for the first time in *Blum's Farmer's and Planter's Almanac* (North Carolina) for 1850 and a second time in the same almanac for the year 1861. The folklorist Addison Barker, who made this invaluable discovery a hundred years later, published it in a barely half-a-page note in the *Journal of American Folklore* with the commentary that "It is possible that an early editor found 'Good fences make good neighbors' in a New England almanac or farm journal. Or he may have gleaned the proverb from oral currency" (1951).

The proverb was most likely in oral use in the first half of the nineteenth century, for by 1859 it made it into the *Transactions of the State Agricultural Society of Michigan:* "Good fences make good neighbors, and enable the farmer when he retires to bed at night, to awake in the morning conscious that his crops are secure, and that the labor of weeks are [*sic*] not destroyed in an hour by his neighbor's or his own stock." This statement is a precise explanation of the basic meaning of this proverb, describing the need of good fences on farm land, where the maintenance of the fence or wall depends on responsible reciprocity among neighbors.

By April 3, 1885, the proverb found its way into the *Home Advocate,* a newspaper published in Union Parish, Louisiana, and on June 16, 1901, finally, the proverb had its debut in an article on "Impressions of the New South" by James C. Bayles in the *New York Times:* "If it be true that good fences make good neighbors, the people of this part of the South must dwell together in great amity." The introductory formula "if it be true" can be understood as a marker indicating the common currency of the "fence" proverb at the end of the nineteenth century.

There is no doubt that the appearance of Robert Frost's celebrated poem "Mending Wall" in the year 1914 was of ultimate significance for the general acceptance of the hitherto rather sporadically employed proverb "Good fences make good neighbors." The proverb, and about a third of the time with reference to Frost's use of it in "Mending Wall," became a proverbial "hit" as of the middle of the twentieth century. It owes this tremendous gain in currency to the fascination with Frost's paradoxical poem that helped to zero in on the strikingly ambivalent interpretation possibility of its folk wisdom. Here then is the text of the poem with the twice repeated phrase that "Something there is that doesn't love a wall" and its juxtaposition to the equally repeated proverb "Good fences make good neighbors":

Mending Wall

Something there is that doesn't love a wall,
That sends the frozen-ground-swell under it,
And spills the upper boulders in the sun;
And makes gaps even two can pass abreast.
The work of hunters is another thing:
I have come after them and made repair
Where they have left not one stone on a stone,
But they would have the rabbit out of hiding,
To please the yelping dogs. The gaps I mean,
No one has seen them made or heard them made,
But at spring mending-time we find them there.
I let my neighbor know beyond the hill;
And on a day we meet to walk the line
And set the wall between us once again.
We keep the wall between us as we go.
To each the boulders that have fallen to each.
And some are loaves and some so nearly balls
We have to use a spell to make them balance:
'Stay where you are until our backs are turned!'
We wear our fingers rough with handling them.
Oh, just another kind of outdoor game,
One on a side. It comes to little more:
There where it is we do not need the wall:
He is all pine and I am apple orchard.
My apple trees will never get across
And eat the cones under his pines, I tell him
He only says, 'Good fences make good neighbors.'

Spring is the mischief in me, and I wonder
If I could put a notion in his head:
'*Why* do they make good neighbors? Isn't it
Where there are cows? But here there are no cows.
Before I built a wall I'd ask to know
What I was walling in or walling out,
And to whom I was like to give offense.
Something there is that doesn't love a wall,
That wants it down.' I could say 'Elves' to him,
But it's not the elves exactly, and I'd rather
He said it for himself. I see him there
Bringing a stone grasped firmly by the top
In each hand, like an old-stone savage armed.
He moves in darkness as it seems to me,
Not of woods only and the shade of trees.
He will not go behind his father's saying,
And he likes having thought of it so well
He says again, 'Good fences make good neighbors.'

Clearly this is a dramatic dialogue with much irony added to it. The complex meaning of the ambiguous poem can be summarized as follows: it is a poem about boundaries, barriers, (in)determinacy, conventions, tradition, innovation, (dis)agreements, individuality, community, property, behavior, communication, knowledge, and folk wisdom, to be sure. It is generally agreed that the speaker of the poem is not Robert Frost, who as the poet intended nothing more or less than to display the confrontation of two neighbors over the maintenance of a wall that, to make things even more difficult, is not really needed any longer for any pragmatic reasons. Commenting on this poem in a letter of November 1, 1927, Frost states that he consciously employed his "innate mischievousness" in setting up the argumentative dialogue "to trip the reader head foremost into the boundless."

On the one hand, the proverb quite literally seems to express the fact that fences create social walls that prevent any type of communication. But are things quite so simple with the meaning of the proverb? After all, it is not the "old-stone savage" who initiates the rebuilding of the seemingly senseless wall but rather the intellectually inclined speaker. In other words, perhaps the old-fashioned neighbor really is not such a stubborn blockhead after all. He does in fact understand the meaning of the proverb quite differently from the speaker. He sees the need of the fence to get along with his neighbor, that is, it is a positive and not a negative barrier or wall. What makes the proverb so difficult to understand in both of its occurrences and different interpretations by the two neighbors is that by its very nature it is a verbal form of indirection. The very fact that the message of the proverb is expressed indirectly through a metaphor makes its dual interpretation possible. Whether the proverb "Good fences make good neighbors" is looked at positively (valid) or negatively (invalid) very much depends on what side of the fence one is on, whether and what one intends to fence in or fence out, and whether any fence is desirable or necessary in any given situation. Perhaps Robert Frost had nothing else in mind when he wrote this poem but to show that proverbs are verbal devices of mischievous indirection, reflecting by their ambiguous nature the perplexities of life itself. In fact, Frost is saying that the wisdom of the proverb "Good fences make good neighbors" is in the eye of the beholder. The argument of the neighbors over the (in)validity of the proverb continues to the present day and will not cease to take place. And to be sure, the proverb "Good fences make good neighbors" with its possible interpretations also implies the obverse claim that "Good neighbors make good fences." As people deal with forms of appropriate separation (personal space, property, territories, etc.), they do well to stress the need for social interaction and communication across the fence. The "fence" proverb, as it appears in Frost's poem "Mending Wall" (with the emphasis perhaps on mending!) and in oral and written communication, is a perfect metaphor for what keeps people apart or together. It is a folkloristic sign for the divergencies and convergencies of life and forces the careful reader, as the German literary scholar Hubert Zapf has remarked, into a "deautomatization of cultural conventions of thought and perception."

The poets who pick up the "fence" proverb after Frost tend to ignore the ambiguous nature of the folk wisdom. Here, for example, is Raymond Souster's four-line poem "The New Fence" (1955) that argues that a fence between good neighbors is simply not necessary:

("Good fences make good neighbors"
*   — Robert Frost)*

Take my next-door neighbor and I,
waiting eight years to put one up,
and now that we've actually done it
wondering why we bothered in the first place.

But here is yet another twist on the proverb and Robert Frost's poem. While the "fence" proverb helps us to preserve our cherished personal independence and freedom, we must be careful not to twist it into the shortsighted and chauvinistic anti-proverb of "Bad neighbors make good fences"—a thought-provoking variation that concludes Richard Eberhart's poem "Spite Fence" (1980):

After years of bickerings
Family one
Put up a spite fence
Against family two.
Cheek for cheek
They couldn't stand it.
The Maine village
Looked so peaceful.
We drove through yearly,
We didn't know.
Now if you drive through
You see the split wood,
Thin and shrill.
But who's who?
Who made it,
One side or the other?
Bad neighbors make good fences.

The "Maine village" that Eberhart speaks of could be anywhere in the world, where disagreeing neighbors put up a fence to cut off communication. There are many examples that take the wisdom of the proverb variant "Bad neighbors make good fences" far beyond the quiet village scene to the loud arena of international politics.

In the second half of the twentieth century the "fence" proverb has repeatedly been employed to comment on U.S. and Canadian relations, two countries that are the best of friends and that maintain this friendship through thousands of miles of a common border. Naturally, there have been periods of friction, but generally the fence has worked well. Joseph Barber's book title *Good Fences Make Good Neighbors. Why the United States Provokes Canadians* (1958) tells some of this story, for even though the two countries are as close in many sociopolitical aspects as any, they both want to retain their separate identities. That is what makes the fence between them such a good one. The mass media illustrates this in numerous reports making use of the metaphorical "fence" proverb, as for example in this account:

"Good Fences" Keeping Us Canadian

Much of the history of Canada can be seen as the establishment, maintenance, and adjustment of our border with the United States. The bor-

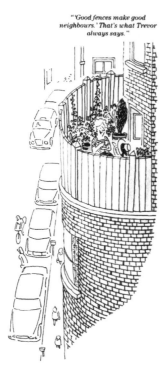

"'Good fences make good
neighbours.' That's what Trevor
always says."

Cited from *Punch* (November 30, 1983),
p. 59. Reproduced with permission of
Punch Ltd.

der is not eroding and the public on both sides may be of a mind to
strengthen "good fences, good neighbors." That same task remains key
in public policy and it remains central to foreign policy. (*Toronto Star,*
2000)

Of course, there are also serious concerns at the U.S. and Mexican border,
primarily dealing with illegal immigrants and drug traffic. Clark Reynolds
discussed these problems in his study *Do Good Fences Make Good Neighbors?
Recent and Prospective U.S.–Mexican Relations* (1973) three decades ago. The
mass media is also filled with numerous articles on the strained relations, sig-
naling that a new iron curtain seems to be falling between the two countries:

Border Watch—Fence Mending

Good fences make good neighbors. That well-known line doesn't always apply to the border between the United States and Mexico: like

the border between any two countries, our fence has some intentional holes. A good deal of the traffic in both directions is legal and beneficial to both sides. But there's truth in the observation that if Mexico City and Washington don't get their border law-enforcement act together, much misery and unhappiness is likely to lie ahead. (*Los Angeles Times,* 1993)

But there is yet another major employment of the "fence" proverb on the international scene, to wit its use as a most fitting metaphor in the Israeli-Palestinian conflict in the Middle East. As the journalist Aviva Cantor put it: "'Good fences make good neighbors,' wrote Robert Frost. If his words apply to any neighbors, it is to Israelis and Palestinians. The two nations are like a couple mired in distrust, fear, and hatred. But each lives in a dream world, because neither is going to get all the property, nor will either succeed in driving the other out. It is time, then, to separate. [...] Here's where the fence idea comes in—not steel, mines, and barbed wire, but a living fence established at an international conference under the umbrella of the United Nations—which has the structure and the experience of maintaining peacekeeping operations—and guaranteed by the world body" (*Christian Science Monitor,* 1989). Five years later, the Israeli journalist Yosef Goell echoed these sentiments by once again using the proverb, albeit as a quotation from Frost: "'Good fences make good neighbors.' (Robert Frost) Nations should separate as much as possible from each other. That is how friction can be reduced" (*Jerusalem Post,* 1994). By the beginning of 1995, Israeli politicians started to think of a real fence that would separate the Israelis from the Palestinians:

Good Fences Make Good Negotiators

Once, the goal of American diplomacy in the Middle East was to help Israel and Palestinians live together. Now, the best aim is to help them live apart. As quickly as possible. Under Ehud Barak's plan, Israel would evacuate three-quarters of the West Bank, abandoning some settlements and annexing others, and build a fence along the border. It would separate Palestinians from the Israeli military and checkpoints, and Israelis from Palestinian suicide bombers. In some cases, good fences make good neighbors or at least non-bleeding ones. (*Newhouse News Service,* 2002)

Separation is perhaps truly the most effective way at the moment to keep Israelis and Palestinians from violent confrontation.

Referring to the new fence and the "fence" proverb, the London *Times* asked two months later on August 17, 2002: "Can you ever a build a bridge by putting up a fence?" The answer ought to be yes, but the necessary bridge-building between Israelis and Palestinians would be much enhanced if both sides were equally committed to building the fence in the first place. Such "good" fences for "bad" neighbors could prove the proverb "Good fences make good neighbors" correct in the case of the Israeli-Palestinian conflict. And yes, communication across the fence could just build a bridge to a better time when the fence could come down again.

This last reference by the journalist Benjamin Forgey on the exhibition "Between Fences" at the National Building Museum in Washington, D.C. is a befitting summary for this investigation of the "fence" proverb. As he reports on the history of fences in the United States, he makes the all too common error of claiming that Robert Frost coined the proverb. Nevertheless, he is aware of its ambiguity in the poem and as a proverb by itself:

The Great Walls of America

"Good fences make good neighbors." Even the poet who coined this most American of proverbs was ambivalent about it. Robert Frost, in "Mending Wall," put the line in his neighbor's mouth, and then proceeded to compare the poor man to "an old-stone savage" moving around in darkness. This ambivalence is doubtless why the saying became so popular—you can see both sides and both seem equally true. Or maybe not quite that. It depends on who is laying the fence, and where and why. Sometimes it simply depends on which side of the fence you're on. (*Washington Post,* 1996)

But it is common knowledge, of course, that there are always two sides to each fence, to that barrier that both separates and connects, if effective communication and serious commitment to common goals like peace, for example, are present. When people work together on not totally dispensable fences, they might just build bridges across them and learn to tolerate each other in a congenial humane way. Fences are a necessary evil in human relationships, and it is better to mend them together than to infringe on each other's territory or privacy. Even though "Something there is that doesn't love a wall," there is ample truth in the proverb that "Good fences make good neighbors."

"A PICTURE IS WORTH A THOUSAND WORDS": AN ADVERTISING SLOGAN TURNED AMERICAN PROVERB

In Ivan Turgenev's well-known novel *Otsy i deti* (*Fathers and Sons,* 1862) the geologist Eugenii Vasil'ich Bazarov is looking at a few drawings of the mountains in Saxony. When Anna Sergeevna Odintsova points out that he as a scientist could learn much more about these mountains from a book than these illustrations, Bazarov gives her the surprising answer "Risunok nagliado predstavit mne to, chto v knige izlozheno na tselykh desiati stranitsakh" (A picture shows me at a glance what it takes dozens of pages of a book to expound). In other words, it is argued that a picture can in fact be worth more than numerous book pages. This is doubtlessly the case also for someone who has difficulty reading or who perhaps cannot read at all. An English proverb from around 1660 expresses this observation only too well as "*Pictures* are the books of the unlearned." While these references claim that pictures can have a greater value than books, they can hardly be considered direct antecedents to the relatively new proverb "A (One) picture is worth a thousand words." Although the predominance of visual communication is stressed, the twentieth-century proverb does not contrast the picture with a book or the number of its pages. Rather it is based on an easily recognizable structure of one picture having the value of a thousand words, a typically proverbial exaggeration to emphasize the discrepancy between visual and verbal communication.

Modern psychological research on perception has shown that the message of this proverb is only too true in light of such visual mass media as television, videos, photographs, advertisements, cartoons, comics, and so on. People communicate more and more through pictures—a fine example being the signs in international airports for the foreign travelers—and there is no doubt that imagery often precedes any verbal process. Alan Dundes, in a fascinating study on this "primacy of vision in American culture," has argued convincingly that "Americans have a deep-seated penchant for the visual sense" since "for Americans the universe is essentially something they can draw a picture or diagram of." Dundes supports this claim by referring to several proverbs and proverbial expressions that reflect this visual metaphorical attitude, his prime example being the proverb "*Seeing* is believing" that has a particularly high frequency in American speech (Dundes 1980). While this proverb dates back to at least the year 1609 in England, it is surprising that Dundes does not cite the American proverb "A picture is worth a thousand words" to support his thesis of the visualization of American culture. From what he and social as well as psycholinguistic scholars have been able to show about the growing preference of visual communication in American society, a strong case could certainly be made that the proverb "A picture is worth a thousand words" had to originate in this country. The fact that it has gained considerable currency since about 1975 as a loan translation in the German language is yet another convincing indication of America's cultural predominance in the Western world where visual media are steadily gaining on the written and even oral word (see Mieder 1989a).

The coiner of the proverb "A picture is worth a thousand words" certainly had an acute knowledge of this shift towards imagery of many kinds. But the insight needed a "catchy" wording and structure in order to gain proverbial currency. The actual structural pattern was definitely not invented by the person who so successfully formulated this new text. For there exists a well-defined international proverb structure of "a,one : hundred,thousand" as can be seen from such texts as "A *friend* is better than a thousand silver pieces" (Greek), "One good *head* is better than a hundred strong hands" (English), "A *moment* is worth a thousand gold pieces" (Korean), "A single *penny* fairly got is worth a thousand that are not" (German), "*Silence* is worth a thousand pieces of silver" (Burmese), and so on. Of particular significance might be the proverb "One *deed* is worth a thousand speeches," which Bartlett Jere Whiting included in his important collection of *Early American Proverbs and Proverbial Phrases* (1977) with only one reference from the year 1767. The "thousand speeches" could easily be changed into "thousand words" and the active "deed" became quite simply the visual "picture." However, the proverb was not included in a proverb collection until 1977, and by that time the "picture" proverb had already gained a considerable age itself. It is doubtful that this rather uncommon text served as a direct basis for the new proverb since it never gained general currency.

To complicate matters a bit more, mention must also be made of such proverbs as "One *laugh* is worth a thousand groans," "One good *deed* is worth a hundred promises," "A *smile* is worth a million dollars," and "One *smile* is worth a thousand tears" that were all collected in oral use in the United States between 1945 and 1985 and that are recorded in Wolfgang Mieder's, Stewart A. Kingsbury's, and Kelsie B. Harder's *A Dictionary of American Proverbs* (1992). No matter whether or not any of these texts were already current when "A picture is worth a thousand words" was formulated, they clearly illustrate the widespread use of the proverbial structure "a,one : hundred,thousand." That being the case, it only took a keen mind to come up with a new text (wording) that caught on quickly since it reflected the growing visualization of the American culture and its worldview.

Although the actual coiner of a proverb is rarely known, in this case the lexicographer Burton Stevenson not only succeeded in 1948 in locating the individual himself, but he also pinpointed the precise date of its first printed version. He had discovered the original text "One look is worth a thousand words" in the American advertising journal *Printers' Ink* of December 8, 1921. There the national advertising manager Fred R. Barnard of the Street Railways Advertising Co. had published a two-page advertisement with the headline "One Look is Worth a Thousand Words." The dry explanatory text, *without* a picture, is an early plea for the desirability of including pictures in effective advertisements:

"One Look is Worth a Thousand Words"

So said a famous Japanese philosopher, and he was right—nearly everyone likes to read pictures.

"Buttersweet is Good to Eat" is a very short phrase but it will sell more goods if presented, with an appetizing picture of the product, to many people morning, noon and night, every day in the year, than a thousand word advertisement placed before the same number of people only a limited number of times during the year.

Good advertising for a trade marked product is nothing more nor less than the delivery of favorable impressions [pictures] for it, and it does not make any difference whether they are delivered through newspapers, magazines or street car advertising.

[...]

It is simply the preponderance of favorable impressions [pictures] for a meritorious product that reminds the consumer to buy it again and again.

From a modern point of view this advertisement is absolutely boring and the fact that a picture is missing makes matters even worse. But that is exactly the purpose of these two pages of text, for Barnard, the shrewd advertising executive, argues innovatively and convincingly that successful advertising is in fact only possible through pictures. How correct he was can be seen in almost all the advertisements that are produced today based on this marketing philosophy and surely also on yet another new American proverb "What you *see* is what you get."

About six years later Fred Barnard repeated his conviction in another two-page advertisement. This time, however, he also included a picture of the happy little boy Bobby, who is looking forward to a piece of cake that his mother has baked with "Royal" baking powder. The picture of the boy, the cake, and the can of baking powder result in an effective visual advertising message:

"Make a Cake for Bobby"

—that's what this car card said *every day* to many millions of women. It reminded all mothers *every day* of a sure way to give a treat to their own children. And hundreds of thousands got an extra thrill with their next cake making because of the happy expression of the boy on the car card.

In addition Barnard also included a small illustration of six Chinese characters with an English translation: "Chinese Proverb: One picture is worth ten thousand words."

Quite obviously Barnard knew about the growing use of proverbs as advertising slogans since they express a message (or truth) with a certain claim of traditional authority and wisdom. It is of interest that Barnard changed his earlier formulation "One look is worth a thousand words" to "One picture is worth ten thousand words." The use of the word "picture" expresses even more precisely the idea that the viewer of an advertisement should react with a mere "look" (glance) at a catchy and somewhat informative picture. The visualization of the advertising message is of utmost importance, and that's why Barnard changed his original text now to the picture that is worth "ten thousand" words.

While Barnard referred to a fictitious "Japanese philosopher" as the originator of his first text, he now claims that his varied advertising slogan is in fact a Chinese proverb. This change of mind alone already indicates that Barnard simply invented the statement for his manipulative marketing purposes. The "Japanese philosopher" and the "Chinese proverb" were only added in order to increase the credibility and authority of the "proverbial" truth. American readers most likely thought of the sayings of Confucius (551–479 B.C.) when they read these references, but Barnard's text is not to be found among his wisdom sayings nor in Asian proverb collections.

In any case, Barnard's advertising slogan caught on quickly. In November of 1934 the Lakeside Press advertising agency produced an advertisement that is based on the same reasoning that Barnard had used to create his slogan in the first place: A picture shows a pretty little girl helping her mother baking a cake. To this appealing illustration the copywriter has attached the varied headline "One picture beats a thousand words" with the following text:

Everyone who has ever planned or published a *food* advertisement knows that while the copy-writer is struggling futilely for flavorous and aromatic adjectives to sell the product, the color photographer accomplishes the whole job with a single click of the shutter.
It's a simple truth that Pictures sell where words can't.

The last sentence, "Pictures sell where words can't," so appropriately called a "simple truth," has what it takes for a slogan to become a proverb—it is short and to the point, it contains a piece of wisdom, it is easily understandable, it uses everyday vocabulary, and it is memorable. However, no other references have been located of this sentence. Hidden away in the copy of an advertisement it probably had no chance to catch on and become proverbial.

But advertisers have without doubt accepted the solid advice of the statement "Pictures sell where words can't," as can be seen in all types of advertisement in the mass media. Barnard's slogan in its original wording or in varied form is heard frequently in oral communication, while at the same time it is effectively used in advertisements, cartoons, and literary works. In 1944 the DuMont Co. of Precision Electronics and Television used the unchanged headline "One Picture is Worth a Thousand Words" with the beginning of the text adding "... and each picture flashing across the screen of your DuMont Television-Radio Receiver will fill your home with a kind of delight you probably have dreamed of many times." Abernathy's Department Store of Burlington, Vermont, quite literally printed only a picture of its establishment with just the caption "One picture is worth a thousand words," obviously taking the proverb at its face value. Fred Barnard would certainly have been pleased to see his advertising philosophy employed in this fashion. And his delight would surely have been at its pinnacle if he had had a chance to look at a newspaper advertisement depicting nothing but four roses and the headline "In whiskey, this picture is worth a thousand words." The name of the distillery is not even mentioned, and the viewer must make the connection with the Four Roses Whiskey Co. by visual means alone. Here the picture truly is worth a lot, for it must communicate the entire advertising message and the name of the whiskey.

There are also a couple of comic strips that play upon the standard form of the proverb. In a *Peanuts* comic strip Lucy is confronted with the task of writing a two thousand–word report. She wittily observes that "I have heard it said that one picture is worth a thousand words...," quickly draws two pictures and smartly proclaims: "What we have here is a couple of pictures." This is pretty clever for a little girl, and it shouldn't be a surprise that a youngster of this visual age would reach that literal interpretation of the proverb. Little wonder that Lucy's cohort Billy from *The Family Circus* cartoons has quite a similar reaction to the proverb: "A picture is worth a thousand words. I guess Shakespeare should have learned to draw." The latter example does indeed convey the unwillingness of the younger generation to read the classics. Shakespeare and other writers of world literature must today be presented in the form of comic strips, cartoons, videos, or major motion pictures to reach the young popu-

Cited from *Time* (September 3, 1984), p. 43.

lation at all. From a pedagogical and cultural literacy point of view the proverb "A picture is worth a thousand words" can take on a rather depressing connotation since it helps to lessen the importance of the written word.

By now this often-quoted proverb has been reduced to the formula "A (One) X is worth a thousand words" to express the importance that this society places on almost anything but the verbal message. Often the variable "X" reflects the materialism that people are eagerly striving for. As early as 1972 the British Jaguar automobile company advertised its luxury sedan with the slogan "One drive is worth a million words." The advertising copy is accordingly very short indeed and merely states that the new model was yet further improved over the already perfect previous Jaguar. Why use a "million words" to inform the consumer properly when all that is needed is the experience of an actual ride?! The Ford Motor Co. eagerly followed suit in 1984 with an extensive advertising campaign for its classic Thunderbird. But predictably

American, the advertisement only showed a picture of the car with the large headline "One drive is worth a thousand words." Any text whatsoever is missing, and why should the copywriters have bothered when the consumer seemingly wants only to see, touch, and experience the Thunderbird?

A variant of the proverb has also been used as a birthday card message above the picture of a furry cat holding a rose: " . . . They say—'One flower can speak a thousand words' . . . " The text on the inside of the card enumerates dozens of wishes with the conclusion "in short, briefly, when it comes down to it, at the end of the day, I really, sincerely hope that your birthday is quite nice!" Equally "cute" is, of course, a large poster depicting a couple of prairie dogs hugging each other with the message "A hug is worth a thousand words." But such messages of friendship and love quickly disappear in such proverbial captions as "And I say one bomb is worth a thousand words" underneath a caricature of two high-level military officers discussing the state of the world at a cocktail party. And how unromantic is the comment by a business executive to another below a second cartoon: "One dollar is worth a thousand words." Power and money have replaced the world of pictures and words, reminding us that the lack of visual and verbal communication alike endanger our very existence.

There also exist variants that are based on the structural formula "A (One) picture is worth a thousand Ys" in which it is the usual noun "words" that has been replaced. The Business Committee for the Arts of the city of Cincinnati got Wendy's fast-food franchise to promote a calendar containing pictures of local artists. A subsequent advertisement in *Time* explained this new way of selling Wendy's hamburgers: It showed one of those pictures and displayed the large headline "One picture is worth a thousand hamburgers." Part of the accompanying copy read as follows:

> Wendy's has discovered there's an art to selling hamburgers. When Wendy's in Cincinnati decided to help local artists, they developed a calendar which featured paintings of scenes of the city, like the one pictured here. The calendar was sold for $1.19 in 26 of its Cincinnati restaurants. Wendy's donated 10 cents to the Cincinnati Commission on the Arts for each calendar sold . . . From Wendy's to Flanigan's Furniture Inc., the Business Committee for the Arts is helping companies of all sizes discover that supporting the arts can paint a nice picture for their business. . . . You'll find your interest repaid a thousand times.

This certainly represents an innovative way of joining forces between business and art, benefiting both the sales of thousands of hamburgers and, at least equally important, the appreciation and sale of artists' works.

Some copywriters have reduced the proverb "A (One) picture is worth a thousand words" even further by replacing both the nouns "picture" and "words" at the same time, the result being the structural formula "A (One) X is worth a thousand Ys." In 1980 the Gulf Oil Co. pushed the idea of gas economy through carpooling by showing a van that transports a number of employees to work each day with the fitting statement "Gulf is van pooling. Because one van is worth 1,000 gallons." And very clever indeed was a British advertisement for Cross fountain pens based on this pattern since it included the product name in the slogan, presented a picture of such a pen, and also played on the traditional custom of placing little crosses at the end of a letter to represent love and kisses: "A Cross says more than a thousand kisses." From a folkloristic point of view this can be considered a slogan masterpiece, and it is to be expected that it was a mercantile success as well. The proverbial ring of the altered proverb and the folkloric message of love must have sent plenty of consumers out on a purchasing spree, indicating once again how folklore and in particular proverbs are effective tools in modern advertising.

A final group of examples illustrates yet another way that advertisers have found to manipulate this proverbial slogan. They can all be reduced to the structural formula "A (One) X is worth a thousand pictures," and they represent a fascinating reversal of the actual proverb. Of particular interest is a large advertising page from a 1980 *Fortune* magazine that in a way goes back to Fred Barnard's original advertisement of 1921. Here too there is no picture and the slogan argues provocatively "Sometimes a word is worth a thousand pictures." The adverb "provocatively" is used intentionally since the reader will obviously juxtapose this variation with the actual proverb "A picture is worth a thousand words" and wonder what has happened to this clear insight. But then follows an interesting line of argumentation by the marketing people of the J. Walter Thompson advertising agency, which has specialized in magazine advertisements for such publications as *Fortune:*

> Whenever it's rumored that the printed word is about to disappear beneath an electronic wave, there are certain things that give us great comfort. The flourishing state of magazines—as witnessed here by *Fortune*'s fiftieth anniversary—is one of them.
>
> Ultimately there is no substitute for print in the transmission of detailed information and complicated ideas. That's as true for advertising as it is for anything else.

It is indeed a refreshing fact to see an advertising agency argue for once that words still count, that is, that informational advertising must rely on the spoken or written word in addition to pictures.

And yet, other advertising agencies have found a way to use even the re-versal formula "A (One) word is worth a thousand pictures" in a way that sup-ports the idea that informational advertisements based on several sentences or even paragraphs are *not* desirable. These copywriters, if one can call them that, simply take the pronoun "a (one)" literally and print just that *one* word together with the slogan and no or only a very short explanatory comment. Thus the Meister Clothes Company printed only its name in large letters and some nondescript fabrics with the telling slogan "One word that's worth a thousand pictures."

The Howard Bank of Vermont also made effective use of this proverb re-versal. Its advertisement contains an empty page with the following message on the bottom that plays beautifully on the word "Vermont" and its almost mystical qualities:

> A word that's worth a thousand pictures.
> Vermont.
> It's more than a state in New England, it's a whole state of mind. A one-word summary of farm houses, foliage, syrup and snow that moves more people than any other word we know.
>
> Vermont. Whether you plow it, paint it, manufacture or market its products, being here means you're part of something very special. And we're very proud to be in the picture.
> The Howard Bank

A last advertising example by the Irish Tourist Board summarizes what has been said about the proverb "A (One) picture is worth a thousand words" and its use and reinterpretation in American society. Besides displaying eight col-orful pictures, the word "Ireland" appears in large print with the slogan "A place that's worth a thousand pictures." And part of the copy reads: "Ireland is indescribable. You've got to see it to believe it. The next best thing to being there is to picture the lush, green, rolling hills, crystal clear lakes and rivers, crisp fresh air and the charming friendly people who speak your language. But that's only part of the picture. Because there's much more to see and do in Ire-land." Yes, it's seeing, hearing, and experiencing Ireland that counts for the tourist. After all, the tourist perhaps is the perfect match for the proverb "*See-ing* is believing." Maybe there will at least be some tourists who might also pay some attention to the oral folklore and the written works of James Joyce, for words ought to be part of a tourist trying to get the complete picture as it were.

All these examples have amply proved that "A (One) picture is worth a thousand words" has become a bona fide proverb in the Anglo-American world and through translations slowly in other countries as well. The fact that conscious variations of it have been recorded as early as the 1950s is yet another indication that Fred Barnard's advertising slogan reached a proverbial status in a relatively short amount of time. With that type of popularity it is not surprising that the proverb has now been registered as such in various language and proverb dictionaries. As a true American proverb it has been disseminated throughout the English-speaking world and elsewhere as, for example, in Germany. The proverb with its emphasis on visual preoccupation represents the worldview of American society in particular. Among a population where "Seeing is believing" is a principle way of communication, the proverb "A picture is worth a thousand words" will doubtlessly retain equal importance, and it is a convincing example that new proverbs are still being coined to reflect the ever changing value system of modern society. One thing is for certain—there is a lot of wisdom in the claim that "A proverb in the hand—is often worth a thousand words."

PROVERBS FROM DIFFERENT CULTURES AND LANGUAGES

The following proverbs were located in numerous proverb collections, but I am listing at least two or three readily available bilingual collections at the end of each group of 35 proverbs so that readers can find texts in their original languages. The full bibliographical information is given in the comprehensive bibliography at the end of the book. The proverbs are arranged alphabetically according to italicized key words, and where appropriate, ethnic identities are provided in parentheses as well.

African Proverbs

Two small *antelopes* can beat a big one. (*Ashanti*)
An *ax* without a handle does not cut firewood. (*Swahili*)
Beans are not equal to meat. (*Ovambo*)
However bad the *bread* it is better than cattle dung. (*Hausa*)
Do not eat your *chicken* and throw its feathers in the front yard. (*Kpelle*)
A *child* that does not cry dies in the cloth it is carried in. (*Shona*)
Two *cocks* do not crow from the same roof. (*Annang*)
Two *crocodiles* do not live in one hole. (*Ga*)
A *dog* with a full mouth will not bark. (*Fulani*)
When two *elephants* jostle, that which is hurt is the grass. (*Swahili*)
All the *flowers* of a tree do not produce fruit. (*Wolof*)
By the time the *fool* has learned the game, the players have dispersed.
   (*Ashanti*)
If you make *friends* on the road, your knife will be lost. (*Oji*)

A *goat* cannot be cooked with the hyena. (*Hausa*)

You cannot shave a man's *head* in his absence. (*Yoruba*)

A *hen* does not break her own egg. (*Swahili*)

Hunger cannot be washed away like dirt. (*Shona*)

When rain beats on a *leopard* it wets him, but it does not wash his spots. (*Ashanti*)

Love is like color which fades away. (*Shona*)

It is the *mouth* that cuts the throat. (*Hausa*)

If the *natives* eat rats, eat rats. (*Swahili*)

The *owner* of the bed knows his bed bug. (*Fulani*)

A *path* has ears. (*Ashanti*)

A *pot* does not boil when not looked after. (*Zulu*)

Rats never sleep on the mat of the cat. (*Jabo*)

Make haste before the *road* gets slippery. (*Bemba*)

The *rope* that is not at hand does not bind the firewood. (*Swahili*)

A *sack* is no load for a goat. (*Hausa*)

When the *snail* crawls, its shell accompanies it. (*Yoruba*)

If a *snake* bites your neighbor, you too are in danger. (*Swahili*)

Noisy *talk* does not bring about a solution. (*Ovambo*)

The *tortoise* is not overburdened by its shell. (*Shona*)

The *vulture* scents the carcass, however high in the air he may be. (*Yoruba*)

Water from a salt well puts out a house on fire. (*Ovambo*)

The best *words* give no food. (*Wolof*)

(see Kuusi 1970; Pachocinski 1996; Scheven 1981; Whitting 1940)

Arabic Proverbs

To *ask* well is to know much.

If the *ass* is summoned to the wedding it is to carry wood.

A handful of *bees* is worth more than a sackful of flies.

The *beetle* in its hole is a sultan.

A *bird* by its note and a man by his talk.

Birth is the messenger of death.

A *book* is like a garden carried in the pocket.

Be *brothers,* but keep accounts.

The *camel* is an open shop.

In the house where there are no *children* they have no light.

When the *cow* falls down, knives are plentiful.

The *dogs* bark, but the caravan passes.

When the *donkey* has eaten his fill he scatters his fodder.

He who *eats* alone, coughs alone.
When *fate* arrives the physician becomes a fool.
Every man thinks his own *fleas* gazelles.
The *flies* know the face of the milkman.
If your *friend* be honey, don't eat him.
If minds were alike *goods* would age in the bazaars.
Keep your tents separate and bring your *hearts* together.
Light your *lamp* before it gets dark.
Life, like fire, begins with smoke and ends with ashes.
Love and pregnancy and riding upon a camel can't be hid.
Nobody is perfect save *Mohammed.*
He who earns *money* earns tears.
Moonlight and oil are the ruin of a house.
It is not every time that the *pitcher* is saved.
Power is sweet to nurse, bitter to wean.
Repetition will teach the donkey.
All *roads* lead to the flour mill.
He who has no *spoon* burns his hand.
The clever *thief* does not steal from his own street.
The *wall* that has support does not fall.
A *well* of sweet water is always empty.
The *world* is a scratching of donkeys.

(see Champion 1938 [1963]: 329–344, Hankí 1998)

Chinese Proverbs

Keep your broken *arm* within your sleeve.
When eating *bamboo sprouts,* remember the man who planted them.
If you cannot pole a *boat,* don't meddle with the pole.
You can't get fat from a dry *bone.*
A load of *books* does not equal one good teacher.
Clean out the *drainpipes* while the weather is good.
If a *family* has an old person in it, it possesses a jewel.
Even the ten *fingers* cannot be of equal length.
Friends should have a high wall between them.
You can't catch two *frogs* with one hand.
One *generation* opens the road upon which another travels.
When the *guests* have gone the host is at peace.
Every *highway* leads to Peking.
Hunger is cured by food, ignorance by study.
Ivory does not grow in the mouth of a dog.

Don't lift off the *lid* too soon.
Sweet-melon *lips,* bitter-melon heart.
No *medicine* can cure a vulgar man.
The *melon-seller* shouts that his melons are sweet.
Money hides a thousand deformities.
To have a good *neighbor* is to find something precious.
An *official* never flogs a bearer of gifts.
You can't beat *oil* out of chaff.
Everyone has a black *pig* in his house.
Little *posts* cannot support heavy weights.
If the *profits* are great, the risks are great.
Don't add *salt* to a boat load of salt fish.
You cannot get two *skins* from one cow.
Speak softly, and be slow to begin your speech.
Leave a little of the *tail* to whisk off the flies.
A good *talker* does not equal a good listener.
Tiger and deer do not walk together.
When the *tree* falls there is no shade.
Distant *water* cannot quench a fire near by.
Words are empty, but the writing-brush leaves traces.
                    (see Rohsenow 2002; Smith 1888 [1965]; Sun 1981)

French Proverbs

It is good to give *advice,* but better to give the remedy.
Be not a *baker* if your head is of butter.
Beauty is eloquent even when silent.
Forbidden *bread* creates an appetite.
Every *cook* makes his own sauce.
The old *cow* thinks she never was a calf.
Death is deaf to our wailings.
A *door* must be either open or shut.
The *dough* of poor people freezes in the oven.
Dress slowly when you are in a hurry.
There's not *enough* if there's not too much.
The shortest *follies* are the best.
Leave off playing when the *game* is at its best.
Hope is the bread of the unfortunate.
Without *jealousy* there is no love.
A fat *kitchen* makes a lean will.
Don't rely on the *label* of the bag.

Life is half spent before we know what life is.
A hard *loaf* needs a sharp tooth.
A crooked *log* makes a good fire.
Old *loves* and old embers soon catch fire.
Everyone must go to the *mill* with his own sack.
Money is a good passport.
Stroke a *nettle* and it will sting you, grasp it and it is as soft as silk.
Precious *ointments* are put in small boxes.
An old *oven* is easier to heat than a new one.
Paris was not built in a day.
Rain always falls on those who are wet.
Rust wears more than use.
The first *step* binds one to the second.
There are *toys* for all ages.
Love *truth*, but pardon error.
Wine and confession reveal everything.
A tiny little *word* can be a clap of thunder.
Youth lives on hope, old age on remembrance.
                    (see Brezin-Rossignol 1997; Flonta 2001a; Mertvago 1996a)

German Proverbs

Who says "*A*" must also say "B."
Old *age* doesn't protect from folly.
A good *anvil* does not fear the hammer.
Don't throw the *baby* out with the bathwater.
Beauty wanes, virtue remains.
In *brevity* there is spice.
Little *children*, little troubles; big children, big troubles.
A clean *conscience* is a soft pillow.
Without *diligence*, no prize.
Fools' hands besmear table and walls.
He who *greases* well, drives well.
Dirty *hands*, clean money.
One's own *hearth* is worth gold.
Idleness is the beginning of all vice.
Ingratitude is the world's reward.
What little *Jack* doesn't learn, big Jack will never learn.
The *last* gets bitten by the dogs.
Lies have short legs.
Old *love* does not rust.

Luck and glass break easily.
Married state, painful state.
The *morning hour* has gold in its mouth.
Order is half of life.
Who does not honor the *penny* is not worthy of the thaler.
Practice makes the master.
He who *rests,* rusts.
A good *rooster* seldom turns fat.
Self-praise stinks.
Better a *sparrow* in the hand than a pigeon on the roof.
First *think,* then dare.
What takes a long *time* turns out well at last.
Time brings counsel.
A good *trade* has a golden foundation.
Old *trees* must not be transplanted.
Who does not love *wine,* women, and song, remains a fool his whole life
    long.

(see Kremer 1955; Mertvago 1997a;
Schemann and Knight 1995; and my own translations)

Indian Proverbs

Giving *advice* to a stupid man is like giving salt to a squirrel. (*Kashmiri*)
A full *belly* makes a heavy head. (*Bihar*)
It is a brave *bird* that makes its nest in the cat's ear. (*Hindi*)
A frisky *bull* carries a good load. (*Telugu*)
A *calf* that goes with a pig will eat excrement. (*Tamil*)
Charity protects you. (*Hindustani*)
Distance promotes close friendship. (*Tamil*)
The *eagle* will not pursue flies. (*Hindi*)
The *frog* perishes by its own mouth. (*Tamil*)
Empty *hands* don't go to the mouth. (*Hindustani*)
Honor and profit are not found in the same dish. (*Hindi*)
Hunger cannot be satisfied by eating froth. (*Tamil*)
Justice is better than worship. (*Kashmiri*)
Labor is bitter, but sweet is the bread which it buys. (*Hindi*)
Where *love* reigns the impossible may be attained. (*Tamil*)
Music has no charms for a buffalo. (*Bihar*)
A good *name* comes after a while, but a bad name is soon obtained.
    (*Kashmiri*)
The *owl* is small, its screech is loud. (*Tamil*)

One blind *ox* will lead a thousand oxen astray. (*Kashmiri*)

What is *play* to one is death to another. (*Bihar*)

A cracked *pot* will hold sugar. (*Tamil*)

Quarrels come of laughter, and disease of coughing. (*Hindi*)

A kind *reception* is better than a feast. (*Telugu*)

If *rice* is thrown on the roof, a thousand crows will come. (*Tamil*)

It is easy to throw anything into the *river,* but difficult to take it out again. (*Kashmiri*)

A *slip* of the tongue is worse than that of the foot. (*Tamil*)

Kill the *snake* as well as save the stick. (*Bihar*)

Soil that is fertile is unfit for the road. (*Hindi*)

A single *stick* upon the hearth does not burn. (*Kashmiri*)

A dog's *tail* can never be straightened. (*Bihar*)

He who planted the *tree* will water it. (*Tamil*)

If *virtue* fails, honor decreases with it. (*Telugu*)

A *word* stirs up anger or love. (*Kashmiri*)

Lack of *work* brings a thousand diseases. (*Hindi*)

The *world* befriends the elephant and tramples on the ant. (*Hindustani*)
  (see Carr 1868 [1988]; Jensen 1897 [1989]; Lazarus 1894 [1991])

Irish Proverbs

It's too late to throw out the *anchor* when the ship is on the rocks.

An empty *barn* needs no roof.

The *beauty* of an old shoe is to polish it.

There is no place like the *bed.*

One *bite* of a rabbit is worth two bites of a cat.

Shallow *brooks* are noisy.

Don't expect a *cherry tree* from an acorn.

It is easier to build two *chimneys* than to keep smoke in one.

Many a white *collar* covers a dirty neck.

Come seldom, come welcome.

A bad *cow* is better than none.

Death is the poor person's cure.

It's not the time to go for the *doctor* when the person is dead.

The *drunkard* will soon have daylight in through the rafters.

It's natural for *ducks* to go barefoot.

Never praise a *ford* till you are over.

Generosity never went to hell.

If you put a silk suit on a *goat,* it is still a goat.

It takes a dirty *hand* to make a clean hearth.

A *herring* in the pan is worth twenty in the sea.
Cleaning the *house* will not pay the rent.
Hunger is a good kitchen.
Good *luck* is better than early rising.
It is not the big *mansion* that makes the happy home.
Good *mearings* [boundaries] make good neighbors.
Big *potatoes* develop from little potatoes.
A dumb *priest* never gets a parish.
It is too late to put a *prop* under a house when it falls.
All are not *saints* that go to church.
There is *skill* in all things, even in making porridge.
It is difficult to take *socks* off a bare-footed man.
You can't teach a *swallow* how to fly.
Time used sharpening a scythe is not time wasted.
It is a poor *village* that has neither smoke nor fire.
There can be no *window* where there is no wall.

(see Gaffney and Cashman 1974; Williams 2000)

Italian Proverbs

Good *bargains* empty the purse.
The *beard* does not make the philosopher.
Beauty is a fading flower.
All is not *butter* that comes from the cow.
Who has no *children* does not know what love is.
The white *coat* does not make the miller.
You cannot hide from your *conscience*.
A *courtesy* is a flower.
Death alone can kill hope.
Diligence is the mother of good fortune.
Every *door* has its knocker.
Better an *egg* today than a hen tomorrow.
When the *feast* is over the saint is forgotten.
The *flame* is not far from the smoke.
Every *flower* loses its perfume in the end.
Fortune is a cow who shows her head to some and her tail to others.
Friends tie their purses with a spider's thread.
Some look for *hair* in new-laid eggs.
Every *horse* scares the flies away with its own tail.
Who *knows* the most believes the least.
It is better to *live* small than to die big.

The *miser* is like the donkey which carries wine and drinks water.
A near *neighbor* is better than distant relatives.
It is better to keep *peace* than to make peace.
The *purse* pays for the eye's mistake.
A young *saint,* an old devil.
A *sin* concealed is half pardoned.
Nothing dries quicker than *tears.*
Time is a file that emits no noise.
Truth can be bent but not broken.
Beware of *vinegar* that is made of sweet wine.
Words and deeds are not weighed in the same balance.
Words do not make flour.
Hasty *work,* double work.
The *world* is a fine book but of little use to those who know not how to
    read.

(see Mertvago 1997b; Flonta 2001b)

Japanese Proverbs

Beauty is but one layer of skin.
A caged *bird* longs for the clouds.
You can't eat the rice *cake* in a picture.
The good *calligrapher* is not choosy about his writing brush.
What is *cheap* may also be bad.
The *cherry tree* is known among others by its flowers.
Confused *crabs* miss their holes.
The *drums* sound according to the way they are struck.
Even *dust* when accumulated makes a mountain.
Eggplants do not grow on melon vines.
The *eyes* speak as much as the mouth.
Large *fish* do not live in a small pond.
Friendship is the marriage of the soul.
A *general* of a defeated army should not talk of tactics.
If the *heart* is right, the deeds will be right.
A *jewel* unless polished will not sparkle.
There is no short cut to *learning.*
Love lives in palaces as well as in thatched cottages.
Money matters make strangers.
Monkeys laugh at the buttocks of other monkeys.
Hot *passion* cools easily.
Wealthy *people* have many worries.

Fast *ripe,* fast rotten.
Early *rising* has seven [many] advantages.
Although *shrimps* may dance around they do not leave the river.
Better a *stitch* now than ten stitches later.
Study well, play well.
A quick *temper* does not bring success.
Unless you enter the *tiger*'s den, you cannot take the cubs.
The *tongue* is mightier than the sword.
The *train* waits for no one.
There are no better *treasures* than children.
Take an *umbrella* before you get wet.
In a *village* do as the village does.
Wisdom and virtue are like the two wheels of a cart.
(see Akiyama 1940; Buchanan 1965; Galef 1987)

Russian Proverbs

Two *bears* don't live together in one den.
Without having tasted the *bitter,* you will not know the sweet.
Don't chop off the *branch* on which you are sitting.
Bread with water is better than a pie with trouble.
As the *call,* so the echo.
Give a *child* seven nannies, and it is sure to be neglected.
The *cow* is giving birth, but the bull's tail hurts.
A frightened *crow* fears even a bush.
To the *drunkard* the sea is knee-deep.
Eggs don't teach the hen.
A small *fish* is better than a large cockroach.
One *fisherman* spots another from afar.
If you don't know the *ford,* don't get into the water.
The farther you go in the *forest,* the more firewood you find.
Each person is the *forger* of his own happiness.
It is too late to worry about your *hair* when you are about to lose your
    head.
Better be born *happy* than pretty.
The *heart* is not a stone.
Learning is light, ignorance is darkness.
Where there is *love,* even a hut will seem like heaven.
A *morsel* looks big in other people's hands.
Moscow wasn't built in an instant.
A bad *peace* is better than a good quarrel.

What's been written with a *pen,* can't be chopped out with an ax.

Allow a *pig* to sit at your table, and it will put its feet on it.

Don't have 100 *rubles,* have 100 friends.

There's no point in taking your *samovar* to Tula [the city where the samovars have traditionally been made].

Seven [the majority] don't wait for one.

If you like to ride, then like pulling the *sled.*

A *tailor* lacks trousers, a shoe-maker lacks shoes.

If everyone gives a *thread,* the naked man will get a shirt.

A *tongue* will get you to Kiev.

Truth stabs the eyes.

If you are afraid of *wolves,* don't go into the forest.

The *word* of the Tsar is a proverb.

(see Lubensky 1995; Margulis and Kholodnaya 2000; Mertvago 1995)

Spanish Proverbs

Admiration is the daughter of ignorance.

Beauty and chastity have a mortal quarrel between them.

When the *bed* is small lie in the center.

Though a *cage* may be made of solid gold, it is still a cage.

Don't look for three feet on a *cat.*

The best *cloth* has uneven thread.

An open *door* tempts a saint.

Faces we see, hearts we don't know.

A *fire* is easily kindled on a warm hearth.

No *fly* dares approach a boiling pot.

If every *fool* carried a stick, firewood would be scarce.

The lame *goat* has no siesta.

A *guest* is beautiful at his back.

The *heart* is no traitor.

Everyone should scratch his own *itch.*

Jealousy bites deeper than fleas.

Who *knows* little soon tells it.

The remedy for *love* is land between.

The *lovers* always think that other people have had their eyes put out.

Marry and grow tame.

Both *melons* and women are hard to know.

Money makes the dog dance.

The *needle* knows what it sows, and the thimble what it pushes.

Take away the *opportunity,* and you take away the sin.
Prosperity forgets father and mother.
Punishment is a cripple, but it does arrive.
Take the middle of the *road* and you won't fall.
A good *rooster* will crow in any chicken coop.
The absent *saint* gets no candle.
With the *spoon* that you choose you will eat.
Sometimes *talking* loses what silence has gained.
He who sows *thistles* should not go barefoot.
Time is gold.
The *tongue* should not say what the head has to pay for.
Words should be weighed, not counted.

    (see Ballesteros 1979; Chen 1998; Flonta 2001e; Mertvago 1996b)

Yiddish Proverbs

A little *advice* can heal a backache.
Age weakens teeth and memory.
You don't need a *calendar* to die.
A *cantor* without a voice is like a sheep without wool.
Chutspeh succeeds.
Even a shelled *egg* won't leap into your mouth.
If there's nothing worth seeing, *eyeglasses* won't help.
It is easy to poke the *fire* with another's hands.
When a *fool* goes to the baths, he forgets to wash his face.
Better a lame *foot* than a lame brain.
The *heart* is half a prophet.
If you stay at *home,* you won't wear out your shoes.
The best *horse* is only a carcass when it dies.
Life is a big headache on a busy street.
If you have no *linen,* you save on laundry bills.
Love is sweet, but tastes best with bread.
Marriage brings much pain but not marrying brings no pleasure.
If you spend *money* for butter, you won't have any for bread.
Pearls around the neck, stones upon the heart.
A full *purse* is not so good as an empty one is bad.
Sitting next to the *rabbi* is no guarantee of becoming one.
Better a *rooster* in the hand than an eagle in the sky.
Keeping the *Sabbath* is easier than preparing it.
Every *sack* is strong until it rips.
Where *salt* is needed shortening won't do.

The *schlemiel* lands on his back and bruises his nose.
A wounded *spirit* is hard to heal.
When the *stomach* is empty so is the brain.
False *teeth* don't hurt.
A nasty *tongue* is worse than a wicked hand.
Half a *truth* is a whole lie.
You can't dance at two *weddings* at the same time.
One cannot live by another's *wits*.
New *worlds,* new troubles.
Worries go down better with soup than without.
      (see Ayalti 1949; Kogos 1970; Kumove 1984 [1986] and 1999)

AUTHENTIC AMERICAN PROVERBS

Many of the proverbs in common use in the United States go back to classical, biblical, and medieval times. They already existed in the English language of Great Britain, and they made their way to North America together with the proverbs of later centuries by way of British immigrants. Such frequently used proverbs include: classical: "One *hand* washes the other" and "*Love* is blind"; biblical: "An *eye* for an eye, and a tooth for a tooth (Exod. 21:24, Lev. 24:20, Deut. 19:21, Matt. 5:38) and "*Man* does not live by bread alone" (Deut. 8:3, Matt. 4:4); medieval: "New *brooms* sweep clean" and "All that glitters is not *gold*"; and later centuries: "*Haste* makes waste" (1346), "Empty *vessels* make the greatest sound" (1430), "Little *pitchers* have large ears" (1546), "*Beauty* is only skin deep" (1606), "A *stitch* in time saves nine" (1732), and "Once *bitten,* twice shy" (1853). They and hundreds more belong to the proverbs that are in continued use in the United States. But they are not American proverbs in the narrower sense, since they did not originate on the soil of this country. Rather they belong to that large stock of proverbs known and used in the various "Englishes" of the world.

In order to shed some light on what proverbs might in fact have been coined in the United States, the American paremiologist Richard Jente (1888–1952) undertook a fascinating study in 1931 based on a compilation of "Proverbs and Proverbial Expressions Current in the United States East of the Missouri and North of the Ohio Rivers" (1929) that Margaret Hardie had published two years earlier. Hardie's list includes 176 individually numbered proverbs with 23 unnumbered variants for a total of 199 texts (Hardie 1929). Since Hardie had provided no annotations, Jente investigated each text for its possible origin in his seminal paper "The American Proverb" (1931–1932), reaching the following conclusions: Approximately 70 percent of these proverbs could be verified by way of English proverb collections to have been in use in England over 200 years earlier, that is, before one can talk of the United States as such. These proverbs are thus of English or even earlier medieval, biblical, or classical origin, having found their way to North America with many other texts. The remaining 30 percent, or about 58 proverbs, Jente could not locate in early English proverb collections. However, for 26 of them he was able to establish at least possible English origins. This means that the English contribution to this list of proverbs current in the United States around 1930 is 84 percent, or 167 of the 199 proverbs. Of the remaining 16 percent, or 32 proverbs, 3.5 percent, or 7 texts, might be adaptations from the English while 6 percent, or 12 proverbs, are from foreign sources other than English. Jente also lists three proverbs of uncertain origin (1.5 percent), which finally leaves the meager number of 10 proverbs, or 5 percent, that are at least with some certainty of American origin. They are as follows:

A setting *hen* never grows fat.
Don't kick a *fellow* when he's down.
Great *minds* run in the same channels.
It pays to *advertise.*
Laugh and the world laughs with you, weep and you weep alone.
Paddle your own *canoe.*
The harder you *fall* the higher you bounce.
The bigger they are the harder they *fall.*
This won't buy the baby's *shoes.*
This won't buy a *dress* for the baby or pay for the one it has on.
(Hardie 1929: 461–465; Jente 1931–1932: 347)

When Jente undertook his task of finding the truly American proverbs in Hardie's list, he did not have the major historical proverb dictionaries of the Anglo-American world available yet. But he was quite correct in his work. The American origin of the first eight proverbs has now been established beyond any doubt. They are all registered with annotations in *A Dictionary of American Proverbs* (1992), where my co-editors Stewart A. Kingsbury and Kelsie B. Harder and I have recorded over 15,000 proverbs collected in use in the United States between 1945 and 1985. It should be noted, however, that "Don't kick a fellow when he's down" is probably a new American variant of the much earlier British proverbial expression "to hit (kick) a *man* when he is down" that goes back to 1551 (see Smith 1935 [1970]: 374; Mieder, Kingsbury, and Harder 1992: 205). "The bigger they are the harder they fall" has traditionally been attributed to the heavyweight boxer Robert Fitzsimmons before his losing fight with James J. Jeffries on July 25, 1900, at San Francisco. But he most likely was varying a British proverb that goes back at least to 1493: "The higher degre [position] the harder is the fal." Some classical antecedents to this formulation have also been found by now (see Stevenson 1948: 749 [no. 2]; Simpson 1982 [1998]: 22–23; Mieder, Kingsbury, and Harder 1992: 51). But be that as it may, both proverbs in the precise formulation as listed by Hardie are in fact American variants that have conquered the English-speaking world. They can safely be called American proverbs as well.

The last two texts about the "baby" are not proverbs per se but rather proverbial expressions along the lines of the popular phrase "That *dog* won't hunt" with the meaning that something is not going to work. The two expressions listed by Hardie might have been regional variants of "This won't buy the baby a new *frock*" (We are achieving nothing like this) for which I have located a reference (see Wilkinson 1993: 276). In any case, both Hardie and Jente were wrong in classifying the two proverbial expressions as proverbs, thus bringing Jente's statistics of American proverbs in Hardie's list down to eight or a mere 4 percent of the total.

All of this shows how difficult it is to establish that a certain proverb is of true American coinage. In fact, for each proverb under consideration, an involved historical investigation would have to be undertaken to find its origin. Fortunately there are now several valuable historical proverb dictionaries available, and dictionaries like *The Oxford English Dictionary* and the possibility of electronic database searches will help such studies along considerably.

The *Dictionary of American Proverbs* is a major resource in the hunt for authentic American proverbs. The following list presents more than a hundred (109) proverbs that for now appear to be American. There is, of course, always the chance that an earlier British reference might be found. In any case, the dates behind the texts (identified by M plus date when available) represent the earliest reference found thus far, one that precedes any British (or Canadian, Australian, etc.) occurrence. For those proverbs without dates, it is at least important to realize that they were registered in the United States between 1945 and 1985. A few additional texts have been added from John A. Simpson's *The Concise Oxford Dictionary of Proverbs* (1982 [1998], identified by S plus date) and from Charles C. Doyle's list of "New Proverbs" (1996, identified by D plus date when available). What these representative proverbs show is that there has been a steady stream of new American proverbs entering the language during the past three centuries. They deserve to be called "American proverbs" rather than "proverbs current in America." And one more thing: owing to the global importance of the American language, many of these proverbs have been spread to other English-speaking countries of the world through the mass media, tourism, popular culture, foreign-language instruction, and so on. Some of these proverbs have also become current in other languages by way of loan translations. Proverbs, and in particular American proverbs, are on the march even today—no doubt about it.

It pays to *advertise.* (M, no date)
Age before beauty. (M1843)
Alcohol and driving don't mix. (M, no date)
There are no *atheists* in foxholes. (M1944, D1944)
No matter how you slice it, it's still *baloney.* (M1931, D1927)
If you can't *beat* them, join them. (M1941, S1941)
Beauty doesn't make the pot boil. (M1860)
Been there, done that. (D, no date)
The blacker the *berry,* the sweeter the juice. (M, no date)
The *bigger* they are (come), the harder they fall. (M1900, corrected date)
You can't judge a *book* by its cover. (M1929, S1929)
You can take the *boy* out of the country, but you can't take the country out of the boy. (M, no date, S1938)
Don't cross the *bridge* till you come to it. (M1850, S1850)
If it ain't *broke,* don't fix it. (S1977)
The *camera* doesn't lie. (D, no date)
Candy is dandy, but liquor is quicker. (M1931, D1931)
Paddle your own *canoe.* (M1802)
Let the *chips* fall where they may. (M1880)
Crime doesn't pay. (M1927, D1927)
Curiosity killed the cat. (M1909, S1921)
The *customer* is always right. (M1928, S1917)
Another *day,* another dollar. (M1957, D1957)
The best *defense* is a good offense. (M1775, S1775)
You can't tell the *depth* of the well by the length of the handle on the pump. (M1940)
Diamonds are a girl's best friends. (D1949)
If you *drink,* don't drive. (M, no date)
Eat, drink, and be merry, for tomorrow you may die. (M1700)
You are what you *eat.* (M1941, S1940)
You can't unscramble *eggs.* (M1928, D1928)
An *elephant* never forgets. (M1937)
Experience keeps (is) a dear school, but fools learn in no other. (M1743, S1743)

Keep your *eye* on the doughnut and not on the hole. (D, no date)

Facts don't lie. (M1748)

All is *fair* in love and war. (M1835, S1845)

Father knows best. (M1931)

Don't kick a *fellow* when he is down. (M1809, corrected date)

Good *fences* make good neighbors. (M1640, S1640, corrected date 1850; see Mieder 2003)

Figures don't lie. (M1739)

Better a big *fish* in a little pond than a little fish in a big pond. (M, no date)

Flattery will get you nowhere. (M1904)

You can't beat a man at his own *game*. (M1756)

Garbage in, garbage out. (M1964, S1964)

What *goes* around, comes around. (S1974)

The *grass* is always greener on the other side of the fence. (M1959, S1959; actually already 1924; see Mieder 1993c)

No *guts,* no glory. (M, no date, D, no date)

Nice *guys* finish last. (D, no date)

The way to a man's *heart* is through his stomach. (M1814, S1814)

If you don't like the *heat,* get out of the kitchen. (S1952)

A setting *hen* never gets (grows) fat. (M, no date)

Hindsight is twenty-twenty. (D, no date)

Last *hired,* first fired. (D1975)

Root, *hog,* or die. (M1834)

Home is where the heart is. (M1870, S1870)

Don't change (swap) *horses* in the middle of the stream (in mid-stream). (M1864, S1864)

Industry pays debts, but despair increases them. (M1742)

Justice delayed is justice denied. (M, no date, D, no date)

The opera (It) isn't over till the fat *lady* sings. (M1978, S1978)

Laziness travels so slowly that poverty soon overtakes him (it). (M1756)

Life begins at forty. (M1932, S1932)

Life is just (but) a bowl of cherries. (M1933, D1933)

Life is just one (damned) thing after another. (M1906, D1906)

There's no such thing as a free *lunch.* (S1967)

You can't keep a good *man* down. (M1900)

Great *minds* run in the same channel. (M, no date)

Money can't buy happiness. (M1792)

Money doesn't grow on trees. (M1750)

Money isn't everything. (M1927, S1927)

Put your *money* where your mouth is. (M, no date, D, no date)

Nobody is perfect. (M1805)

A *picture* is worth a thousand words. (M1921, see Mieder 1990)

It's better to be *pissed* off than pissed on. (D, no date)

Politics makes strange bedfellows. (M1839, S1839)

Put up or shut up. (M1924)

Three *removes* are as bad as a fire. (M1736, S1758)

There is no royal *road* to learning. (M1824, S1824)

There's always *room* at the top. (M1900, S1900)

Hoe your own *row*. (M1844)

It's a poor *rule* that won't work both ways. (M1837)

What you *see,* is what you get. (S1971)

Don't give up the *ship*. (M1814)

From *shirtsleeves* to shirtsleeves in three generations. (M1907, S1907)

Shit happens. (D, no date)

Shit or get off the pot. (D1952)

Every man must skin his own *skunk*. (M1813)

There will be *sleeping* enough in the grave. (M1741)

Sloth makes all things difficult, but industry makes all things easy. (M1734)

Small is beautiful. (S1973)

If you're not part of the *solution,* you're part of the problem. (S1968)

Speak softly and carry a big stick. (M1901)

Three *strikes* and you're out. (D1942)

Different *strokes* for different folks. (M, no date, S1973; actually 1968, and in oral use in the 1950s; see Mieder 1989: 317–332; McKenzie 1996).

Don't sweat the small *stuff.* (D, no date)

If at first you don't *succeed,* try, try again. (M1840, S1840)

Nothing succeeds like *success*. (M1867, S1867)

There's a *sucker* born every minute. (M1850)

Talk is cheap. (M1843, S1843)

It takes two to *tango*. (S1952)

One *thing* at a time. (M1702)

The best *things* in life are free. (M1940)

Things are tough all over. (M, no date, D, no date)

No *tickee*, no washee. (M1931, D1931; in oral use perhaps already at the end of the nineteenth century; see Mieder 1996)

When the going gets *tough,* the tough get going. (S1962)

Two can live as cheaply as one. (M1921, D1921)

Use it or lose it. (D, no date)
Variety is the spice of life. (M1778, S1785)
Hitch your *wagon* to a star. (M1870)
Water seeks its own level. (M1778)
You can't *win* them all. (S1953)
You're only *young* once. (M1941, D1929)
   (see Mieder, Kingsbury, and Harder 1992; Simpson 1982 [1998];
                                                    Doyle 1996)

Many proverbs could be added to this list, but they would not necessarily be known throughout the United States and beyond. The proverbs cited here from *A Dictionary of American Proverbs* are all identified there as having general currency throughout the country. From John A. Simpson's *The Concise Oxford Dictionary of Proverbs* (1982 [1998]) and other English-language proverb collections it is clear that these American proverbs have in fact made their way to Great Britain and doubtlessly also to Canada, Australia, and so on.

REGIONAL AMERICAN PROVERBS

Many proverbs in *A Dictionary of American Proverbs* are listed with only one or two designations of states where they were recorded between 1945 and 1985. They are thus regional proverbs or variants of common proverbs. But these geographical indicators must be taken with a proverbial grain of salt. It is obviously very difficult to establish the precise and restricted location where certain proverbs are used or even coined. This is not the place to present extended lists of regional proverbs from the different American states, but here are at least two samples from Vermont and Texas, one a small state in the Northeast, the other a large state in the Southwest. A few examples of Mexican American proverbs from the Southwest are included as well.

Among the local proverbs current in Vermont without being limited to that small state is the proverb "*Talk* less and say more." I have not been able to find it in any proverb collection, and it does indeed characterize the alleged taciturnity of native Vermonters. But here are a few more examples that fit well for this rural state. I collected them in oral use during more than 30 years living in Vermont, appropriately entitling my small popular book *"Talk Less and Say More": Vermont Proverbs* (1986):

Never *cackle* unless you lay.
Every *cow* needs a tail in fly time.
You can't judge a *cow* by her looks.

It's a rare *farm* that has no bad ground.
You can't mow *hay* where the grass doesn't grow.
The early *robin* looks for worms behind the early plow.
Keep a *thing* seven years and it will sort of do.
The *time* to pick berries is when they're ripe.
You can't get *wool* off a frog.
The *world* is your cow, but you have to do the milking.

(Mieder 1986; Mieder 1993a)

The proverbs from Texas also indicate the rural life, but this time it is not so much dairy farming but rather the work with cattle on the ranch. Perhaps one might even recognize a bit of the stereotypical Texan in these forceful texts:

A *bastard* always looks like his father.
He who watches the *clock* will only be a hand.
Don't *kick* until you're spurred.
Man is the only animal that can be skinned more than once.
Misfortune, like the rattler, does not always give a warning before striking.
A fool's *mouth* is his destruction.
There is little *rust* on a useful tool.
Steel will not bend, but it will break.
The *track* of evil thought is crooked and has no end.
The *world* owes you a living, providing you earn it.

(Atkinson 1954; Smith and Eddins 1937)

But speaking of Texas brings to mind the many Mexican American immigrants who live primarily in the Southwest of the United States. They have brought many of their proverbs with them, using them in their native Spanish language and, at times, also translating them into English. Eventually some of these proverbs will gain currency in English as well, just as other immigrant proverbs have been transplanted into the American multicultural environment. Here are a few examples from two collections based on actual field research among Mexican Americans:

La *ambición* rompe el saco.
Ambition will tear your coat.

No le *busques* tres pies al gato.
Don't look for three feet on a cat.

El que no oye *consejos,* no llegará a viejo.
He who does not listen to advice, will not grow old.

Caras vemos, coraznes no sabemos.
Faces we see, hearts we don't know.

Con *dinero* baila el perro.
Money makes the dog dance.

Un buen *gallo* en cualquier gallinero canta.
A good rooster will crow in any chicken coop.

Al *nopal* nomás lo van a ver cuando tiene tunas.
People go to the cactus only when it bears fruit.

Las *piedras* rodando se encuentran.
Rolling stones often cross paths.

El *tiempo* es oro.
Time is gold.

Quien tiene buen *vecino* tiene buen amigo.
A good neighbor is a good friend.

(see Ballesteros 1979; Glazer 1987)

Shirley Arora, the leading expert on Spanish proverb use in the United States, has pointed out that the various Spanish-speaking immigrant groups make considerable use of their traditional proverbs for didactic purposes, the regulation of social relationships, child rearing, cultural identification (ethnicity), and lending metaphorical expressiveness to verbal communication. Obviously some of the proverbs get translated into English as well, while English proverbs find their way into Spanish (Arora 1982; Briggs 1985). It is exactly this bilingual proverb use that is of great sociolinguistic importance during inculturation processes of the Mexican American population and all other immigrants.

NATIVE AMERICAN PROVERBS

While proverbs abound in the thousands in most cultures of the world, it remains a riddle why the Native Americans have hardly any proverb tradition at all. Members of the many Indian tribes in North, Central, and South America have but a very few proverbs. Even though anthropologists, folklorists, and linguists have tried to find at least some proverbs, the fact remains that the Native Americans are quite unique in their lack of large numbers of proverbs. No satisfactory answer has been found for this dearth of proverbs, and one cannot help but wonder whether scholars have simply not tried hard enough to find and collect the proverbs. When I called for a scholarly prize competition in 1988 to encourage the collection of Native American proverbs, not a single scholar responded to my offer of publishing lists of proverbs together with awarding a monetary prize (Mieder 1989b). The problem at least in part seems to be a certain disinterest, perhaps because of the difficulty of spotting the proverbs in linguistically difficult languages.

In any case, some proverbs have been recorded in a very few scholarly publications. I am aware of perhaps 200 true Native American proverbs and proverbial expressions, having tried for 30 years to find more texts. This is indeed a sad state of affairs. The following small number of texts is, however, a clear indication that there must be more proverbs in circulation still today in the numerous Indian languages. All of this does not, of course, explain why proverbs would not be more popular. Perhaps it is because Indian languages appear to be less metaphorical, but recent scholarship has shown that the apparent lack of metaphors has been overstated (see Boas 1940: 232–239; Basso 1976: 93–121). However, Native Americans have a long tradition of handing on collective wisdom by means of narratives, and this might at least somewhat explain the small amount of proverbs. And yet, such didactic and explanatory narratives also exist in other oral cultures. Why is it then that African tribes have a wealth of proverbs while Indian tribes have very few to hand on wisdom in short and memorable form? Nobody really knows, and one can only wish that renewed interest in the proverbs of Native Americans might yield some satisfactory answers.

Here then are at least a few texts from the best scholarship on the proverbial wisdom of Native Americans. The first group was collected by O. Morison during field research in the 1880s among the Tsimshian Indians from the coastal region of British Columbia. Most of Morison's but 16 annotated texts are proverbial expressions, but some of the following might be looked at as proverbs:

Tsimshian Proverbs

It is not good to be too *covetous.*
(While the Tsimshian Indians esteem wealth and prowess, they still advise people to regard only their own interests or to rely solely on their own resources.)

A *deer,* although toothless, may accomplish something.
(The basic meaning is that one should not judge another person by outward appearances.)

He is just sleeping on a *deerskin*.
(He is now enjoying a comfortable rest, but soon he will have to endure
   hardships and privations.)

Go where your *ears* will be full of grubs.
(Said to a person who goes foolhardily to his own destruction. The saying means: Your head will be full of grubs like that of salmon that has
   been thrown away by wasteful people without having served any
   good purpose [not having been eaten].)

You think you are as *handsome* as the sun's (moon's) child.
(This expression is cited to signify a vain person [sun and moon have
   the same name].)

You mistake the corner of the *house* for the door.
(Through this expression a gross mistake is signified.)

What will you eat when the *snow* is on the north side of the tree?
(This proverbial question refers to the end of the winter, when food is
   scarce. It is a reproach to the careless and wasteful.)

He is enjoying the *water lilies* for a short time.
(A person is enjoying the good things in life but will be soon faced with
   hardships and privations. The expression relates to a hunter, aiming
   at a bear, who is feeding on water lilies,—a parable of the transient-
   ness of life's pleasures.)

(Morison 1889)

Anthropologist Robert H. Lowie collected at least the following six proverbial
expressions from the Crow Indians of Montana in the early 1930s. It is to be assumed that he would have included bona fide proverbs had he but found them:

Crow Proverbial Expressions

When *cottontails* have long tails (or: when they are dragged).
(A proverbial phrase characterizing an impossibility.)

He is like the poor *helper*.
(This is applied to a person who proffers his assistance but who turns
   out to be a bungler.)

When *pine needles* turn yellow.
(A proverbial phrase characterizing an impossibility.)

He is like the one who wanted to catch the *porcupine*.
(The expression applies to a person who persists in a hopeless enterprise.)

He is like a man who did not run away until after he had been *scalped.*
(This expression refers to a person who is belated in his actions.)

He is like the *turtle* that was thrown into the water.
(The turtle pretends to be afraid of the water. The expression is there-
    fore applied to a person feigning not to like what he really craves.)
(Lowie 1932)

Finally, there is a third richly annotated list of 12 proverbs collected by anthropologist Gary H. Gossen during the late 1960s among the Tzotzil Indians from Chamula, a community of Mayan Indians in southern Mexico:

Tzotzil Proverbs

The *burro* eats and always brays.
(This proverb is usually said by adults to children, particularly their own
    children when they eat too much or want to take more than their fair
    share of food. The proverb also accuses the greedy person of being lazy.)

The *man* does not see (people) well, but he kicks (them) well.
(This proverb applies to old men who still have a strong interest in sex.)

The *ram* always throws himself around.
(This proverb is usually said by adult men and women to ridicule the
    behavior of drunks and to comment on drunkenness in general.)

It is going to *rain;* the cow is bawling.
(One meaning of the proverb is that of a weather aphorism, i.e., that the
    cows somehow sense the atmospheric conditions that precede a rain
    and bawl unusually long and loudly several hours before the shower.
    But the proverb is also frequently used by male relatives and neigh-
    bors for ridiculing a woman when she cries in public.)

The *road* is still open, but it will close.
(The proverb is addressed to people who foul the road or path by defe-
    cating or urinating there. This emphasizes the principle of proper eti-
    quette that requires one to go to a little-frequented place to eliminate.)

If one *talks* loudly, the cave will answer.
(The proverb may be said either by men or women to anyone who
    passes wind audibly and excessively in a public place. It may also be
    addressed to one who talks too much or too loudly when he is drunk.
    The text ridicules antisocial behavior. Anybody that acts in such a
    fashion does not deserve to live in a house but rather in a cave.)
(Gossen 1973)

AFRICAN AMERICAN PROVERBS

In comparison to the dearth of Native American proverbs, there is a plethora of African American proverbs with considerable scholarship on them. Some proverbs current among African Americans can be traced back to African and Caribbean sources (see Abrahams 1968). These early texts date back to the time of the slave trade and some contain wisdom to deal with the inhuman condition of slavery. The proverbs were used to teach common sense for everyday survival, and at times they were employed as an indirect way of criticizing the white landlords (see Daniel 1973). Joel Chandler Harris included a section of "Plantation Proverbs" in his classic book *Uncle Remus: His Songs and Sayings* (1881 [1895]), of which the following texts might serve as telling examples:

> Termorrow may be de *carriage-driver's* day for ploughin'.
> *Crow* en corn can't grow in de same fiel'.
> De howlin' *dog* know w'at he sees.
> Dem w'at *eats* kin say grace.
> Lazy *fokes'* stummacks don't git tired.
> Better de *gravy* dan no grease 'tall.
> *Mole* don't see w'at his naber doin'.
> De *proudness* un a man don't count w'en his head's cold.
> *Rooster* makes mo' racket dan de hen w'at lay de aig.
>
> (Harris 1881 [1895])

But there are also important studies and collections of African American proverbs from more recent times, indicating how they are used to express values, ethics, wit, and traditional wisdom in families (Daniel, Smitherman-Donaldson, and Jeremiah 1987; see also Prahlad 1996). While African Americans quite naturally make use of the general proverb stock in common circulation in the United States, they also have some proverbs that are more unique to their cultural experiences, as for example:

> Your *backyard* should look as pretty as your front yard.
> The blacker the *berry*, the sweeter the juice.
> Don't die with the *dead*.
> If you dig a *ditch* for your brother, dig two.
> Smiling *faces* sometimes lie.
> Don't let anyone outpick you in your own *field*.
> What *goes* around, comes around.

A hard *head* makes a soft behind.
Leave half of what you know in your *head*.
One *monkey* don't stop no show.
Your *word* is your bond.
                    (Daniel, Smitherman-Donaldson, and Jeremiah 1987)

Of 50 proverbs collected among African Americans in Pittsburgh and Detroit, only these nine texts do not belong to the common American proverbs. After all, the two declaredly African American proverbs "The blacker the *berry*, the sweeter the juice" and "What *goes* around, comes around" have become part of the general American proverb stock by now. But here are a few more interesting texts collected by Alene Barnes-Harden around 1980 in Buffalo, New York. Included is the most universally known African American proverb, namely "Different *strokes* for different folks" (my favorite proverb of all, I might add):

Black is beautiful.
Don't knock on your own *door*.
Dreams die first.
Keep your *dress* down and your draws (panties) up.
If it don't *fit*, don't force it.
Don't *forget* where you came from.
Don't let your *head* start something that your ass can't handle.
If you don't *know* much, you can't do much.
Money talks and bullshit walks.
It takes *one* to know one.
You have to *pay* to play.
Always save a *penny* so you can buy a pot to piss in.
There is always a *person* greater or lesser than yourself.
Different *strokes* for different folks.
                    (Barnes-Harden 1980: 61–72)

Only this last proverb made it into the *Dictionary of American Proverbs* (1992). Some of these texts might already have been in circulation during the four decades from 1945 until 1985 when the data was collected for this large compilation. But most likely people did not do field research at the time in the inner city environments, thus missing important and differentiated material. There might also have been some censoring of sexual and scatological texts. This puritan attitude on behalf of collectors has plagued proverb collections for centuries. Too many suggestive texts were left unrecorded, giving the impression that proverbs are at all times trim and proper. But nothing could be further from the truth, as can be seen by just some of these fascinating proverbs listed here. There is clearly still much work to be done by the paremiographers of the future. Regarding the United States, two major efforts should certainly be to publish annotated proverb collections of Native Americans and African Americans. Their rich contents would assuredly reveal many unique and welcome proverbs that have hitherto not been recorded, studied, and treasured by scholars and the general public.

SELECTED BIBLIOGRAPHY

Book-length studies are listed in the major bibliography at the end of this book. Cross-references at the ends of entries correspond to collections listed in the bibliography.

Abrahams, Roger D. 1968. "British West Indian Proverbs and Proverb Collections." *Proverbium,* no. 10: 239–243.

Arora, Shirley L. 1982. "Proverbs in Mexican American Tradition." *Aztlán* 13: 43–69.

Atkinson, Mary. 1954. "Familiar Sayings of Old-Time Texas." In *Texas Folk and Folklore,* ed. by Mody C. Boatright, Wilson M. Hudson, and Aiken Maxwell, 213–218. Dallas, Tex.: Southern Methodist University Press.

Barnes-Harden, Alene L. 1980. *African American Verbal Arts: Their Nature and Communicative Interpretation (A Thematic Analysis).* Diss. University of New York at Buffalo (proverbs on pp. 61–72).

Basso, Keith. 1976. "'Wise Words' of the Western Apache: Metaphor and Semantic Theory." In *Meaning in Anthropology,* ed. by K. Basso and Henry Selby, 93–121. Albuquerque: University of New Mexico Press.

Boas, Franz. 1940. "Metaphorical Expression in the Language of the Kwakiutl Indians." In *Language and Culture,* by F. Boas, 232–239. New York: The Free Press.

Briggs, Charles L. 1985. "The Pragmatics of Proverb Performances in New Mexican Spanish." *American Anthropologist* 87: 793–810; also in Mieder 1994: 317–349.

Daniel, Jack L. 1973. "Towards an Ethnography of Afroamerican Proverbial Usage." *Black Lines* 2: 3–12.

Daniel, Jack L., Geneva Smitherman-Donaldson, and Milford A. Jeremiah. 1987. "'Makin' a Way outa no Way': The Proverb Tradition in the Black Experience." *Journal of Black Studies* 17: 482–508.

Doyle, Charles C. 1996. "On 'New' Proverbs and the Conservativeness of Proverb Dictionaries." *Proverbium* 13: 69–84; also in Mieder 2003: 85–98.

Dundes, Alan. 1980. "Seeing Is Believing." In *Interpreting Folklore,* ed. by A. Dundes, 86–92. Bloomington: Indiana University Press.

Ek, Sven B. 1964. *Den som kommer först till kvarns – ett ordspåk och dess bakgrund.* Lund, Sweden: Gleerup.

Gossen, Gary H. 1973. "Chamula Tzotzil Proverbs: Neither Fish nor Fowl." In *Meaning in Mayan Languages. Ethnolinguistic Studies,* ed. by Munro S. Edmonson, 205–233. The Hague: Mouton; also in Mieder 1994: 351–392.

Hardie, Margaret. 1929. "Proverbs and Proverbial Expressions Current in the United States East of the Missouri and North of the Ohio Rivers." *American Speech* 4: 461–472.

Harris, Joel Chandler. 1881 (1895). "Plantation Proverbs." In *Uncle Remus: His Songs and Sayings,* by J.C. Harris, 173–177. New York: D. Appleton.

Jente, Richard. 1931–1932. "The American Proverb." *American Speech* 7: 342–348.

Lowie, Robert H. 1932. "Proverbial Expressions Among Crow Indians." *American Anthropologist* 34: 739–740.

McKenzie, Alyce M. 1996. "'Different Strokes for Different Folks': America's Quintessential Postmodern Proverb." *Theology Today* 53: 201–212; also in Mieder 2003: 311–324.

Mieder, Wolfgang. 1987. "History and Interpretation of a Proverb about Human Nature: 'Big Fish Eat Little Fish.'" In *Tradition and Innovation in Folk Literature,* by W. Mieder, 178–228 and 259–268 (notes). Hanover, N.H.: University Press of New England.

———. 1989a. "'Ein Bild sagt mehr als tausend Worte': Ursprung und Überlieferung eines amerikanischen Lehnsprichworts." *Proverbium* 6: 25–37, also in Mieder 1992: 191–201.

———. 1989b. "Proverbs of the Native Americans: A Prize Competition." *Western Folklore* 48: 256–260.

———. 1990. "'A Picture Is Worth a Thousand Words': From Advertising Slogan to American Proverb." *Southern Folklore* 47: 207–225; also in Mieder 1993: 135–151.

———. 1993a. "'Good Proverbs Make Good Vermonters': The Flavor of Regional Proverbs." In *Proverbs Are Never Out of Season: Popular Wisdom in the Modern Age,* by W. Mieder, 173–192. New York: Oxford University Press.

———. 1993b. "'The Apple Doesn't Fall Far from the Tree': History of a German Proverb in the Anglo-American World." *Midwestern Folklore* 19: 69–98; also in Mieder 2000b, 109–144.

———. 1993c. "'The Grass Is Always Greener on the Other Side of the Fence': An American Proverb of Discontent." *Proverbium* 10: 151–184; also in Mieder 1994: 515–542.

———. 1993d. "'The Only Good Indian Is a Dead Indian': History and Meaning of a Proverbial Stereotype." *Journal of American Folklore* 106: 38–60; also in Mieder 1997: 138–159 and 221–227 (notes).

———. 1996. "'No Tickee, No Washee': Subtleties of a Proverbial Slur." *Western Folklore* 55: 1–40; also in Mieder 1997: 160–189 and 227–235 (notes).

———. 2000a. "'First come, First Served': Proverbial Wisdom from the World of the Millers and the Mills." In *The Mills at Winooski Falls: Winooski and Burlington, Vermont,* ed. by Laura Krawitt, 128–134 and 203 (references). Winooski, Vt.: Onion River Press.

———. 2003. "'Good Fences Make Good Neighbors': History and Significance of an Ambiguous Proverb." *Folklore* (London) 114: 155–179.

Morison, O. 1889. "Tsimshian Proverbs." *Journal of American Folklore* 2: 285–286.

Nicolaisen, W.F.H. 1994. "The Proverbial Scot." *Proverbium* 11: 197–206.

Robinson, F.N. 1945. "Irish Proverbs and Irish National Character." *Modern Philology* 43: 1–10; also in Mieder and Dundes 1981 (1994): 284–299.

Smith, Morgan, and A.W. Eddins. 1937. "Wise Saws from Texas." In *Straight Texas,* ed. by J. Frank Dobie and Mody C. Boatright, 239–244. Dallas, Tex.: Southern Methodist University Press.

Taylor, Archer. 1971. "'Leave no Stone Unturned' or an Afternoon with a Historical Dictionary of Proverbs." *Proverbium,* no. 16: 553–556.

Three
Scholarship and Approaches

A description of the present state of proverb scholarship and its future direction must also consider past accomplishments. The interest in proverbs can, after all, be traced back to Sumerian cuneiform tablets and the Greek and Roman philosophical and rhetorical writings. Humanists like Erasmus of Rotterdam and later scholars have all built on previous research as they put forth their own collections and studies of proverbs. There exists an impressive history of the two major aspects of proverb scholarship, that is, the collection of proverbs (paremiography) and the study of proverbs (paremiology). Naturally these two branches are two sides of the same coin, and some of the very best research on proverbs combines the two most convincingly. Although the identification of traditional texts as proverbs and their arrangement in collections of various types are of paramount importance, proverb scholars have always known that the interpretation of proverbs in oral or written speech is of equal significance.

The remarks in this section can only scratch the proverbial surface of the retrospective and prospective aspects of modern paremiology. At least some major issues of past, present, and future proverb research will be discussed together with representative examples of recent scholarship that can serve as models for what lies ahead. My remarks are divided into three major categories: (1) fundamental resources, such as special journals, essay volumes, and bibliographies dedicated to proverb research; (2) the status of extant proverb collections and the direction of paremiography in the future; and (3) the impressive results of twentieth-century proverb scholarship and a glimpse at the desiderata for paremiology during the twenty-first century. While the first two categories are not subdivided, the third is actually made up of 12 sections: comprehensive overviews of paremiology; empiricism and paremiological minima; linguistic and semiotic considerations; performance (speech acts) in social contexts; issues of culture, folklore, and history; politics, stereotypes, and worldview; sociology, psychology, and psychiatry; use in folk narratives and literature; religion and wisdom literature; pedagogy and language teaching; iconography: proverbs as art; and mass media and popular culture. These headings certainly indicate that paremiology is a multifaceted and fascinating enterprise that in its complexity encompasses many fields of study (for the following discussions see also Mieder 1997).

PROVERB JOURNALS, ESSAY VOLUMES, AND BIBLIOGRAPHIES

The widespread interest in proverbs throughout the world is thoroughly documented in a number of international bibliographies as well as the 25 issues of the "old" *Proverbium,* edited by Matti Kuusi from 1965 to 1975 in Helsinki and available in my two-volume reprint (1987); the short-lived *Proverbium Paratum,* edited by Vilmos Voigt from 1980 to 1989 in only four issues in Budapest; the "new" *Proverbium: Yearbook of International Proverb Scholarship,* edited by me since 1984 in Burlington, Vermont; the Spanish annual *Paremia,* edited by Julia Sevilla Muñoz since 1993 in Madrid; and the innovative, electronically published *De Proverbio,* edited by Teodor Flonta from 1995 to 2000 in Tasmania, Australia. It is a shame that *De Proverbio* ceased publication with the retirement of Teodor Flonta, since it made invaluable articles available on the Internet. But together these annual publications have established a close net of international scholars, and it is to be hoped that additional yearbooks might be started in other countries. A yearly publication devoted to African proverbs is doubtlessly needed, and the same holds true for the rich field of Asian proverbs. The particularly active proverb scholars in the Baltic States would also be well served to have their own periodic publications with valuable interpretive essays, collections, bibliographies, and book reviews. In any case, these yearbooks would enhance the regional, national, and international study of proverbs and result in a comparatively oriented synchronic and diachronic proverb scholarship of the highest quality in a global environment.

Numerous informative volumes of proverb essays by different authors have also been published. In fact, there is a plethora of them in the broader area of phraseology that includes all types of collocations (see the numerous entries in the third section of the bibliography). In the narrower field of paremiology, there are essay volumes that give a convenient overview of various aspects, ranging from definitional, structural, and semiotic studies to analyses of the origin, history, and dissemination of individual proverbs, and from their use in literary works or psychological testing to their depiction in art as well as the modern mass media. Alan Dundes and I edited such a volume entitled *The Wisdom of Many: Essays on the Proverb* (1981 [1994]) that included English-language essays primarily from the first half of the twentieth century. On the other hand, my edited volume of *Wise Words: Essays on the Proverb* (1994) features only essays that were published after 1970, and now there is also my third edited essay collection of the most recent scholarship entitled *Cognition, Comprehension, and Communication: A Decade of North American Proverb Studies (1990–2000)* (2003). Together these three "casebooks" present 67 of the most important and representative essays written in English on a broad array of anthropological, folkloristic, historical, linguistic, literary, philological, psychological, and sociological subjects. While the scope of eight additional volumes edited by Naiade Anido, *Des proverbes...à l'affut* (1983), Grigorii L'vovich Permiakov, *Paremiologicheskie issledovaniia: Sbornik statei* (1984), François Suard and Claude Buridant, *Richesse du proverbe,* 2 vols. (1984), Annette Sabban and Jan Wirrer, *Sprichwörter und Redensarten im interkulturellen Vergleich* (1991), Cristina Vallini, *La pratica e la grammatica: Viaggio nella linguistica del proverbio* (1989), Peter Ďurčo, *Europhras 97: Phraseology and Paremiology* (1998), Rupprecht S. Baur, Christoph Chlosta, and Elisabeth Piirainen, *Wörter in Bildern—Bilder in Wörtern: Beiträge zur Phraseologie und Sprichwortforschung* (1999), and Dietrich Hartmann and Jan Wirrer, *"Wer A sägt, muss auch B sägen": Beiträge zur Phraseologie und Sprichwortforschung* (2002) is also deliberately interdisciplinary and comparative, there are others that address proverbs from particular cultures and languages, as for example the essay volumes edited by Wolfgang Mieder, *Ergebnisse der [deutschen] Sprichwörterforschung* (1978), Willem Saayman, *Embracing the Baobab Tree: The African Proverb in the 21st Century* (1997), and Salvatore C. Trovato, *Proverbi locuzioni modi di dire nel dominio linguistico italiano* (1999). It would be quite useful to have other such volumes available, and essay volumes containing articles dealing on a cross-cultural level with misogyny, stereotypes, religion, animals, and so on in proverbs are also needed. Such studies would be welcome research tools for students and scholars of proverbs alike and would make largely inaccessible publications available in thematically packaged casebooks. Naturally such essay volumes should contain informative introductions and useful bibliographies that list special collections and additional analytical studies.

Turning to bibliographical matters, it can be stated that of all verbal folklore genres, the bibliographies regarding proverbs are the most comprehensive. Previous bibliographies of proverb collections were subsumed by Wilfrid

Bonser's still valuable *Proverb Literature: A Bibliography of Works Relating to Proverbs* (1930 [1967]) and Otto Moll's superb *Sprichwörterbibliographie* (1958), with the latter registering over 9,000 references. My own annual "International Bibliography of New and Reprinted Proverb Collections" that has appeared in *Proverbium: Yearbook of International Proverb Scholarship* since 1984 has by now cited well over 1,500 publications, among them some extremely important reprints of earlier collections as well as a large number of significant new national and comparative collections. There are, however, also numerous smaller collections intended for the popular book market. Scholars must not forget that the general reader enjoys the proverbial wisdom of certain national, ethnic, religious, occupational, or thematic (animals, love, women) groups. The phenomenon of popular proverb collections for the mass market (general readers, tourists, etc.) deserves a serious analysis, since it definitely plays an influential role in disseminating proverbs.

As helpful as these yearly bibliographies have been, there is a definite need to assemble updated national bibliographies of proverb collections with explanatory annotations. A superb two-volume example is Anatolii Mikhailovich Bushui's *Paremiologiia Uzbekistana* (1978–1980). It registers 840 annotated paremiographical and paremiological publications of Uzbekistan in central Asia. Bushui includes books and articles on proverbs, proverbial expressions, proverbial comparisons, clichés, idioms, and phraseology in general. But there is yet another incredible bibliographical masterpiece, namely the two massive volumes by Joachim Lengert, *Romanische Phraseologie und Parömiologie* (1999), which has registered and annotated over 17,000 phraseological and paremiological publications of all Romance languages on 2,132 pages. Both of these bibliographies are models to be emulated for other regions and languages. There are, of course, also smaller but valuable bibliographies dealing with collections of ethnic proverbs, stereotypical expressions, proverbs about women, and so on. Many more restricted bibliographies of this type are needed, but it is also high time that a critically annotated international bibliography of the world's major proverb collections be put together. As paremiographers work more and more comparatively, they need to know which collections are the most reliable and inclusive for as many languages as possible.

The bibliographical status of paremiology is by comparison with that of paremiography in an even better state. There is my *International Proverb Scholarship: An Annotated Bibliography*, 4 vols. (1982–2001), in which 7,368 books, dissertations, and articles have been registered with detailed and critical comments as well as extensive name, subject, and proverb indices. These massive volumes contain the major accomplishments of proverb scholars during the past 200 years, and the most recent publications are listed in my yearly "International Proverb Scholarship: An Updated Bibliography" in *Proverbium: Yearbook of International Proverb Scholarship* with the impressive number of well over 300 entries per year. But this is not to say that specialized annotated bibliographies are not needed, for which the *Catalogo de bibliografía paremiologica española* (1992) by José de Jaime Gómez and José María Jaime Lorén, and my *African Proverb Scholarship: An Annotated Bibliography* (1994) might serve as examples and models. There are also some specialized bibliographies for certain specific areas or subject matters, for example the three annotated bibliographies that I have coauthored with George B. Bryan, *Proverbs in World Literature: A Bibliography* (1996), with Janet Sobieski, *Proverb Iconography: An International Bibliography* (1998), and once again with Janet Sobieski, *Proverbs and the Social Sciences: An Annotated International Bibliography* (2003). But many additional specialized bibliographies on such matters as misogyny in proverbs, worldview expressed through proverbs, the weather in proverbs, and God (or religion) in proverbs would be welcome. The list of possibilities is endless. In the meantime the indices included in my volumes of *International Proverb Scholarship* will help scholars to find those publications that include rich bibliographical information (check under the entry "bibliography"). It will always be a worthwhile service to put together additional bibliographies, even in the age of Web sites and electronic databases.

PROVERB COLLECTIONS AND FUTURE PAREMIOGRAPHY

While there is a steady stream of new proverb collections, diachronically oriented scholars are also well served by the invaluable reprints of major collections of earlier centuries. Especially for some of the major European languages, proverb collections from the late fifteenth century onwards are available as reprints. This is not the place to comment on individual reprinted volumes of these and other languages, since they are all listed in my annual bibliographies of *Proverbium: Yearbook of International Proverb Scholarship* (for additional information see Mieder 1990). Instead, two European multivolume proverb collections should be mentioned. There is the gargantuan effort of Hans Walther and Paul Gerhard Schmidt, who have assembled approximately 150,000 Latin proverbs and their variants from the Middle Ages through the seventeenth century in their seminal nine-volume *Proverbia sententiaeque latinitatis medii aevi. Lateinische Sprichwörter und Sentenzen des Mittelalters* (1963–1986). Since many of the proverbs were common throughout Europe either in the Latin original or through loan translations into the vernacular languages, these volumes represent a unique research tool for all historical and comparative paremiographers. For the vernacular languages of the Middle Ages another giant paremiographical project has been completed. A team of scholars under the direction of Ricarda Liver worked for 40 years at Berne, Switzerland, on a 13-volume *Thesaurus proverbiorum medii aevi. Lexikon der Sprichwörter des germanisch-romanischen Mittelalters* (1995–2002) based on the materials of the Swiss paremiographer Samuel Singer (1860–1948). While the major language of this lexicon is German, texts in Greek, Latin, French, Provençal, Italian, Catalan, Spanish, Portuguese, Icelandic, Swedish, Danish, English, and Dutch are cited. This multivolume research tool has unlocked the intricacies of medieval proverbs, leaving paremiographers with the hope that similar mammoth projects might be undertaken on a comparative basis for the proverbs of later centuries and other linguistic families of the world. With the use of the computer and proper funding, teams of scholars might be able to accomplish such desirable tasks in the future.

In the meantime there is a great need for single-language historical proverb dictionaries based on the lexicographical classification system developed by the American paremiographer par excellence Bartlett Jere Whiting in his celebrated and massive *Proverbs, Sentences, and Proverbial Phrases from English Writings Mainly Before 1500* (1968) and his many subsequent Anglo-American proverb collections (see Taylor and Whiting 1958; Whiting 1977, 1989). Whiting actually adapted the methodology of Morris Palmer Tilley's *A Dictionary of the Proverbs in England in the Sixteenth and Seventeenth Centuries* (1950), and both were followed by an unequalled four-volume Polish collection, *Nowa ksiega przysłów i wyrazen przysłowiowych polskich* (1969–1978) edited by Julian Krzyzanowski and Stanisław Swirko. These collections are historical dictionaries in which the individual proverbs and proverbial expressions are arranged alphabetically according to key words. For each proverb the editors supply historical references from the Middle Ages on, often including the earlier classical and/or biblical references. At the end of such historical monographs on individual proverbs, cross-references to other proverb collections of the language involved are cited as well. Even though this methodology for major historical proverb collections has been long established, it is being followed more or less exclusively only in the Anglo-American world and has resulted in several major proverb dictionaries (in addition to Whiting, see Dent 1981, 1984; Simpson 1982 [1998]; Smith 1935 [1970, 3rd ed. by F.P. Wilson]).

A definite goal of serious paremiographers must be the establishment of national proverb compendia, preferably based on historical principles. The time-consuming effort is best dealt with by scholars working in teams, as can be seen by two industrious research groups in the Baltic States. Arvo Krikmann, Ingrid Sarv, and their colleagues have published the seminal five-volume national Estonian proverb collection *Eesti vanasõnad* (1980–1988). A similar five-volume venture is well on its way in Lithuania, formerly under the directorship of the recently deceased Kazys Grigas. When finished, the Lithuanian people will have the superb national proverb collection *Lietuviu patarles ir priežodžiai* (2000–) at their disposal. The Germans already have a massive five-volume *Deutsches Sprichwörter-Lexikon* (1867–1880 [1964]) by Karl Friedrich Wilhelm Wander available to them. All existing proverb collections of a national language, including regional and dialect collections, should be integrated into such large compendia, adding almost automatically a historical component. But of special importance would be to include as many historical references from the print media as possible.

European paremiographers have published several major international proverb collections in the past few years. Matti Kuusi, in cooperation with seven other scholars, took the lead with the exemplary collection *Proverbia Septentrionalia: 900 Balto-Finnic Proverb Types with Russian, Baltic, German and Scandinavian Parallels* (1985). This significant synchronic and comparative volume registers the common proverbs of the six Balto-Finnic peoples of Finno-Ugrian origin (the Finns, Karelians, Estonians, Votes, Vespians, and Livonians), who form a linguistically and geographically unified group between the Scandinavians, Balts, and Russians. The proverb types are cited in English, and the proverbs in their original languages under each type are arranged on the basis of their distribution in the Balto-Finnic languages, always beginning with those proverbs occurring in all six languages and ending with those found in only one. Where possible, a Russian, Baltic, German, and Scandinavian parallel of the proverb type is cited. After the Balto-Finnic variants, bibliographical sources are listed. Of much value are also Gyula Paczolay's *European Proverbs in 55 Languages with Equivalents in Arabic, Persian, Sanskrit, Chinese and Japanese* (1997) with 106 monographs citing the proverbs in their original languages with English translations, and Emanuel Strauss's massive three-volume *Dictionary of European Proverbs* (1994) with its 1804 proverbs in dozens of languages (see also the "Multilingual Proverb Collections" section in the bibliography). There exist many similar comparative collections where English is not the base language, and, of course, there are also dozens of bilingual proverb collections that are of special use to translators and foreign-language students (see section five of the bibliography).

So much for the Euro-American picture, but how do matters look for the many languages of the African continent? Missionaries and anthropologists have long collected proverbs indigenous to certain African tribes, and this work has resulted in many valuable collections. Of special merit are Cyril L. Nyembezi, *Zulu Proverbs* (1963); M.A. Hamutyinei and A.B. Plangger, *Tsumo-Shumo: Shona Proverbial Lore and Wisdom* (1974); Albert Scheven, *Swahili Proverbs* (1981); and Oyekan Owomoyela, *"A Ki i": Yoruba Proscriptive and Prescriptive Proverbs* (1988). Special mention, however, must be made of Matti Kuusi's collection *Ovambo Proverbs with African Parallels* (1970), since this scholar has provided comparative African commentaries to the Ovambo proverbs. Kuusi observes that "The number of common African proverbs appears proportionally smaller than that of common European or Eurasian proverbs, but the establishment of a common Bantu tradition and that of the most general African proverbs provides a necessary basis for the determination of whether or not the peoples of the three ancient continents have a common heritage of proverbs" (p. 13). The time has surely come to assemble major comparative proverb collections based on the numerous previously published collections of small linguistic groups. Research teams need to work on this major task making use of computer technology. Only through such work will questions regarding the geographical distribution and commonality of African proverbs be answered. What proverbs are known throughout Africa? How old are they? Are they indigenous to that continent? How do they relate to the common stock of European proverbs that were disseminated by missionaries? A step in the right direction is Ryszard Pachocinski's *Proverbs of Africa: Human Nature in the Nigerian Oral Tradition* (1996) with its exposition and analysis of 2,600 proverbs from 64 African peoples. The first step should be the establishment of a computer bank of all African proverbs collected thus far. While valuable individual collections and studies of African proverbs exist, a comparative analysis of all these African texts is highly desirable. The good news is that such an "African Proverbs Project" is now in progress under the tutelage of Joseph Healey and Stan Nussbaum (see Saayman 1997).

A similar picture arises for the Arabic, Asian, Indic, and other major language groups, which also have a long and complex history of a rich common proverb stock. There are clearly numerous proverb collections in the native languages that are, unfortunately, inaccessible to most Western scholars. But such collections as Young H. Yoo's *Wisdom of the Far East* (1972) and the many bilingual collections (see bibliography) have shown that related languages of Asia, India, or the Middle East have many proverbs in common just as there are general European proverbs. Such synchronic (and possibly also diachronic) comparative collections with their scholarly apparatus of indices, frequency analyses, sources, geographical distribution, and so on are of great importance in trying to find international proverb types. Collections of this scope advance the structural, semantic, and semiotic studies of comparative paremiographers like Grigorii L'vovich Permiakov (see Grzybek 2000), Matti Kuusi, Outi Lauhakangas, and Gyula Paczolay (Permiakov 1970 [1979]; Kuusi 1972; Lauhakangas 2001; Paczolay 1997) in their search for and creation of an international type system of proverbs.

COMPREHENSIVE OVERVIEWS OF PAREMIOLOGY

Any interest in proverbs whatsoever leads quite naturally to the question of what makes proverbs "click," that is, what differentiates these short texts from normal utterances or such subgenres as proverbial expressions, proverbial comparisons, twin formulas, and wellerisms. When inquiring about the definition, origin, history, dissemination, language, structure, meaning, use, and function of such phraseological units or phraseologisms, one enters the realm of proverb scholarship or paremiology, as it is called by its Greek technical term (the Greek "paremia" is equivalent to the Latin "proverbium") in differentiation from the more limited concerns of proverb collecting or paremiography. While there exist one-volume comprehensive surveys of the two areas of proverb studies for many languages and cultures, it is perhaps fair to say that the great German paremiographer Karl Friedrich Wilhelm Wander (1803–1879), acclaimed compiler of the *Deutsches Sprichwörter-Lexikon* (1867–1880 [1964]) with its five large volumes and 250,000 proverbs and proverbial expressions with sources and parallel texts from other European languages, was also the first "modern" paremiologist with his encompassing study *Das Sprichwort, betrachtet nach Form und Wesen, für Schule und Leben, als Einleitung zu einem volksthümlichen Sprichwörterschatz* (1836 [1983]). Not quite 20 years later, Richard Chenevix Trench (1807–1886) published a similar English-language volume *On the Lessons of Proverbs* (1853 [2003]), which in its many English and American editions became a standard work for paremiologists interested in the definition, origin, form, style, content, morality, and theology of proverbs. Two outstanding inclusive studies of the proverb in the early part of the twentieth century are F. Edward Hulme's *Proverb Lore: Being a Historical Study of the Similarities, Contrasts, Topics, Meanings, and Other Facets of Proverbs, Truisms, and Pithy Sayings, as Expressed by the People of Many Lands and Times* (1902 [1968]) and Friedrich Seiler's *Deutsche Sprichwörterkunde* (1922 [1967]). Similar books exist for other languages and cultures, to be sure: Jacques Pineaux, *Proverbes et dictons français* (1956); Louis Combet, *Recherches sur le "refranero" castillan* (1971); Matti Kuusi, *Parömiologische Betrachtungen* (1957); Lutz Röhrich and Wolfgang Mieder, *Sprichwort* (1977); Jean Cauvin, *Comprendre: Les Proverbes* (1981); Cezar Tabarcea, *Poetica proverbului* (1982); Maria Conca, *Paremiologia* (1987); Julia Sevilla Muñoz, *Hacia una aproximación conceptual de las paremias francesas y españolas* (1988); Katsuaki Takeda, *Kotowaza no Retorikku* (1992); and Agnes Szemerkényi, *"Közmondás nem hazug szólás": A proverbiumok használatának lehetöségei* (1994). But paremiologists are fortunate in having a seminal study dedicated to international paremiology in an accessible language that must be regarded as a "classic" and hitherto unsurpassed treatise of the subject. If there ever were a bible of proverb scholarship, this book would be it by any standard of comparison.

Archer Taylor's (1890–1973) book *The Proverb* (1931; repr. as *The Proverb and an Index to "The Proverb"* in 1962; and repr. again in 1985 with an introduction and bibliography by Wolfgang Mieder), comprised of a mere 223 small pages, has guided scholars and students around the world in their proverb studies. In short but pregnant chapters with many suggestions for further research, Taylor presents a complete overview of the rich field of international paremiology. The first section concerns itself with the origins of the proverb, and the individual chapters deal with the problems of definition, metaphorical proverbs, proverbial types, variations, proverbs based on narratives, proverbs and folk-verse, proverbs and literature, loan translations, biblical proverbs, and classical proverbs. In the second section on the content of proverbs, Taylor analyzes customs and superstitions reflected in proverbs, historical proverbs, legal proverbs, *blasons populaires* (i.e., stereotypes), weather proverbs, medical proverbs, conventional phrases, and proverbial prophecies. The third section addresses primarily the style of proverbs (meter, metaphor, personification, parallelism, rhyme, pun, etc.), but there are also chapters on dialogue proverbs, epigrammatic proverbs, national and ethnic traits, ethical values, obscene proverbs, and a review of proverbs in European literature. The fourth section is divided into three chapters devoted to various aspects of proverbial phrases, wellerisms, and proverbial comparisons. The book, filled with examples from many languages, contains generous bibliographical references, and three years after its publication, Taylor published an invaluable 105-page *An Index to "The Proverb"* (1934), which has been included in both the 1962 and 1985 reprints. There can be no doubt that this book belongs in every research library of the world and on the bookshelf of every paremiologist.

With Taylor as doyen of proverb studies in the United States in the 1930s and beyond, paremiology flourished there to a remarkable degree. Taylor's many additional publications were at least in part republished in two essay volumes, namely *Comparative Studies in Folklore: Asia–Europe–America* (1972) and *Selected Writings on Proverbs* (1975). Taylor's friend and at times coauthor, Bartlett Jere Whiting (1904–1995), rose to equal heights both as a paremiographer and paremiologist. His fundamental studies on the origin (1931), nature (1932), and study (1939) of proverbs have been edited in one volume by Joseph Harris and me under the title of *When Evensong and Morrowsong Accord: Three Essays on the Proverb* (1994; a bibliography of Whiting's publications is appended). The three articles in this book comprise yet another major treatise on the proverb, with Taylor's as well as Whiting's insights into the complexities and intricacies of proverbs being as valid today as they were some decades ago. They certainly represent the cornerstone of modern international paremiology and its future. It is of little wonder, then, that basically every serious publication on proverbs throughout the world pays homage in some form or another to these two great scholars.

For me to do the same to all the many outstanding scholars, colleagues, and friends who are presently at work as paremiologists in all corners of the world is patently impossible. But in the remaining pages of this section of my book, I will attempt to summarize some of the major trends of recent scholarship with brief references to major publications, while at the same time focusing on some innovative studies that need to be undertaken in the future. My comments are somewhat selective, and no slight to any scholar, culture, or language is intended by these remarks. The emphasis remains on English-language publications, since this book is intended for a wide, general, and global readership.

EMPIRICISM AND PAREMIOLOGICAL MINIMA

As Peter Grzybek and Christoph Chlosta have shown in their pioneering essay on "Grundlagen der empirischen Sprichwortforschung" (1993, Foundations of Empirical Proverb Study), scholars must base their studies on demographic research methods utilizing questionnaires and sophisticated statistical analyses in order to establish lists of those proverbs that are actually known and continue to be in current use (see Levin 1968–1969; Mieder 1985). This research methodology will also help to establish the proverbiality of the new proverbs of the modern age (see Doyle 1996). There is thus a definite need for increased global field research, from highly technological societies to those parts of the world where life continues to be based on traditional and rural life. Such empirical work will, of course, also help to establish "proverbial minima" for many languages and cultures, as Grigorii L'vovich Permiakov (1919–1983), one of the greatest theoretical paremiologists of the twentieth century, suggested already in the early 1970s.

Utilizing his paremiological experiment conducted in Moscow in 1970, Permiakov was able to establish the general currency of 1,494 phraseological units among modern inhabitants of that city. Included were 268 proper proverbs, and the rest of the texts were proverbial expressions, proverbial comparisons, wellerisms, fables, anecdotes, riddles, slogans, weather signs, superstitions, allusions to fairy tales, oaths, and so on. Permiakov's list shows clearly that many long folk narratives have currency as short phraseological remnants (allusions). All of these texts are part of the general cultural literacy of Russians (Permiakov 1971). Native as well as foreign speakers of Russian need to know them in order to communicate effectively in that language. Permiakov subsequently established a so-called paremiological minimum of 300 such texts based on this experiment (Permiakov 1982 [1989]) and published it with an explanatory introduction and many notes as *300 obshcheupotrebitel'nykh russkikh poslovits i pogovorok* (1985; see Grzybek and Eismann 1984: 351–358). German and Bulgarian translations have appeared that enable foreign-language instructors to teach their students the most frequently used Russian proverbs, proverbial expressions, proverbial comparisons, and so on.

Similar paremiological minima of such common phraseological units of other national languages are now being established by paremiographers, to wit the very useful results for Croatian, Czech, English, German, and Hungarian. Many proverbs of classical, biblical, or medieval origin will belong to the paremiological minima of European languages. But there will still be room for national proverbs among a list of about 300 texts. Since these texts are identified by statistical frequency studies of actual use in oral and written communication, they become a very useful list for foreign-language instruction. After all, it is important to teach the most well-known and current proverbs to foreign-language learners rather than obscure and seldom used texts. The proverbs that belong to the paremiological minimum of a language are clearly part of the cultural literacy of native speakers, and it behooves foreign-language teachers to include them in their instruction of language and culture (Mieder 1992; Tóthné Litovkina 1998). Demoscopic research will also finally give scholars a much better idea as to which of the thousands of proverbs listed in the older collections are still in actual use today. Paremiography cannot remain a science that looks primarily backwards and works only with texts of times gone by. Modern paremiographers can and should also assemble proverb collections that include the texts of the twentieth and twenty-first centuries, as is the case at least in part with *A Dictionary of American Proverbs* (Mieder, Kingsbury, and Harder 1992).

Regarding the English language, no precise paremiological minimum has been established thus far. However, some empirically oriented work has been done (Mieder 1992: Tóthné Litovkina 1994), indicating that the following seventy-five proverbs are certainly used with high frequency in the United States today:

Absence makes the heart grow fonder.
An *apple* a day keeps the doctor away.
The *apple* doesn't fall far from the tree.
Beauty is in the eye of the beholder.
Beauty is only skin deep.
Early to *bed* and early to rise, makes a man healthy, wealthy, and wise.
Beggars can't be choosers.
A *bird* in the hand is worth two in the bush.
Birds of a feather flock together.
The early *bird* catches the worm.
Don't judge a *book* by its cover.
Don't cross the *bridge* till you come to it.
New *brooms* sweep clean.
Business before pleasure.
You cannot have your *cake* and eat it too.
Chickens come home to roost.
Don't count your *chickens* before they're hatched.
Spare the rod and spoil the *child*.
Every *cloud* has a silver lining.
Easy *come*, easy go.
First *come*, first served.
Too many *cooks* spoil the broth.
Curiosity killed the cat.
Do unto others as you would have them do unto you.
Let sleeping *dogs* lie.
You can't teach an old *dog* new tricks.
Don't put all your *eggs* in one basket.
All's well that *ends* well.
Like *father*, like son.
Big *fish* eat little fish.
A *fool* and his money are soon parted.
A *friend* in need is a friend indeed.
Don't look a *gift horse* in the mouth.
All that glitters is not *gold*.
The *grass* is always greener on the other side of the fence.
Many *hands* make light work.

One *hand* washes the other.
Haste makes waste.
Make *hay* while the sun shines.
Two *heads* are better than one.
He who *hesitates* is lost.
Honesty is the best policy.
Don't change *horses* in the middle of the stream (mid-stream).
You can lead a *horse* to water, but you can't make him drink.
Strike while the *iron* is hot.
Better *late* than never.
He who *laughs* last, laughs best.
Live and let live.
Look before you leap.
Love is blind.
Misery loves company.
Money talks.
A *penny* saved is a penny earned.
Penny wise and pound foolish.
A *picture* is worth a thousand words.
A watched *pot* never boils.
Practice makes perfect.
An ounce of *prevention* is worth a pound of cure.
When it *rains,* it pours.
When in *Rome,* do as the Romans do.
Easier *said* than done.
If the *shoe* fits, wear it.
Out of *sight,* out of mind.
Where there's *smoke,* there's fire.
A *stitch* in time saves nine.
A rolling *stone* gathers no moss.
If at first you don't *succeed,* try, try again.
It takes two to *tango.*
Time is money.
Never put off till *tomorrow* what you can do today.
Waste not, want not.
Still *waters* run deep.
The squeaky *wheel* gets the grease.
Where there's a *will,* there's a way.
Two *wrongs* don't make a right.

These texts would represent 25 percent of an Anglo-American paremiological minimum of 300 texts, and I am quite convinced that every one of these proverbs would be on the minimum list in a wide-scale demographic study with frequency analysis.

In the meantime there is also the fascinating study that Kimberly J. Lau carried out by making use of the LEXIS/NEXIS computer database of over 2,300 full-text information sources from U.S. and overseas newspapers, magazines, journals, newsletters, and the like (Lau 1996). She established a list of 188 proverbs for which frequent citations are listed in the four major Anglo-American proverb dictionaries. She then took these proverbs and checked how many "hits" would be registered on this large electronic database that goes back to the early 1970s. Thus the results cover a time frame of about 25 years. Here are the "top 10" proverbs with the number of hits for each text:

Enough is enough.	(15,808)
Time will tell.	(14,226)
First *come,* first served.	(13,050)
Forgive and forget.	(5,097)
Time is money.	(3,770)
History repeats itself.	(3,713)
Time flies.	(3,673)
Better *late* than never.	(3,493)
Out of *sight,* out of mind.	(2,902)
Boys will be boys.	(2,103)

Lau goes on to present the "hit" numbers for the remaining 178 proverbs, with her list basically including the 75 proverbs listed above. Of course, these texts from the print media do not necessarily show anything about their currency in oral speech. While care should be taken not to interpret these texts too quickly as indicators of American values or worldview (see Winick 2001), they certainly include most of the common Anglo-American proverbs in actual use today. Until a nationwide research project with questionnaires is started to establish an American paremiological minimum, the materials summarized here present a good idea of the favorite proverbs in the English language.

LINGUISTIC AND SEMIOTIC CONSIDERATIONS

Theoretical proverb scholarship has been influenced to a large degree by the semiotic studies of Grigorii L'vovich Permiakov, notably by his Russian book *Ot pogovorki do skazki: Zametki po obshchei teorii klishe* (1970) and its English translation *From Proverb to Folk-Tale: Notes on the General Theory of Cliché* (1979), Peter Grzybek and Wolfgang Eismann (eds.), *Semiotische Studien zum Sprichwort. Simple Forms Reconsidered I* (1984), and Zoltán Kanyó, *Sprichwörter—Analyse einer Einfachen Form: Ein Beitrag zur generativen Poetik* (1981). Peter Grzybek has summarized this linguistic approach to proverbs in his seminal article on "Foundations of Semiotic Proverb Study" (1987, see also Grzybek 2000). As scholars investigate the hetereo-situativity, poly-functionality, and poly-semanticity of proverbs as "einfache Formen" (simple forms), it is of great significance that they pay attention to the paradigmatic, syntagmatic, logical, structural, pragmatic, and semantic aspects of these traditional utterances as communicative and strategic signs. Structural analyses of texts will certainly gain in value if semiotic aspects of proverbs as linguistic and cultural signs are added to them with a special focus on actual proverb performance in speech acts (Goodwin and Wenzel 1979).

This is not to say that the purely linguistic approach to proverbs lacks in value, as David Cram has clearly shown in his article on "The Linguistic Status of the Proverb" (1983). Cram and other linguists argue that the proverb should be viewed as a lexical element with a quotational status. The proverb is a lexical element in the sense that it is a syntactic string of words that is learned and reused as a single unit with a fixed internal and external structure. Its quotational status derives from the fact that proverbs are typically invoked or cited rather than straightforwardly asserted. In fact, proverbs often are quoted with such introductory formulas as "my grandfather used to say," "it is true that," "everybody knows that," and even more directly "the proverb says."

Structural proverb studies continue to be of interest, with Beatrice Silverman-Weinreich's essay "Towards a Structural Analysis of Yiddish Proverbs" (1978) being of special interest. The author concentrates on grammatical patterns in those proverbs that are based on conditional, comparative, imperative, and interrogative sentences. In addition she discusses such markers as parallelism, ellipsis, assonance, alliteration, rhyme, and meter. Robert A. Rothstein's paper on "The Poetics of Proverbs" (1969) based his linguistic analysis on proverbs from many languages, stressing ellipsis, parallelism, rhyme, and other poetic devices. Of much importance is also Robert M. Harnish's analysis of "Communicating with Proverbs" (1993) that emphasizes the form (sential, phrasal, declarative, imperative) and the force (explanatory, attitudinal, directive) of English and Hungarian proverbs in speech acts.

In any case, linguists of various schools have investigated the language, grammar, structure, syntax, and form of proverbs, and they have created an entire new field of inquiry called "phraseology" that deals with all formulaic language or phraseological units (phraseologisms), from proverbs to literary quotations, from proverbial expressions to idioms, from greeting formulas to phrasal superstitions, and so on (see the numerous books on phraseology in the bibliography). It behooves narrowly focused paremiologists to pay attention to such publications as Aleksandr K. Zholkovskii's "At the Intersection of Linguistics, Paremiology and Poetics" (1978) and Dmitrij Dobrovol'skij's *Phraseologie als Objekt der Universalienlinguistik* (1988). The relationship between paremiology and phraseology is indeed a very close one, especially when dealt with from linguistic and semiotic viewpoints (Fleischer 1997).

PERFORMANCE (SPEECH ACTS) IN SOCIAL CONTEXTS

The vexing problem of proverb meaning continues to occupy semantic studies. Linguists and folklorists have repeatedly attempted to explain the semantic ambiguity of proverbs, which results to a large degree from their being used in various contexts with different functions (Jason 1971). But proverbs also act as analogies, which adds to the complexity of understanding their precise meaning in a particular speech act. Some semantic and semiotic studies along this line are Barbara Kirshenblatt-Gimblett's "Toward a Theory of Proverb Meaning" (1973), Richard P. Honeck's and Clare T. Kibler's "The Role of Imagery, Analogy, and Instantiation in Proverb Comprehension" (1984), and Michael D. Lieber's "Analogic Ambiguity: A Paradox of Proverb Usage" (1984). In fact, linguist Neal R. Norrick dedicated his entire book on *How Proverbs Mean: Semantic Studies in English Proverbs* (1985) to this problem. He deals, of course, primarily with both the literal but usually figurative meaning of proverbs, emphasizing the ambiguity of metaphorical proverbs. In trying to understand the meaning of proverbs in certain contexts, one must keep in mind that they are usually employed to disambiguate complex situations and events. Yet they are paradoxically inherently ambiguous, because their meaning depends on analogy. Proverbs as devices of disambiguation, the paradox of analogic ambiguity in proverb usage, and the sociocultural use of proverbs in oral and written communication still require further study by paremiologists as they map out the strategies used in the appropriate employment of seemingly simple and yet so complex proverbial utterances.

Clearly the meaning and purpose of proverbs are best revealed by actual usage in social situations. Their strategic use in communication has been effectively analyzed by Kenneth Burke in his enlightening essay on "Literature [i.e., proverbs] as Equipment for Living" (1941) and in Peter Seitel's article on "Proverbs: A Social Use of Metaphor" (1969). When one considers proverbs in context, it should not be surprising that there are such contradictory proverb pairs as "*Birds* of a feather flock together" and "*Opposites* attract." After all, proverbs are not universal truths but rather limited pieces of folk wisdom that are valid only in certain situations. As Kwesi Yankah explains in his article "Do Proverbs Contradict?" (1984), the problem of contradictory proverbs exists primarily because people ignore their social context. If one deals with proverbs only as a concept of a cultural fact or truism, contradictions are easily found in any proverb repertoire. In contextual usage, however, proverbs function effectively as social strategies. In fact, the meaning of any proverb is actually evident only after it has been contextualized. Proverbs in normal discourse are not contradictory at all, and they usually make perfect sense to the speaker and listener. After all, people don't speak in proverb pairs, unless they are "dueling" with proverbs as a verbal contest, as Yankah shows in his invaluable study on *The Proverb in the Context of Akan Rhetoric: A Theory of Proverb Praxis* (1989).

Today it has almost become a cliché to point out that proverbs must be studied in context, but it took a long time for anthropologically oriented proverb collectors to go beyond mere texts and look at the use and function of the proverbial materials in actual speech acts. The noted anthropologist Edward Westermarck (1862–1939) began to look at proverbs from this contextual point of view in his *Wit and Wisdom in Morocco. A Study of Native Proverbs* (1930), and Cyril L. Nyembezi followed suit with his *Zulu Proverbs* (1963). Modern scholars trained in the theoretical aspects of speech acts or performance look at proverbs as part of active verbal communication. E. Ojo Arewa and Alan Dundes laid the groundwork for this type of analysis with their study on "[Yoruba] Proverbs and the Ethnography of Speaking Folklore" (1964), in which they looked at such questions as "What rules govern the use of proverbs? Who is using them and to whom? On what occasions? In what places?" (see also Penfield 1983; Fabian 1990). The study by anthropologist Charles L. Briggs on "The Pragmatics of Proverb Performances in New Mexican Spanish" (1985) is exemplary in this respect. Briggs studied the oral proverb performance in Córdova, a community of about 700 inhabitants located in the mountains of northern New Mexico in the United States. From transcriptions of recorded performances, Briggs isolates eight features of proverb use: tying phrase (i.e., introductory formula), identity of owner, quotation-framing verb, proverb text, special association, general meaning or hypothetical situation, relevance of context, and validation of the performance. Most speakers have never thought of all of this when expressing a proverb during an actual speech act, but these linguistic strategies definitely exist as proverbs are cited as signs of commonly understood and accepted folk wisdom.

ISSUES OF CULTURE, FOLKLORE, AND HISTORY

Folklorists, cultural historians, and philologists have occupied themselves for a long time with tracing the origin, history, dissemination, and meaning of individual proverbs and their variants. One could go so far as to say that there is a "story" behind every proverb, and it is usually a sizable task to deal with just one text in this diachronic and semantic fashion. About some proverbs entire books have been written, but there are also numerous lengthy articles and small notes on specific expressions, to wit the listing in my *International Bibliography of Explanatory Essays on Individual Proverbs and Proverbial Expressions* (1977). The German folklorist and paremiologist Lutz Röhrich has put together a three-volume *Das große Lexikon der sprichwörtlichen Redensarten* (1991–1992), in which he discusses the history and meaning of hundreds of German texts. There are also a number of helpful dictionaries that include explanatory comments on English proverbs and proverbial expressions (see Ammer 1992, 1997; Brewer 1870 [1970]; Flavell 1993; Funk 1948, 1950, 1955, 1958, 1993; Rees 1984, 1987, 1990, 1995, 1996; Titelman 1996). While there exist exemplary studies on such proverbs as "When *Adam* delved and Eve span, who was then the gentleman?" (Friedman 1974), "Don't throw the *baby* out with the bathwater" (Mieder 1993: 193–224), and "It is an ill *bird* that fouls its own nest" (Kunstmann 1939), much remains to be done for obscure regional and dialectical texts (see Hain 1951) as well as for globally disseminated proverbs.

But folklorists and cultural historians do not concern themselves only with the history and meaning of individual proverbs. They are also very much interested in looking at how proverbs were used in different historical periods. Proverbs do, at least to a degree, reflect the attitudes or worldview (mentality) of various social classes at different periods. This has been shown by Donald McKelvie in his article on "Proverbial Elements in the Oral Tradition of an English Urban Industrial Region" (1965), by Natalie Z. Davis in her book chapter "Proverbial Wisdom and Popular Error" (1975) in French society and culture, and by J.O.J. Nwachukwu-Agbada in his paper on the "Origin, Meaning and Value of Igbo Historical Proverbs" (1990). The latter is a significant article on the origin and importance of Igbo historical proverbs to an understanding of the cultural history of Nigeria. Although the texts might not be precise history, they contain important information concerning the folk interpretation of colonialism, wars, and other events. The fact that these matters were crystallized into proverbial form brought about the remembrance and memorability of such historical facts in a primarily oral culture. Of major interest is also James Obelkevich's essay on "Proverbs and Social

History" (1987), in which he discusses the users and uses of proverbs in Europe during different historical periods. He deals with various meanings of proverbs in their historical and social context, emphasizing their significance as expressions of "mentalities" or worldview. The article is primarily a social history of proverb usage in England and shows that historians ought to join literary scholars, folklorists, and anthropologists in studying proverbs as socially relevant wisdom.

Another area of interest for folklorists and cultural historians are proverbs that belong to a particular group or that can be grouped together under a theme, showing, for example, the traditional wisdom about gender issues and misogyny in particular over the centuries (Kerschen 1998; Rittersbacher 2002). At their best, studies of this type should be comparatively oriented, that is, they should look at proverbs from different cultural and linguistic groups (see Petrova 2003). Thus, when A.A. Parker investigated *The Humour of Spanish Proverbs* (1963) in a small pamphlet, it would have been of interest to know whether the proverbs of other countries have similar texts. Of much interest is also folklorist Sw. Anand Prahlad's study on "'No Guts, No Glory': Proverbs, Values and Image among Anglo-American University Students" (1994), since he based it on actual field research among young informants and their proverbs. A group can of course also be just a family, and folklorists have been eager to find out how proverbs function in these small social units. Three revealing accounts of familial proverb use based once again on field research and informants are given by Isaac Jack Lévy and Rosemary Lévy Zumwalt in "A Conversation in Proverbs: Judeo-Spanish *Refranes* in Context" (1990), Dan Ben-Amos in "Meditation on a Russian Proverb ['Don't say *hop* before you have jumped and landed'] in Israel" (1995), and Derek A. Williams, "'Everything that Shine Ain't Gold': A Preliminary Ethnography of a Proverb in an African American Family" (2003). But the group studied can, of course, also be as complex as the multi-ethnic society of Israel. Galit Hasan-Rokem has dealt with the use and function of proverbs in Israeli discourse in her enlightening paper on "Proverbs as Inter-Ethnic Dialogue in Israel" (1992), showing that proverbs can take on an important role in conflict solutions. Finally, one might ask what the proverb repertoire of one particular person might be. In order to answer this question, Stanley Brandes interviewed an elderly Spanish widow and presented his findings in an intriguing article on "The Selection Process in Proverb Use: A Spanish Example" (1974). Brandes compares her proverbs with the total inventory of proverbs collected in her village, he examines how the proverb content may reflect or relate to her direct experience, he evaluates whether her proverbs express consistent or contradictory notions, and he determines the functions and goals of her proverb use. Above all, Brandes shows that there is always a selection process going on whereby each person seizes upon or rejects the proverbs he or she has heard, depending upon his or her momentary outlook, status, or lifestyle. All of this is yet another indication that proverbs are no simple matter. Being acquainted with a number of proverbs is one thing, knowing when and how to use what proverb is quite another. Any person speaking a foreign language is well aware of this communicative difficulty with proverbs.

As can be seen, folklorists, and many paremiologists are folklorists, occupy themselves with all aspects of proverbs discussed in this section of the book. This continues to include the vexing problem of the definition of proverbs and the creation of new texts, to wit Stephen D. Winick's superb article on "Intertextuality and Innovation in a Definition of the Proverb Genre" (2003). More than other scholars, folklorists and cultural historians are also interested in the content of proverbs, to wit what cultural realia are contained in individual proverbs and how they differ from culture to culture in proverbs that might mean the same. Many proverbs refer to old measurements, obscure professions, outdated weapons, unknown tools, plants, animals, names, and various other traditional matters. Often it is not clear any longer what exactly is meant by certain words in a proverb, even though its actual sense is understood. That is why people so often ask what a proverb really means, where it comes from, and so on. Folklorists and cultural historians together with historically minded linguists are the ones who provide answers to these fascinating questions.

POLITICS, STEREOTYPES, AND WORLDVIEW

Care must be taken when looking at proverbs as expressing aspects of a certain worldview or mentality of a people that no stereotypical conclusions about a so-called national character are drawn. There are so many popular proverbs from classical, biblical, and medieval times current in various cultures that it would be foolish to think of them as reflecting some imagined national character, as for example Chinese or Finnish (Lister 1874–1875; Kuusi 1967). Nevertheless, the frequent use of certain proverbs in a particular culture could be used together with other social and cultural indicators to formulate valid generalizations. Thus, if the Germans really do use the proverbs "*Morgenstunde* hat Gold im Munde" (The morning hour has gold in its mouth, i.e., The early *bird* catches the worm) and "*Ordnung* ist das halbe Leben" (Order is half of life) with high frequency, then they do mirror at least to some degree the German attitude towards getting up early and keeping things in good order (see Dundes 1984). In any case, proverb studies looking for national character traits should be undertaken with much care.

Proverbs can be quite negative when they express, as many of them do, slurs or stereotypes, as Lynne Ronesi has illustrated on a global scope in her important paper on "'Mightier than the Sword': A Look at Proverbial Prejudice" (2000). Such negative proverbial texts appear in the earliest proverb collections, and they are still used today despite attempts to be open-minded towards ethnic, religious, sexual, national, and regional differences. Two special collections are Otto von Reinsberg-Düringsfeld's *Internationale Titulaturen* (1863) and Abraham A. Roback's *A Dictionary of International Slurs* (1944). Folklorist Alan Dundes presents an excellent study of national slurs, or "*blasons populaires,*" in his "Slurs International: Folk Comparisons of Ethnicity and National Character" (1975), dealing with such topics as stereotypes, national character, ethnocentrism, and prejudice. Shirley L. Arora contributed a revealing article on "Proverbs and Prejudice: *El Indio* in Hispanic Proverbial Speech" (1994), outlining the proverbial stereotypes that the Spanish colonizers invented against the native populations of Central and South America. I have described the use of anti-Semitic proverbs by the National Socialists in their murderous campaign of the destruction of the European Jews in my chilling article on "Proverbs in Nazi Germany: The Promulgation of Anti-Semitism and Stereotypes through Folklore" (1982), and J.O.J. Nwachukwu-Agbada has studied the historical and social background of proverbs against the white colonizers in "'Bèkeè' [the white man] in Igbo Proverbial Lore" (1988). The sad story of just one such hateful proverb I have shown in my analysis of "'No *Tickee,* No Washee'" (1996) and also in my book-length study *"Call a Spade a Spade": From Classical Phrase to Racial Slur* (2002). These proverbial stereotypes against the Chinese Americans and African Americans, respectively, have done much harm in the American society, and they should not be used any longer. Many additional studies need to be undertaken to show the danger and harm that such proverbial invectives can inflict on innocent people.

Finally, folklorists, historians, and political scientists have also looked at the use of proverbs in politics as most effective rhetorical devices (Louis 2000). Shirley L. Arora published an intriguing study of the role that the Greek proverb "The *fish* rots from the head first" with its major variant "The *fish* begins to stink at the head" played during the American presidential campaign in the summer of 1988 in the mass media (Arora 1989). In my book on *The Politics of Proverbs* (1997) I was able to illustrate that politicians from classical to modern times have deployed proverbs effectively in their rhetoric. Adolf Hitler, for example, used proverbs in his propagandistic and prophetic book *Mein Kampf* (*My Battle,* 1925–1926) to advocate the military and deadly goals of Nazism (see also Doerr 2000). Winston S. Churchill employed proverbs in his speeches and letters to convince the British people and the rest of the world that Nazi Germany had to be overcome by all means (Mieder and Bryan 1995). And, as expected, the plain-speaking Harry S. Truman added many proverbs and proverbial expressions to his verbal messages in order to communicate in a language that the average folk could understand (Mieder and Bryan 1997).

But speaking of presidents, John Adams, Abraham Lincoln, Teddy Roosevelt, Franklin D. Roosevelt, and also John F. Kennedy were all quite proverbial in their communications with the American people. Basically all presidents try to express their political messages in a language that is accessible to all the American people, no matter what their ethnic, social, or intellectual background might be. Proverbs are so to speak the "common denominator" of wisdom of a nation, and little wonder that even inaugural addresses are replete with proverbs. They add colorful metaphors to speeches that are often filled with setting political agendas, thus giving them a "folksy" touch with which people can identify (Mieder 2000). But proverbs in political use are not without their problems. While they can do much good in creating solid communication based on generational wisdom, they can also be misused to manipulate people into following the wrong leaders. Nazi Germany is a warning of how proverbs, especially anti-Semitic proverbs, became dangerous verbal weapons. People followed such proverbial invectives blindly, forgetting that proverbs are not absolute truths. As Joseph Raymond signaled in his article on "Tensions in Proverbs: More Light on International Understanding" (1956), proverbs can cut both ways in the political realm—as stereotypical invectives they can lead to tensions, but as metaphors of indirection they can in fact relax tensions. My later study on "'Raising the Iron Curtain': Proverbs and Political Cartoons of the Cold War" (Mieder 1997: 99–137 and 214–221 [notes]) showed clearly that world leaders like Leonid Brezhnev, Mikhail Gorbachev, Margaret Thatcher, Helmut Kohl, François Mitterand, and Ronald Reagan as well as international journalists employed such proverbs as "Hear no *evil*, see no evil, speak no evil," "Big *fish* eat little fish," "The *pen* is mightier than the sword," and "It takes two to *tango*" to deal with serious political issues. As the world continues its struggle towards peace and democracy, people might well keep in mind the American proverb of democracy: "Government of the *people*, by the people, for the people" (Mieder 2003).

SOCIOLOGY, PSYCHOLOGY, AND PSYCHIATRY

The social sciences have contributed a wealth of scholarship about the multifaceted characteristics, uses, functions, and meanings of proverbs. Janet

Sobieski and I have put together a 1,169-item review of these publications in our book *Proverbs and the Social Sciences: An Annotated Bibliography* (2003). The large subject index shows that some of the major areas of inquiry are abstraction, attitude, behavior, cognition, communication, community, ethnicity, experience, gender, intelligence, memory, mental health, perception, schizophrenia, socialization, transmission, validity, wisdom, and so on. The work of anthropologists like Charles Briggs and Edward Westermarck has already been mentioned in other sections on culture, folklore, performance, and social contexts, but Ruth Finnegan's chapter on "Proverbs" in her celebrated book on *Oral Literature in Africa* (1970) must be added here. It represents a detailed anthropological survey of the concept of proverbs in African societies, especially among the Jabo, Zulu, and Azande peoples. While Finnegan deals in general with the language, style, content, use, and function of the proverbs as part of social life, there is also Samuel Gyasi Obeng's much more specific study on "The Proverb as a Mitigating and Politeness Strategy in Akan Discourse" (1996). This paper is a superb example of how anthropologists study proverbs as performance in social contexts. In this case it is the indirection of the proverbial message that brings about a congenial communicative process that otherwise might have been confrontational. But it should be stressed that proverbs are used as mitigating strategies in modern discourse as well, once again owing their effectiveness to the indirect and less threatening way of expressing something that must be said.

While social anthropologists have dealt with proverbs since the nineteenth century, basing their research on impressive field research, sociologists regrettably have had much less interest in proverbs. And yet, as they study the social organizations and the behavior of people in them, it would make eminent sense to take a look at how proverbs relate and participate in social structures and life. But there is exciting new scholarship available, as for example Paul Hernadi's and Francis Steen's "The Tropical Landscapes of Proverbia: A Crossdisciplinary Travelogue" (1999) with its look at proverbs as socially sanctioned advice. Marilyn A. Nippold, Linda D. Uhden, and Ilsa E. Schwarz looked at the ability of understanding and interpreting proverbs at different age stages in "Proverb Explanation Through the Lifespan: A Developmental Study of Adolescents and Adults" (1997), and Alyce McKenzie published a fascinating study on "'Different *Strokes* for Different Folks': America's Quintessential Postmodern Proverb" (1996), explaining that while this modern proverb does advocate the freedom of choice (especially in behavioral matters), it must not be interpreted from a relativistic point of view lacking any moral and social obligations. The liberating thoughts of the proverb regarding individual choices obviously should go only so far as they conform with ethical concepts of society at large.

Proverbs have also been studied and used by social psychologists to help people deal with various behavioral problems including alcohol or drug addictions. Tim B. Rogers has shown in his article on "The Use of Slogans, Colloquialisms, and Proverbs in the Treatment of Substance Addiction: A Psychological Application of Proverbs" (1989) that proverbs like "No *pain, no gain*" can be used on posters in treatment centers as a constant reminder that it is a worthwhile struggle to overcome an addiction in order to live a normal life. Such proverbs have also been used during discussions in group therapeutic sessions where they help to create a common ground for the addicts. There is also a follow-up paper by Bryan B. Whaley with the proverbial title "When 'Try, Try Again' Turns to 'You're Beating a Dead Horse': The Rhetorical Characteristics of Proverbs and Their Potential for Influencing Therapeutic Change" (1993), indicating that the therapeutic use of proverbs is not without its problems and that they should not be overused as simplistic remedies of folk speech.

Psychologists and psychiatrists have long been interested in proverbs for testing intelligence, attitudes, aptitudes, and various mental illnesses. Numerous so-called "proverbs tests" have been devised for this purpose, the best known and most commonly used of which is the Gorham Proverbs Test. It was developed by Donald R. Gorham in 1956 as a tool for diagnosing schizophrenia, since schizophrenics have difficulty in understanding the metaphors of proverbs by interpreting them literally (Gorham 1956). Obviously psycho- and sociolinguistic aspects of normal comprehension of metaphors by, for instance, children versus adults, native versus foreign speakers, or white-collar versus blue-collar workers, enter into this. Of greatest importance is, however, that proverbs tests usually exclude any contextualization of the proverbs, even though it has long been established that proverbs can only be understood properly in social contexts (Mieder 1978; Rogers 1986).

But it is in the area of psycholinguistics that the true cutting-edge work is going on in theoretical paremiology. Psycholinguists have employed proverbs to study the mental development of children and the whole question of cognition and comprehension of metaphors (see Lakoff and Johnson 1980; Cacciari and Tabossi 1993; Everaert et al. 1995; Katz et al. 1998; Glucksberg 2001). Diana Van Lancker's seminal article on "The Neurology of Proverbs" (1990) looks at the complex mental processes that must take place in the brain of healthy people to understand abstract (i.e., metaphorical) proverbs, and Raymond W. Gibbs and his colleague Dinara Beitel have looked in great detail at "What Proverb Understanding Reveals about How People Think" (1995), discussing various theories of metaphor understanding based on proverbs. The psycholinguist Richard P. Honeck has dedicated his entire scholarly career to finding solutions to the vexing problems of cognition and figurative (metaphorical) language. In his superb book on *A Proverb in Mind: The Cognitive Science of Proverbial Wit and Wisdom* (1997) he reviews all relevant previous scholarship on metaphor comprehension and then examines proverbs in particular, looking at such matters as cognition, comprehension, communication, indirection, memory, and metaphor. As Honeck and his psycholinguistic colleagues have shown, proverbs might appear to be simple truths, but they certainly demand complex brain transactions to be properly understood and effectively used.

USE IN FOLK NARRATIVES AND LITERATURE

The interrelationship of proverbs with other verbal folklore genres has been of great interest to paremiologists for a long time. Classical Greek and Latin writers commented on the obvious interrelationship between fables and proverbs, theorizing, as it were, about which of the genres came first. In other words, does the proverb that adds a bit of moralizing or ethical wisdom at the end of a fable summarize its content, or is the fable nothing but an explanatory comment on the original proverb? This scholarship has been splendidly edited by Pack Carnes in his volume entitled *Proverbia in Fabula: Essays on the Relationship of the Fable and the Proverb* (1988). The use and function of proverbs in German fairy tales has been studied by Lothar Bluhm and Heinz Rölleke in their book on *Das Sprichwort in den "Kinder- und Hausmärchen" der Brüder Grimm* (1988), and there is also my essay on "Wilhelm Grimm's Proverbial Additions in the Fairy Tales" (1986), showing that the Brothers Grimm changed the style of the fairy tales they had collected from oral sources to make them sound even more "folksy" and ready-made for children. Galit Hasan-Rokem's valuable study on *Proverbs in Israeli Folk Narratives: A Structural Semantic Analysis* (1982) is also of much interest. The connections between proverbs and riddles, proverbs and jokes, and wellerisms and tall tales have also been studied in smaller articles and notes, and both Bartlett Jere Whiting and Richard Sweterlitsch have looked at the significance of proverbs in the narrative texts of ballads (Whiting 1934; Sweterlitsch 1985; see also Harris 1933). Much work remains to be done in this area, especially regarding etiological tales that serve the purpose of explaining the origin and meaning of proverbs and proverbial expressions (Hood 1885; Taylor 1971–1973; Röhrich 1991–1992).

Much has also been accomplished regarding the use and function of proverbs in literature, as can be seen from the 2,654 entries in George B. Bryan's and my *Proverbs in World Literature: A Bibliography* (1996). Early scholarship consists primarily of annotated lists of the proverbs found in literary works, while more recent publications address the problems of identification and interpretation of proverbial language in poetry, dramas, and prose. As Roger D. Abrahams and Barbara A. Babcock have noted in their essay on "The Literary Use of Proverbs" (1977), there are hundreds of literary proverb studies centering primarily on European and American authors ranging from the Middle Ages through the nineteenth century, but there are now also investigations of the proverbs in modern writers of Africa, Asia, and elsewhere (see Adéékó 1998). While the many monographs on famous writers as J. Alan Pfeffer's *The Proverb in Goethe* (1948), María Cecilia Colombi's *Los refranes en el Quijote: Texto y contexto* (1989), Daniel Calvez's *Le langage proverbial de Voltaire dans sa correspondance (1704–1769)* (1989), Marjorie Donker's *Shakespeare's Proverbial Themes: A Rhetorical Context for the "Sententia" as "Res"* (1992), George B. Bryan's *Black Sheep, Red Herrings, and Blue Murder: The Proverbial Agatha Christie* (1993), Susan E. Deskis's *"Beowulf" and the Medieval Proverb Tradition* (1996), and my *"No Struggle, No Progress": Frederick Douglass and His Proverbial Rhetoric for Civil Rights* (2001) are of importance, there are also more inclusive literary proverb studies of a national literature or a certain historical period, as for example Elisabeth Schulze-Busacker's *Proverbes et expressions proverbiales dans la littérature narrative du moyen âge français* (1985), Adéékè Adéékó's *Proverbs, Textuality, and Nativism in African Literature* (1998), and Kevin McKenna's edited volume *Proverbs in Russian Literature: From Catherine the Great to Alexander Solzhenitsyn* (1998). Rather than writing yet another study on Chinua Achebe or William Shakespeare, more such inclusive investigations are in order to draw valid conclusions regarding the use and function of proverbs during the different literary periods of various cultures and languages. The many specific analyses of literary works ought to add up to a better understanding of the poetics of proverbs in literature, also indicating, of course, what proverbs were in frequent use at what time.

All of this scholarship shows that there exists an impressive tradition of folklorists and literary historians looking at and interpreting the proverbial language in literary texts. Although authors differ in the frequency with which they employ proverbs, proverbial expressions, proverbial comparisons, and wellerisms, their works become important repositories of proverbial language. Whatever the number of proverbial texts in a literary work might be, locating them and interpreting their meaning can be a significant twofold task. Identification serves primarily paremiographical goals in that it deals with the texts. Since the oral use of proverbs in former centuries can no longer be investigated through field research, scholars depend on the written word as sources of them. Every literary investigation of proverbs should, ideally, include an index of all proverbial material with proper verification of their proverbiality (as far as this is possible) by means of standard proverb dictionaries. Such annotated proverb lists are of great importance for the preparation of both expanded and new historical proverb dictionaries.

However, this is only the paremiographical side of the coin. In addition to the identification of proverbial texts there should also be a detailed interpretation of their contextual function. Literary critics, folklorists, and paremiologists want to know when, why, how, by whom, and to whom proverbs are used in literary works. They will thus consider each example in its context to determine what effect it has on the style and message of the entire work. Of much interest is also whether introductory formulas are used to integrate the proverb into the text, whether the formulaic standard structure of the proverb has been changed for stylistic effect, whether a proverb is merely alluded to in an ironic twist, whether a proverb is intentionally parodied or questioned, and so on. The answers to such queries reveal the function and meaning of proverbial wisdom in literary works. In summary then, the ideal literary proverb investigation consists of a proverb index and an interpretive essay.

RELIGION AND WISDOM LITERATURE

Proverbs derived from the sacred writings of the world's religions have also gained wide circulation and have been studied as international expressions of wisdom. Selwyn Gurney Champion has put together a comparative proverb collection entitled *The Eleven Religions and Their Proverbial Lore* (1945), followed by Albert Kirby Griffin's *Religious Proverbs: Over 1600 Adages from 18 Faiths Worldwide* (1991), and there is also my small book *Not by Bread Alone: Proverbs of the Bible* (1990) with its 425 biblical proverbs current in the Anglo-American language. A vast international scholarship centers on wisdom literature that has found its way into traditional proverbs (see O'Connor 1993). Of particular importance are the studies by Clifford Henry Plopper, *Chinese Religion Seen through the Proverb* (1926); John Mark Thompson, *The Form and Function of Proverbs in Ancient Israel* (1974); Carole R. Fontaine, *Traditional Sayings in the Old Testament: A Contextual Study* (1982); Alan P. Winton, *The Proverbs of Jesus: Issues of History and Rhetoric* (1990); Theodore A. Perry, *Wisdom Literature and the Structure of Proverbs* (1993); and Claus Westermann, *Roots of Wisdom: The Oldest Proverbs of Israel and Other Peoples*

(1995). But much more comparative work is needed to point out the similarities and dissimilarities of the proverbial wisdom of the various religions. There is also not enough known yet about the influence that biblical proverbs had on the African or Asian population because of the missionary work. An exemplary and massive study (767 pp.) along these lines is Philippe Dinzolele Nzambi, *Proverbes bibliques et proverbes kongo: Étude comparative de "Proverbia 25–29" et de quelques proverbes kongo* (1992). But such indigenous studies as Gerald J. Wanjohi's *The Wisdom and the Philosophy of the Gikuyu Proverbs* (1997) are also of great value in understanding the religious and ethical value systems of various peoples.

There have been many attempts to discover links between wisdom and science. Some of this fascinating scholarship has been collected into an essay volume by Warren S. Brown with the title *Understanding Wisdom: Sources, Science, and Society* (2000). Evidence of verbal wisdom, much of it in the form of proverbs, can be seen both in the perception and performance of it, in religious writings, and certainly in everyday communication on all levels. Scholars from such diverse fields as theology, philosophy, medicine, psychology, and linguistics continue to look at the sources of wisdom (ancient wisdom literature, cultural traditions, moral values), the science of wisdom (cognition, comprehension, psycholinguistics), and the learning of wisdom (pedagogy, memorization, communication). John Marks Templeton published an uplifting book on *Worldwide Laws of Life: Two Hundred Eternal Spiritual Principles* (1997) based on wisdom drawn from major sacred scriptures of the world and different philosophies. The book is intended to help people to acquaint themselves with and hopefully to practice universally accepted moral truths, often expressed in the form of proverbs, as for example "Love thy *neighbor* as yourself" (Matt. 19:19), "Hitch your *wagon* to a star" (Ralph Waldo Emerson), "*Honesty* is the best policy," "A healthy *mind* in a healthy body," and, of course, the so-called golden rule of "*Do* unto others, as you would have them do unto you" (Matt. 7:12). There is also the ever expanding area of "self-help" books that draw on the wisdom of religious and folk proverbs to assist people in coping with the many challenges of modern life. Such books are meant to be therapeutic both from a sociological and psychological point of view, being based to a considerable extent on such proverbs as "If at first you don't *succeed,* try, try again," "No *pain,* no gain," and "Don't put off until *tomorrow* what you can do today." These matters have been studied by Jeffrey D. Arthurs in his article on "Proverbs in Inspirational Literature: Sanctioning the American Dream" (1994). Dylan Eret followed up with his essay on "'The Past Does Not Equal the Future': Anthony Robbins' Self-Help Maxims as Therapeutic Forms of Proverbial Rhetoric"

(2001), showing clearly that some of the "gurus" of the self-help phenomenon also create their very own maxims in the style of proverbs to spread their message among their eager readers.

Finally, but certainly not of less importance, there is the long tradition of the sermonic use of proverbs. Preachers in all religions frequently base their sermons on religious as well as folk proverbs to teach moral values for an upright life. From the folk preachers of the Middle Ages via Martin Luther (see Cornette 1942 [1997]) to the nineteenth-century American preacher Henry Ward Beecher and on to such internationally acclaimed preachers like Martin Luther King, proverbs have played a central role in their religious and social messages. At times the proverbs were simply used in an exegetic way to clarify certain Bible passages, but a much more important function of proverbs in sermons is to employ them as a sapient leitmotif. Alyce M. McKenzie has summarized this significant use of proverbial wisdom in her book on *Preaching Proverbs: Wisdom for the Pulpit* (1996).

PEDAGOGY AND LANGUAGE TEACHING

Proverbs have been used as teaching tools for centuries to teach moral values and social skills. In fact, there exist special proverbs that deal with such matters as the mind, wisdom, experience, learning, authority, and the teacher, as Dumitru Stanciu has shown in his article on "The Proverb and the Problems of Education" (1986). Proverbs contain much educational wisdom, and they have long been used as didactic tools in child rearing, in linguistic and religious instruction in schools, and in teaching about general human experiences. Such proverbs continue to play a major role as a pedagogical tool in modern societies, especially among family members and at school. They deserve to be taught as part of general education, and since they belong to the common knowledge of basically all native speakers, they are indeed very effective devices to communicate wisdom and knowledge about human nature and the world at large. Felix Boateng reaches similar conclusions in his significant paper on "African Traditional Education: A Tool for Intergenerational Communication" (1985), calling for a return to traditional education in Africa with an emphasis on the rich heritage of oral literature as expressed in fables, myths, legends, folk tales, and proverbs. Clearly the educational and communicative power of proverbs in African societies lies in their use as validators of traditional ethics, procedures, and beliefs in teaching children as well as adults. Further studies will certainly show that the value and power of proverbs as educational tools have not diminished in traditional or technological societies.

Proverbs have also been employed in native language instruction and to bring cultural traditions to foreign-language classes. Textbooks on both the teaching of native and foreign languages usually include at least some lists of proverbs and accompanying exercises. For English this began in the Middle Ages when Latin proverbs were used for translation exercises and to teach children moral precepts. This pedagogical and didactic use of proverbs continued well into the sixteenth and seventeenth centuries, as Martin Orkin explains in his article on "The Poor Cat's Adage and Other Shakespearian Proverbs in Elizabethan Grammar-School Education" (1978). But this tradition has by no means come to an end, as Deborah Holmes and I explain in our book on *"Children and Proverbs Speak the Truth": Teaching Proverbial Wisdom to Fourth Graders* (2000). The study shows that the developmental stage of fourth graders might be the perfect time to confront students with the character-building values of proverbial laws of life. The fact that they learned proverbs, that they can employ them in meaningful contexts, and that they act according to their wisdom is proof that children age 9 to 10 can cope with abstract and metaphorical proverbs as rules of moral conduct.

But proverbs also play a major role in the teaching of English as a second language, where they are included as part of metaphorical and cultural learning. Obviously it behooves new speakers of English to be acquainted with proverbs and other phraseological units for effective communication. As instructors plan the curriculum and devise textbooks for teaching English as a second language, they should choose those proverbs for inclusion that are part of the Anglo-American paremiological minimum. It is the proverbs that are in use today that ought to be taught, as Michael C. Abadi has argued in his survey of "Proverbs as ESL [English as Second Language] Curriculum" (2000). All of this also holds true for foreign language instruction in general, where proverbs have always been included as fixed cultural expressions. There is much scholarship on how to integrate proverbs into the teaching of foreign languages, notably Kevin J. McKenna's article on "'Na poslovitsu ni suda ni raspravy': The Role of Proverbs in the Russian Language Curriculum" (1991), Frank Nuessel's survey of "Proverbs and Metaphoric Language in Second-Language Acquisition" (1999), and above all Anna Tóthné Litovkina's book *A Proverb a Day Keeps Boredom Away* (2000). While the latter volume is intended primarily for Hungarian students learning English, it could easily be adapted for other language classes. The aim of the book is to familiarize language students with over 450 Anglo-American proverbs by providing a series of activities and exercises that will help the learner to discover what each proverb means and how to apply it in particular situations. The exercises bring the proverbs alive with short illustrative references from books, magazines, and newspapers, as well as from poems, fables, and folk narratives. The book also focuses on proverb humor, including anti-proverbs and wellerisms. The fact that the author has also provided 60 proverb illustrations from such well-known artists as Hieronymus Bosch and Pieter Bruegel the Elder as well as woodcuts, engravings, emblems, caricatures, cartoons, and advertisements makes it a most attractive and useful textbook for proverb acquisition in language classes.

ICONOGRAPHY: PROVERBS AS ART

There exists a long tradition of iconographic interpretations of proverbs, ranging from medieval woodcuts to misericords, from book illustrations to emblems, from tapestries to oil paintings, and from broadsheets to modern caricatures, cartoons, comic strips, and advertisements. Much attention has been paid to the Dutch painter Pieter Bruegel the Elder (1520–1569), who produced many proverb pictures, his most celebrated one being the *Netherlandish Proverbs* (1559), an oil painting illustrating over 100 proverbial expressions as well as some proverbs like "Big *fish* eat little fish" or "Two *dogs* over one bone seldom agree." Numerous books and articles have been written on this picture alone, three more recent publications being Alan Dundes and Claudia A. Stibbe, *The Art of Mixing Metaphors: A Folkloristic Interpretation of the "Netherlandish Proverbs" by Pieter Bruegel the Elder* (1981); Margaret A. Sullivan, "Bruegel's Proverb Painting: Renaissance Art for a Humanist Audience" (1991); and Mark Meadow, *Pieter Bruegel the Elder's "Netherlandish Proverbs" and the Practice of Rhetoric: Studies in Netherlandish Art and Cultural History* (2002).

As valuable as this preoccupation with Bruegel is, a detailed survey of the history of proverb iconography shows that he is but one major figure in the long tradition of proverbial art that in addition to paintings and drawings also includes such other artistic media as ceramics, textiles, T-shirts, sculptures, gold weights, coins, stamps, playing cards, and posters. The impressive scholarship concerning this fascinating area of paremiology has been put together by Janet Sobieski and me in *Proverb Iconography: An International Bibliography* (1999). The 378 annotated entries are proof that since proverbial metaphors are verbal images, artists have long delighted in translating these images into various art forms.

Before Pieter Bruegel, another Dutch painter by the name of Hieronymus Bosch had already included numerous proverbial scenes in his well-known oil paintings *The Hay Wain* (1485) and *The Garden of Earthly Delights* (1500). Pieter Brueghel the Younger made a number of copies of his father's cele-

Cited from Max J. Friedländer, *Pieter Bruegel.* Berlin: Propyläen Verlag, 1921, plate 44.

brated proverb picture in the early seventeenth century, and there is also the less ambitious oil painting *Dutch Proverbs* (1646/47) by David Teniers II. Francisco Goya prepared 22 etchings entitled *Los Proverbios* (1824; also called *Los Disparates*), and many other artists followed suit, including Albrecht Dürer, Jacob Jordaens, and Paul Klee. There is even a proverb tapestry from the fifteenth century in the Isabella Stewart Gardner Museum in Boston, and mention must also be made of 182 woodcuts with didactic eight-line stanzas from the same time that have been edited with explanatory comments by Grace Frank and Dorothy Miner as *Proverbes en Rimes: Text and Illustrations of the Fifteenth Century from a French Manuscript in the Walters Art Gallery, Baltimore* (1937). But while much is known about secular proverbial carvings on wooden choir stalls (i.e., misericords) in late medieval churches (Jones 1989), very little work has been done on proverbs in plastic art otherwise. There are, however, at least some studies on African gold weights, drums, tribal spokesman staffs, and textiles that depict proverbial wisdom (Yankah 1989: 71–116).

Many proverb illustrations are satirical depictions of foolishness in an ab- surd or so-called world-upside-down (Kunzle 1977). The satirical intent is usually coupled with didactic messages, as can be seen in hundreds of illustrated books that include woodcuts, engravings, and emblems. For some proverbs and proverbial expressions like "*Pandora's* box," "The *pitcher* goes to the well so often until at last it breaks," and "Hear no *evil,* see no evil, speak no evil" and the figures of the three monkeys attached to it, art historians, folklorists, and paremiologists have assembled various types of iconographic representations that span several centuries (see Panofsky 1956; Zick 1969; Mieder 1981). Other diachronic studies with numerous illustrations are needed, and care should be taken to include modern depictions as well. After all, these traditional and common proverbs continue to be illustrated in caricatures, cartoons, and comic strips. In addition, they appear on posters, billboards, postcards, greeting cards, buttons, banners, plaques, bookmarks, bumper stickers, coffee mugs, decorative plates, and T-shirts as well as in numerous advertisements. The images might be modern, but the idea of transposing verbal proverbs into art is old, and one is inclined to state proverbially that "There is nothing new under the *sun.*" (Eccles. 1:9).

MASS MEDIA AND POPULAR CULTURE

While it is perfectly appropriate for paremiologists to look backwards for the use of proverbs, they must not forget to investigate their traditional and innovative use in modern times. With the growing interest in popular culture, the mass media, and cultural literacy, paremiologists ought to look at which traditional proverbs survive today and which have actually been coined in the twentieth and twenty-first centuries. Nigel Rees offers useful information on *Sayings of the Century: The Stories Behind the Twentieth Century's Quotable Sayings* (1984), and I have dealt with the modern German scene in a number of books (Mieder 1983, 1985, 1995a, 1995b) and with Anglo-American materials in my book on *Proverbs Are Never Out of Season: Popular Wisdom in the Modern Age* (1993). People do not necessarily consider proverbs to be sacrosanct, and the "fun" of parodying, manipulating, and perverting them has become quite widespread. While such parodies might be humorous, they also often express serious sociopolitical satire in the form of slogans and graffiti, as Jess Nierenberg has convincingly shown in his article on "Proverbs in Graffiti: Taunting Traditional Wisdom" (1983). There is, of course, also the well-established tradition of intentionally rephrased anti-proverbs in all types of modern communication, from books of witticisms to T-shirt inscriptions and on to advertising slogans (see Mieder 1989: 239–275; Valdaeva 2003). While such play is not absolutely new, humorous or satirical proverb parodies certainly abound in modern literature, the mass media, and the popular culture of television, film, and music. Richard Sweterlitsch looked at the American comic writer "Josh Billings: His Anti-Proverbs and Comic Aphorisms" (2001), Anna Tóthné Litovkina and I have assembled over 3,000 parodied proverbs in *Twisted Wisdom: Modern Anti-Proverbs* (1999), and I have also issued a small popular collection of *Wisecracks! Fractured Proverbs* (2003). As I list but a few expressive anti-proverbs that include humor as well as social comments, the traditional proverb text is cited first. It is, after all, the juxtaposition of the original proverb with the innovative variation that adds even more spice to this play with proverbial language:

Absence makes the heart grow fonder.
Absence makes the heart go wander.

An *apple* a day keeps the doctor away.
A condom a day keeps the doctor away.

Too many *cooks* spoil the broth.
Too many legislators spoil reform.

Experience is the best teacher.
Expedience is the best teacher.

A *miss* is as good as a mile.
A Ms. is as good as a male.

Nobody is perfect.
No body is perfect.

Different *strokes* for different folks.
Different Volks for different folks.

The last anti-proverb was a popular advertising slogan for various Volkswagen models in the 1970s (see Mieder 1989: 293–315). In fact, copywriters know very well that advertising slogans built on proverbial structures bring with them that familiar and authoritative ring that is so crucial to the actual message. My wife, Barbara Mieder, and I looked at this phenomenon in a paper on "Tradition and Innovation: Proverbs in Advertising" (1977). There have been many additional studies ever since, including Jean Michel Massing's fascinating study "From Greek Proverb to Soap Advert: Washing the Ethiopian" (1995). The author traces the proverbial expression "To wash an Ethiopian (Blackamoor) white" based on the dual biblical proverb "Can the *Ethiopian* change his skin, or the *leopard* his spots?" (Jer. 13:23) from ancient times through various European languages and literatures and shows that it has been used in soap advertisements with racist overtones.

Much work has also been accomplished on the manipulative use of proverbs in the mass media as well as their (mis)use in political discourse. In their traditional or fittingly changed wording, proverbs are frequently used by journalists as attention-getting headlines, as Kevin J. McKenna has indicated in his article on "Proverbs and *Perestroika:* An Analysis of *Pravda* Headlines, 1988–1991" (1996). Of equal importance are his papers on "Politics and the Russian Proverb: A Retrospective of *Pravda* Political Cartoons in the 1990s" (2002) and "A Nation Adrift: The Russian 'Ship of State' in *Pravda* Political Cartoons during the Decade of the 1990s" (2003). Most of my studies in German or English on the modern use of proverbs in the mass media include numerous caricatures and cartoons as well (see especially Mieder 1989: 277–292), and Lutz Röhrich's *Das große Lexikon der sprichwörtlichen Redensarten* (1991–1992) contains over 1,000 illustrations, among them many with sociopolitical messages. Stephen D. Winick's unpublished dissertation features an intriguing chapter on "From Common Sense to Nonsense: Proverbial Language and Intertextuality in Gary Larson's *The Far Side*" (Winick 1998: 217–283) that should serve as a model for similar studies of *Peanuts, Dennis the Menace,* and other long-running comic strips and cartoons. There is no doubt that proverbs and proverbial expressions are very much alive in this visual type of communication. Usually the text of the proverb appears as a caption, and the topics range from political to sexual matters. Comic strips are also filled with proverbs, often questioning their wisdom and changing them into anti-proverbs.

The use and function of proverbs in film and music have also been studied, but this area definitely needs more attention. Donald Haase in his article on "Is Seeing Believing? Proverbs and the Film Adaptation of a Fairy Tale" (1990) has at least looked at the appearance of proverbs in Angela Carter's and Neil Jordan's film version of her tale *The Company of Wolves* (1979) that is based on the fairy tale *Little Red Riding Hood.* Of special value is also yet another chapter from Stephen D. Winick's dissertation on "Proverb Is as Proverb Does: Forrest Gump, the Catchphrase, and the Proverb" (Winick 1998: 83–162), in which he analyzes proverbial statements in the film *Forrest Gump* (1994), including such "Gumpisms" as "*Life* is like a box of chocolates: you never know what you're gonna get" that has become a proverb owing to the incredible popularity of this Hollywood film with its thousands of screenings. In the area of music, George B. Bryan in his article on "The Proverbial W.S. Gilbert: An Index to Proverbs in the Works of Gilbert and Sullivan"

(1999) shows how pervasive proverbs in fact are in popular music, and Steven Folsom has done the same in his paper on "Proverbs in Recent American Country Music: Form and Function in the Hits of 1986–87" (1993). And I have discussed "Proverbs in Popular Songs" (Mieder 1989: 195–221) as well, including such popular proverbial hits as Bob Dylan's *Like a Rolling Stone* (1965), Cher's *Apples Don't Fall Far from the Tree* (1973), and, of course, also the Beatles' song *[Money] Can't Buy Me Love* (1964).

At the end of this review of scholarship and approaches with an emphasis on publications in English, it is obvious that the ubiquitous proverbs enable and empower paremiologists to study them literally everywhere at any time. Modern paremiology is an absolutely open-ended phenomenon with many new challenges lying ahead. There is no doubt that proverbs, those old gems of generationally tested wisdom, help people in everyday life and communication to cope with the complexities of the modern human condition. The traditional proverbs and their value system provide some basic structure, and if their worldview does not fit a particular situation, they are quickly changed into revealing and liberating anti-proverbs. And there are, of course, the new proverbs of modern times, such as "Different *strokes* for different folks," that express a liberated worldview. Proverbs don't always have to be didactic and prescriptive; they can also be full of satire, irony, and humor. As such, the thousands of proverbs that make up the stock of proverbial wisdom of all cultures represent not a universally valid but certainly a pragmatically useful treasure. In retrospect, paremiologists have amassed a truly impressive body of proverb scholarship upon which prospective paremiology can build in good faith. Modern theoretical and empirical paremiology will doubtlessly lead to new insights about human behavior and communication, and by comparing these research results on an international basis, paremiologists might add their bit to a humane and enlightened world order based on common sense and experienced wisdom.

SELECTED BIBLIOGRAPHY

Book-length studies are listed in the major bibliography at the end of this book. Cross-references at the ends of entries correspond to collections listed in the bibliography.

Abadi, Michael C. 2000. "Proverbs as ESL [English as Second Language] Curriculum." *Proverbium* 17: 1–22.

Abrahams, Roger D., and Barbara A. Babcock. 1977. "The Literary Use of Proverbs." *Journal of American Folklore* 90: 414–429; also in Mieder 1994: 415–437.

Arewa, E. Ojo, and Alan Dundes. 1964. "[Yoruba] Proverbs and the Ethnography of Speaking Folklore." *American Anthropologist* 66, part 2: 70–85.

Arora, Shirley L. 1989. "On the Importance of Rotting Fish: A Proverb and Its Audience." *Western Folklore* 48: 271–288.

———. 1994. "Proverbs and Prejudice: *El Indio* in Hispanic Proverbial Speech." *Proverbium* 11: 27–46; also in Mieder 2003: 17–36.

Arthurs, Jeffrey D. 1994. "Proverbs in Inspirational Literature: Sanctioning the American Dream." *Journal of Communication and Religion* 17: 1–15; also in Mieder 2003: 37–52.

Ben-Amos, Dan. 1995. "Meditation on a Russian Proverb ['Don't say *hop* before you have jumped and landed'] in Israel." *Proverbium* 12: 13–26.

Boateng, Felix. 1985. "African Traditional Education: A [Proverb] Tool for Intergenerational Communication." In *African Culture: The Rhythms of Unity,* ed. by Molefi Kete Asante and Kariamu Welsh Asante, 109–122. Westport, Conn.: Greenwood Press.

Brandes, Stanley H. 1974. "The Selection Process in Proverb Use: A Spanish Example." *Southern Folklore Quarterly* 38: 167–186.

Briggs, Charles L. 1985. "The Pragmatics of Proverb Performances in New Mexican Spanish." *American Anthropologist* 87: 793–810; also in Mieder 1994: 317–349.

Bryan, George B. 1999. "The Proverbial W.S. Gilbert: An Index to Proverbs in the Works of Gilbert and Sullivan." *Proverbium* 16: 21–35.

Burke, Kenneth. 1941. "Literature [i.e., proverbs] as Equipment for Living." In *The Philosophy of Literary Form: Studies in Symbolic Action,* by K. Burke, 253–262. Baton Rouge: Louisiana University Press.

Cram, David. 1983. "The Linguistic Status of the Proverb." *Cahiers de lexicologie* 43: 53–71; also in Mieder 1994: 73–98.

Davis, Natalie Z. 1975. "Proverbial Wisdom and Popular Error." In *Society and Culture in Early Modern France,* by N.Z. Davis, 227–267 and 336–346 (notes). Palo Alto, Calif.: Stanford University Press.

Doerr, Karin. 2000. "'To Each His Own' (*Jedem das Seine*): The (Mis-)Use of German Proverbs in Concentration Camps and Beyond." *Proverbium* 17: 71–90.

Doyle, Charles Clay. 1996. "On 'New' Proverbs and the Conservativeness of Proverb Collections." *Proverbium* 13: 69–84; also in Mieder 2003: 85–98.

Dundes, Alan. 1975. "Slurs International: Folk Comparisons of Ethnicity and National Character." *Southern Folklore Quarterly* 39: 15–38; also in Mieder 1994: 183–209.

Eret, Dylan. 2001. "'The Past Does not Equal the Future': Anthony Robbins' Self-Help Maxims as Therapeutic Forms of Proverbial Rhetoric." *Proverbium* 18: 77–103.

Finnegan, Ruth. 1970. "Proverbs." In *Oral Literature in Africa,* by R. Finnegan, 389–425. Oxford: Clarendon; also in Mieder and Dundes 1981 (1994): 10–42.

Folsom, Steven. 1993. "Proverbs in Recent American Country Music: Form and Function in the Hits of 1986–87." *Proverbium* 10: 65–88.

Friedman, Albert. 1974. "'When Adam Delved…': Contexts of an Historic Proverb." *Harvard English Studies* 4: 213–230; also in Mieder 1994: 495–513.

Gibbs, Raymond W., and Dinara Beitel. 1995. "What Proverb Understanding Reveals about How People Think." *Psychological Bulletin* 118: 133–154; also in Mieder 2003: 109–162.

Goodwin, Paul D., and Joseph W. Wenzel. 1979. "Proverbs and Practical Reasoning: A Study in Socio-Logic." *The Quarterly Journal of Speech* 65: 289–302; also in Mieder and Dundes 1981 (1994): 140–160.

Gorham, Donald R. 1956. "A Proverbs Test for Clinical and Experimental Use." *Psychological Reports* 2: 1–12.

Grzybek, Peter. 1987. "Foundations of Semiotic Proverb Study." *Proverbium* 4: 39–85; see also Mieder 1994: 31–71.

Grzybek, Peter, and Christoph Chlosta. 1993. "Grundlagen der empirischen Sprichwortforschung." *Proverbium* 10: 89–128.

Haase, Donald. 1990. "Is Seeing Believing? Proverbs and the Film Adaptation of a Fairy Tale." *Proverbium* 7: 89–104.

Harnish, Robert M. 1993. "Communicating with Proverbs." *Communication & Cognition* 26: 265–290; also in Mieder 2003: 163–184.

Harris, Clement A. 1933. "Music in the World's Proverbs." *Musical Quarterly* 19: 382–392.

Hasan-Rokem, Galit. 1992. "Proverbs as Inter-Ethnic Dialogue in Israel." *Jewish Folklore and Ethnology Review* 14: 52–55.

Hernadi, Paul, and Francis Steen. 1999. "The Tropical Landscapes of Proverbia: A Crossdisciplinary Travelogue." *Style* 33: 1–20; also in Mieder 2003: 185–204.

Honeck, Richard P., and Clare T. Kibler. 1984. "The Role of Imagery, Analogy, and Instantiation in Proverb Comprehension." *Journal of Psycholinguistic Research* 13: 393–414.

Jason, Heda. 1971. "Proverbs in Society: The Problem of Meaning and Function." *Proverbium,* no. 17: 617–623.

Jones, Malcolm. 1989. "The Depiction of Proverbs in Late Medieval Art." In *Europhras 88: Phraséologie contrastive,* ed. by Gertrud Gréciano, 205–223. Strasbourg, France: Université des Sciences Humaines.

Kirshenblatt-Gimblett, Barbara. 1973. "Toward a Theory of Proverb Meaning." *Proverbium,* no. 22: 821–827; also in Mieder and Dundes 1981 [1994]: 111–121.

Kunstmann, John G. 1939. "'The Bird that Fouls Its Nest.'" *Southern Folklore Quarterly* 3: 75–91; also in Mieder and Dundes 1981 (1994): 190–210.

Kunzle, David. 1977. "Bruegel's Proverb Painting and the World Upside Down." *The Art Bulletin* 59: 197–202.

Kuusi, Matti. 1967. "Fatalistic Traits in Finnsih Proverbs." In *Fatalistic Beliefs in Religion, Folklore and Literare,* ed. by Helmer Ringgren, 89–96. Stockholm: Almqvist & Wiksell; also in Mieder and Dundes 1981 (1994): 275–283.

Lau, Kimberly J. 1996. "'It's about Time': The Ten Proverbs Most Frequently Used in Newspapers and Their Relation to American Values." *Proverbium* 13: 135–159.

Levin, Isidor. 1968–1969. "Überlegungen zur demoskopischen Parömiologie." *Proverbium,* no. 11: 289–293 and no. 13: 361–366.

Lévy, Isaac Jack, and Rosemary Lévy Zumwalt. 1990. "A Conversation in Proverbs: Judeo-Spanish *Refranes* in Context." *Proverbium* 7: 117–132; also in Mieder 2003: 255–269.

Lieber, Michael D. 1984. "Analogic Ambiguity: A Paradox of Proverb Usage." *Journal of American Folklore* 97: 423–441; also in Mieder 1994: 99–126.

Lister, Alfred. 1874–1875. "Chinese Proverbs and Their Lessons." *The China Review* 3: 129–138; also in Mieder and Dundes 1981 (1994): 242–256.

Louis, Cameron. 2000. "Proverbs and the Politics of Language." *Proverbium* 17: 173–194; also in Mieder 2003: 271–292.

Massing, Jean Michel. 1995. "From Greek Proverb to Soap Advert: Washing the Ethiopian." *Journal of the Wartburg and Courtauld Institutes* 58: 180–201.

McKelvie, Donald. 1965. "Proverbial Elements in the Oral Tradition of an English Urban Industrial Region." *Journal of the Folklore Institute* 2: 244–261.

McKenna, Kevin J. 1991. "'Na poslovitsu ni suda ni raspravy': The Role of Proverbs in the Russian Language Curriculum." *Russian Language Journal* 45: 17–37.

———. 1996. "Proverbs and *Perestroika:* An Analysis of *Pravda* Headlines, 1988–1991." *Proverbium* 13: 215–233; also in Mieder 2003: 293–310.

———. 2002. "Politics and the Russian Proverb: A Retrospective of *Pravda* Political Cartoons in the 1990s." *Proverbium* 19: 225–252.

———. 2003. "A Nation Adrift: The Russian 'Ship of State' in *Pravda* Political Cartoons During the Decade of the 1990s." *Proverbium* 20: 237–258.

McKenzie, Alyce M. 1996. "'Different Strokes for Different Folks': America's Quintessential Postmodern Proverb." *Theology Today* 53: 201–212; also in Mieder 2003: 311–324.

Mieder, Barbara and Wolfgang. 1977. "Tradition and Innovation: Proverbs in Advertising." *Journal of Popular Culture* 11: 308–319; also in Mieder and Dundes 1981 (1994): 309–322.

Mieder, Wolfgang. 1978. "The Use of Proverbs in Psychological Testing." *Journal of the Folklore Institute* 15: 45–55.

———. 1981. "The Proverbial Three Wise Monkeys: 'Hear No Evil, See No Evil, Speak No Evil.'" *Midwestern Journal of Language and Folklore* 7: 5–38; also in Mieder 1987: 157–177 and 255–259 (notes).

———. 1982. "Proverbs in Nazi Germany: The Promulgation of Anti-Semitism and Stereotypes through Folklore." *Journal of American Folklore* 95: 435–464; also in Mieder 1993: 225–255.

———. 1985. "Neues zur demoskopischen Sprichwortforschung." *Proverbium* 2: 307–328.

———. 1986 (1988). "Wilhelm Grimm's Proverbial Additions in the Fairy Tales." *Proverbium* 3: 59–83; also in *The Brothers Grimm and Folktale,* ed. by James McGlathery et al., 112–132. Urbana: University of Illinois Press.

———. 1990. "Prolegomena to Prospective Paremiography." *Proverbium* 7: 133–144.

———. 1992. "Paremiological Minimum and Cultural Literacy." In *Creativity and Tradition in Folklore: New Directions,* ed. Simon J. Bronner, 185–203. Logan:

Utah State University Press; also in Mieder 1993: 41–47 and Mieder 1994: 297–316.

———. 1996. "'No Tickee, No Washee.'" *Western Folklore* 55: 1–40; also in Mieder 1997: 160–189 and 227–235 (notes).

———. 1997. "Modern Paremiology in Retrospect and Prospect." In *Embracing the Baobab Tree: The African Proverb in the 21st Century,* ed. by Willem Saayman, 3–36. Pretoria: University of South Africa; also in Mieder 2000b: 7–36.

———. 2000. "'It's Not a President's Business to Catch Flies': Proverbial Rhetoric in Inaugural Addresses of American Presidents." *Southern Folklore* 57: 188–232; also in Mieder 2003: 325–366.

———. 2003. "'Government of the People, by the People, for the People': The Making and Meaning of an American Proverb of Democracy." *Proverbium* 20: 259–308.

Nierenberg, Jess. 1983. "Proverbs in Graffiti: Taunting Traditional Wisdom." *Maledicta* 7: 41–58; also in Mieder 1994: 543–561.

Nippold, Marilyn A., Linda D. Uhden, and Ilsa E. Schwarz. 1997. "Proverb Explanation Through the Lifespan: A Developmental Study of Adolescents and Adults." *Journal of Speech, Language, and Hearing Research* 40: 245–253; also in Mieder 2003: 367–383.

Nuessel, Frank. 1999. "Proverbs and Metaphoric Language in Second-Language Acquisition." *Studies in Applied Psychosemiotics* 16: 157–178; also in Mieder 2003: 395–412.

Nwachukwu-Agbada, J.O.J. 1988. "'Bèkeè' [the white man] in Igbo Proverbial Lore." *Proverbium* 5: 137–144.

———. 1990. "Origin, Meaning and Value of Igbo Historical Proverbs." *Proverbium* 7: 185–206.

Obelkevich, James. 1987. "Proverbs and Social History." In *The Social History of Language,* ed. by Peter Burke and Roy Porter, 43–72. Cambridge: Cambridge University Press; also in Mieder 1994: 211–252.

Obeng, Samuel Gyasi. 1996. "The Proverb as a Mitigating and Politeness Strategy in Akan Discourse." *Anthropological Linguistics* 38: 521–549; also in Mieder 2003: 413–442.

Orkin, Martin. 1978. "The Poor Cat's Adage and Other Shakespearian Proverbs in Elizabethan Grammar-School Education." *English Studies in Africa* 21: 79–88.

Parker, A.A. 1963. *The Humour of Spanish Proverbs.* London: The Hispanic & Luso-Brazilian Councils; also in Mieder and Dundes 1981 (1994): 257–274.

Permiakov, Grigorii L'vovich. 1971. *Paremiologicheskie eksperiment. Materialy dlia paremiologicheskogo minimuma.* Moskva, Russia: Nauka.

———. 1982 (1989). "K voprosu o russkom paremiologicheskom minimume." In *Slovari i lingvostranovedenie,* ed. by E.M. Vereshchagina, 131–137. Moskva, Russia: Russkii iazyk. Translated into English by Kevin J. McKenna as "On the Question of a Russian Paremiological Minimum." *Proverbium* 6: 91–102.

———. 1985. *300 obshcheupotrebitel'nykh russkikh poslovits i pogovorok.* Moskva, Russia: Russkii iazyk.

Petrova, Roumyana. 2003. "Comparing Proverbs as Cultural Texts." *Proverbium* 20: 331–344.

Prahlad, Sw. Anand. 1994. "'No Guts, No Glory': Proverbs, Values and Image among Anglo-American University Student." *Southern Folklore* 51: 285–298; also in Mieder 2003: 443–458.

Raymond, Joseph. 1956. "Tensions in Proverbs: More Light on International Understanding." *Western Folklore* 15: 153–158; also in Mieder and Dundes 1981 (1994): 300–308.

Rogers, Tim B. 1986. "Psychological Approaches to Proverbs: A Treatise on the Import of Context." *Canadian Folklore Canadien* 8: 87–104.

———. 1989. "The Use of Slogans, Colloquialisms, and Proverbs in the Treatment of Substance Addiction: A Psychological Application of Proverbs." *Proverbium* 6: 103–112.

Ronesi, Lynne. 2000. "'Mightier than the Sword': A Look at Proverbial Prejudice." *Proverbium* 17: 329–347.

Rothstein, Robert A. 1969. "The Poetics of Proverbs." In *Studies Presented to Professor Roman Jakobson by His Students,* ed. by Charles Gribble, 265–274. Cambridge, Mass.: Slavica Publications.

Seitel, Peter. 1969. "Proverbs: A Social Use of Metaphor." *Genre* 2: 143–161; also in Mieder and Dundes 1981 (1994): 122–139.

Silverman-Weinreich, Beatrice. 1978. "Towards a Structural Analysis of Yiddish Proverbs." *Yivo Annual of Jewish Social Science* 17: 1–20; also in Mieder and Dundes 1981 (1994): 65–85.

Stanciu, Dumitru. 1986. "The Proverb and the Problems of Education." *Proverbium* 3: 153–178.

Sullivan, Margaret A. 1991. "Bruegel's Proverb Painting: Renaissance Art for a Humanist Audience." *The Art Bulletin* 73: 431–466; also in Mieder 1994: 253–295.

Sweterlitsch, Richard. 1985. "Reexamining the Proverb in the Child Ballad." *Proverbium* 2: 233–256.

———. 2001. "Josh Billings: His Anti-Proverbs and Comic Aphorisms." *Proverbium* 18: 319–327.

Taylor, Archer. 1971–1973. "The Collection and Study of Tales and Proverbs." *Béaloideas* 39–41: 320–328.

Tóthné Litovkina, Anna. 1994. "The Most Powerful Markers of Proverbiality: Perception of Proverbs and Familiarity with Them Among 40 Americans." *Semiotische Berichte,* nos. 1–4: 227–353.

———. 1998. "An Analysis of Popular American Proverbs and Their Use in Language Teaching." In *Die heutige Bedeutung oraler Tradition: Ihre Archivierung, Publikation und Index-Erschließung,* ed. by Walther Heissig and Rüdiger Schott, 131–158. Opladen, Germany: Westdeutscher Verlag.

Valdaeva, Tatiana. 2003. "Anti-Proverbs or New Proverbs: The Use of English Anti-Proverbs and Their Stylistic Analysis." *Proverbium* 20: 379–390.

Van Lancker, Diana. 1990. "The Neurology of Proverbs." *Behavioural Neurology* 3: 169–187; also in Mieder 2003: 531–554.

Whaley, Bryan B. 1993. "When 'Try, Try Again' Turns to 'You're Beating a Dead Horse': The Rhetorical Characteristics of Proverbs and Their Potential for Influencing Therapeutic Change." *Metaphor and Symbolic Action* 8: 127–139; also in Mieder 2003: 555–570.

Whiting, Bartlett Jere. 1934. "Proverbial Material in the Popular Ballad." *Journal of American Folklore* 47: 22–44.

Williams, Derek A. 2003. "'Everything that Shine Ain't Gold': A Preliminary Ethnography of a Proverb in an African American Family." *Proverbium* 20: 391–406.

Winick, Stephen D. 2001. "'Garbage in, Garbage out,' and Other Dangers: Using Computer Databases to Study Proverbs." *Proverbium* 18: 353–364.

———. 2003. "Intertextuality and Innovation in a Definition of the Proverb Genre." In *Cognition, Comprehension, and Communication: A Decade of North American Proverb Studies* (1990–2000), ed. by Wolfgang Mieder, 571–601. Baltmannsweiler, Germany: Schneider Verlag Hohengehren.

Yankah, Kwesi. 1984. "Do Proverbs Contradict?" *Folklore Forum* 17: 2–19; also in Mieder 1994: 127–142.

Zholkovskii, Aleksandr K. 1978. "At the Intersection of Linguistics, Paremiology and Poetics." *Poetics* 7: 309–332.

Zick, Gisela. 1969. "Der zerbrochene Krug als Bildmotiv des 18. Jahrhunderts." *Wallraf-Richartz Jahrbuch* 31: 149–204.

Four

Contexts

There are again two parts to this fourth section. The first six subsections show how proverbs function in literary works, letters, speeches, and political writings. There are two analyses from the eighteenth century dealing with Lord Chesterfield's arguments against the use of proverbs and Benjamin Franklin's opposing view of seeing a high ethical value in these traditional bits of wisdom. The next two discussions are concerned with the nineteenth-century use of proverbs by Abraham Lincoln in his fight against slavery and Charles Dickens's desire to depict social realities through language. The final couple of subsections look at two major figures of the twentieth century, namely Winston S. Churchill, who masterfully employed proverbs in his war rhetoric, and Bertolt Brecht, whose dialectical use of proverbs dealt with the worrisome human condition. Once again these six accounts are based on my much longer former publications that contain many more references and detailed bibliographical information. These studies have been stripped of their scholarly apparatus to enhance their readability and to present a general understanding of the effective integration of proverbs into all sorts of communication during the past three centuries. The original publications are listed under my name in the selected bibliography of this fourth section of the book for those readers who wish to get more detailed information.

The second part of this section is comprised of five groups of texts that show how proverbs function in particular contexts. The first deals with Benjamin Franklin's famous essay "The Way to Wealth" (1758) that includes over 100 proverbs to instruct people in solid work ethics and a commonsense approach to life's trials and tribulations. The second subsection presents poems and songs that include proverbs as didactic and sapient messages. These poetic texts also indicate that poets and songwriters do not look at proverbs as sacrosanct statements. In fact, they do enjoy questioning or parodying them in order to get their readers to think critically about their purported wisdom. This is also the intent of the caricatures, cartoons, and comic strips that are based on proverbs. While some of them cite the proverbs in their original wording, most of them alter them satirically, ironically, or humorously into revealing anti-proverbs. Copywriters of advertisements also employ proverbs either traditionally or innovatively to get the attention of consumers, and the same is true for journalists using proverbs or anti-proverbs in newspaper and magazine headlines. And, of course, there are also graffiti, bumper stickers, and T-shirts that exhibit (un)altered proverbs as old or new messages of the modern age. The three subsections on proverbs in the mass media contain numerous illustrations that indicate how metaphorical proverbs as headlines and captions work hand in hand with pictures to bring about meaningful communication. Together, all contextualized proverbs are solid proof that proverbs are by no means out-of-date. If traditional texts do not seem to fit a particular context, they can always be twisted into shape by changing a word or two. And, to be sure, modern people from poets to slogan writers are perfectly capable of creating statements based on proverbial structures that over time might well become the new proverbs of modernity.

"A MAN OF FASHION NEVER HAS RECOURSE TO PROVERBS": LORD CHESTERFIELD'S TILTING AT PROVERBIAL WINDMILLS

Certain unfounded generalizations and unproven claims exist in all intellectual attempts to draw sweeping conclusions. Even Archer Taylor as the grand master of proverb studies fell into this trap in a chapter on "Proverbs in Literature" in his celebrated and classic book on *The Proverb* (1931). Commenting on the fact that "different attitudes [exist] toward proverbs in different ages," he observes correctly that the sixteenth and seventeenth centuries exhibit a widespread interest in folk wisdom, but he goes too far in his claim that "during the eighteenth century a reaction set in: the rationalistic temper found little to admire in proverbs." While such eighteenth-century authors as William Blake, Denis Diderot, Henry Fielding, Johann Wolfgang von Goethe, Gotthold Ephraim Lessing, Jonathan Swift, and François Marie Voltaire do in fact question or ridicule the wisdom of proverbs at times, they also see their communicative value as strategically placed moral and didactic statements. In the United States, one glance at the writings of Benjamin Franklin will clearly show what ethical significance proverbs had in this young democracy. In addition, it must not be forgotten that enlightened scholars with interest in folklore put together major proverb collections at this time, thus indicating that there was a persuasive interest in registering and preserving proverbs and proverbial expressions. Proverbs did not die out in the Age of Reason even though there were forces that argued vigorously against their commonsense philosophy. There is then merely a certain ambivalence towards proverbs that is somewhat reminiscent of the critical view of proverbs today. But no zealous spirit, no matter how convinced of the absolute invalidity and stupidity of proverbs, could possibly have succeeded in ridding the language, both written and oral, of this formulaic treasure of wisdom.

Yet there was such an individual who tried his very best to do exactly that. It was Philip Dormer Stanhope, fourth Earl of Chesterfield (1694–1773), who in two letters to his illegitimate son Philip Stanhope (1732–1768) argued vehemently against the value and use of proverbs. Always the teacher of proper social behavior in upper society, he instructed his son in a letter of July 25, 1741, to make sure that he would follow the manners and speech of people of fashion:

> There is, likewise, an awkwardness of expression and words, most carefully to be avoided; such as false English, bad pronunciation, old sayings, and common proverbs; which are so many proofs of having kept bad or low company. For example, if, instead of saying that tastes are different, and that every man has his own peculiar one, you should let off a proverb, and say, That what is one man's meat is another man's poison; or else, Everyone as they like, as the good man said when he kissed his cow, everybody would be persuaded that you had never kept company with anybody above footmen and housemaids.

It is of interest to note that in his eagerness to explain his point, Lord (appointed 1730) Chesterfield lowers himself to cite something as crude as a wellerism, albeit in a somewhat "cleansed" variant. The more vulgar version would be "'Every *man* where he likes,' quoth the goodman when he kissed his cow." In typical folk humor, the "where of the kiss" might well include the tail end of that animal. And how disheartened would the Earl be if he could have known that his sentence that " *Tastes* are different" has been registered as a proverb as early as 1803. In any case, these few epistolary lines are a definite sign that even a proverb despiser can't escape the occasional and unintentional use of proverbial wisdom.

But be that as it may, the *summum bonum* of his two tirades against proverbs appears in a lengthy letter of September 27, 1749. Always interested in instructing his son in the proper and sophisticated use of language, Lord Chesterfield gets quite carried away on his rhetorical soapbox. Of special importance is his preoccupation with the words "vulgar" and "vulgarism," the latter of which is for him synonymous with "proverb":

> DEAR BOY: A vulgar, ordinary way of thinking, acting, or speaking, implies a low education, and a habit of low company. Young people contract it at school, or among servants, with whom they are too often used to converse; but after they frequent good company, they must want attention and observation very much, if they do not lay it quite aside; and, indeed, if they do not, good company will be very apt to lay them aside. The various types of vulgarisms are infinite; I cannot pretend to point them out to you; but I will give some examples, by which you may guess the rest. [...]
>
> Vulgarism in language is the next and distinguishing characteristic of bad company and a bad education. A man of fashion avoids nothing with more care than that. Proverbial expressions and trite sayings are the flowers of the rhetoric of a vulgar man. Would he say that men differ in their tastes; he both supports and adorns that opinion by the good old saying, as he respectfully calls it, that WHAT IS ONE MAN'S MEAT, IS ANOTHER MAN'S POISON. A man of fashion never has recourse to proverbs and vulgar aphorisms; uses neither favorite words nor hard words; but takes great care to speak very correctly and grammatically, and to pronounce properly; that is, according to the usage of the best companies.

While repeating the proverb "One man's *meat* is another man's poison" from his previous letter, Lord Chesterfield drops the "tasteless" wellerism from his denunciation. Yet this time he also includes explicitly proverbial expressions among his scorned "vulgarisms."

But who then was this Lord Chesterfield about whom all of this proverbial fuss has and is being made? He was an extremely dedicated and diligent public servant as a member of the House of Lords and as Viceroy of Ireland as well as Ambassador at The Hague, who nevertheless found the time to study his contemporaries and to reflect upon the attitudes and mores of his age in countless letters, essays, and speeches. In particular, he expended much energy in the education both of his son and his godson of the same name, albeit primarily through a never-ending stream of didactic and edifying letters (about 430 letters to his son). And it is exactly these letters as an exemplification of how to become a perfect member of upper society for which Lord Chesterfield gained so much notoriety as well as fame.

The basis of Lord Chesterfield's educational philosophy and pedagogical program consisted above all of the conviction that there are the social graces, which include good manners, moderation, civility, self-control, politeness, and the proper behavior in all settings. Driven by his own "pedagogomania," Chesterfield never tired of insisting on these behavioral graces. Basically he was teaching the pragmatic skills of social life, and adding a good deal of general knowledge to this for good measure. On October 9, 1746, he writes to his son:

> Your destination is the great and busy world; your immediate object is the affairs, the interests, and the history, the constitutions, the customs, and the manners of the several parts of Europe. In this, any man of common sense may, by common application, be sure to excel. Ancient and modern history are, by attention, easily attainable. Geography and chronology the same, none of them requiring any uncommon share of genius or invention. Speaking and Writing [*sic*], clearly, correctly, and with ease and grace, are certainly to be acquired, by reading the best authors with care, and by attention to the best living models. [...]
>
> If care and application are necessary to the acquiring of those qualifications, without which you can never be considerable, nor make a figure in the world, they are not less necessary with regard to the lesser accomplishments, which are requisite to make you agreeable and pleasing in society. In truth, whatever is worth doing at all, is worth doing well; and nothing can be done well without attention.

There then is the program of social and intellectual education with two proverbial statements to drive home the point. Chesterfield is positively obsessed with the proverbial expression "to make a *figure*" (i.e., to show proper social behavior) and the proverb "Whatever is worth *doing* at all, is worth doing well." These are two leitmotifs that reoccur throughout these instructive letters based on "good sense and good taste." As can be seen, there are natural lapses back into good old plain English with its expressive proverbs and proverbial expressions. Neither Chesterfield nor his age could live without them!

But it is time to take a look first at such textual references, where Chesterfield employs proverbs as "vulgar" expressions. And what a surprise one finds already with the first example! Even though Chesterfield wants to interpret proverbs as negative verbal and behavioral signs that should be avoided, he must admit that there is wisdom in some of them too good to be ignored. Giving his son once again numerous commonsense lessons on life, he summarizes them with a fitting proverb in his letter of July 20, 1748: "All those things, in the common course of life, depend entirely upon the manner; and, in that respect, the vulgar saying is true, That one man can better steal a horse, than another look over the hedge." Chesterfield is even capable of declaring one of these despicable vulgar proverbs as absolutely true in order to drive home a point: "It is a vulgar, ordinary saying, but it is a very true one, that one should always put the best foot foremost." He simply seems to have the need of distancing himself from these preformulated expressions of the lower class. That is, of course, where his fundamental error lies. Proverbs express traditional wisdom shared by all people of a culture. After all, Chesterfield knows them only too well and is clearly incapable and yes, unwilling, to avoid them completely. If proverbs can express matters so effectively, then why label them as vulgar at all?

And sure enough, more often than not Chesterfield fails to include this superfluous and incorrect label, clearly indicating that proverbial language is part of his written style and quite certainly of his oral speech. He frequently

"So's vice."

Cited from *Playboy* (March 1977), p. 177.

employs proverbs in a very straightforward traditional fashion as a valuable and didactic piece of advice. In those cases, proverbs are not at all questioned or labeled as inappropriate for the elegant upper class. In fact, they become major instruments for the proper education of his son, serving an absolutely legitimate purpose:

> A man of sense knows how to make the most of his time, and put out his whole sum either to interest or to pleasure; he is never idle, but constantly employed either in amusements or in study. It is a saying, that idleness is the mother of all vice. At least, it is certain that laziness is the inheritance of fools; and nothing is so despicable as a sluggard.

> For though people should not do well for the sake of rewards, yet those who do well ought in justice to be rewarded. One should do well for the sake of doing well, and virtue is its own reward; that is, the consciousness of having done right makes one happy enough even without any other reward.

These short statements give solid moral or behavioral advice, and the proverbs serve to underscore the intended lesson. Here and there, but seldom indeed, does Chesterfield argue against a proverb as in the following two examples:

> I knew once a very covetous, sordid fellow, who used frequently to say, "Take care of the pence; for the pounds will take care of themselves." This was a just and sensible reflection of a miser. I recommend to you to take care of the minutes; for hours will take care of themselves.

> Those who aim at perfection will come infinitely nearer it than those desponding or indolent spirits, who foolishly say to themselves: Nobody is perfect; perfection is unattainable; to attempt it is chimerical; I shall do as well as others; why then should I give myself trouble to be what I never can, and what, according to the common course of things, I need not be, PERFECT?

But such quibbles are rare and indicate a perfectly normal ambivalent reaction to proverbs. It will be an unusual person who would buy into the wisdom of every proverb in every situation! And these few negative reactions on the part of Chesterfield certainly cannot be regarded as a convincing proof of his fundamental dislike of proverbs.

How much he actually likes and believes in traditional folk wisdom becomes evident in his use of two favorite proverbs. Being the pragmatic expounder of solid work ethics, he definitely has a predilection towards the proverb "Never put off till *tomorrow* what you can do today." Chesterfield employed it several times in his letters, obviously advocating its plain truth:

> Many people lose a great deal of their time by laziness; they loll and yawn in a great chair, tell themselves that they have not time to begin anything then, and that it will do as well another time. This is a most unfortunate disposition, and the greatest obstruction to both knowledge and business. [...] You are but just listed in the world, and must be active, diligent, indefatigable. If ever you propose commanding with dignity, you must serve up to it with diligence. Never put off till tomorrow what you can do to-day.

> Use yourself, therefore, in time to be alert and diligent in your little concerns; never procrastinate, never put off till to-morrow what you can do to-day; and never do two things at a time; pursue your object, be it what it will, steadily and indefatigably; and let any difficulties (if surmountable) rather animate than slacken your endeavors. Perseverance has surprising effects.

But there is yet another proverb that served Chesterfield as a leitmotif for teaching his son the most basic principle of human behavior, namely the biblical golden rule of "*Do* unto others as you would have them do unto you" (Matt. 7:12) in its various forms. On September 27, 1748, he summarized the entire purpose of his moral teaching thus: "Pray let not quibbles of lawyers, no refinements of casuists, break into the plain notions of right and wrong, which every man's right reason and plain common sense suggest to him. To do as you would be done by, is the plain, sure, and undisputed rule of morality and justice. Stick to that." Nowhere is there an argument with this moral rule, and Chesterfield also quite expectedly by now accepted other biblical proverbs as invaluable truisms.

Yet another group of proverbs stands out in these fascinating letters, namely the proverbial wisdom from other languages like Latin, French, Italian, and Spanish. As a man of the political world, the polyglot Chesterfield had lived and traveled widely in Europe. Again and again he advises his son to study French, Italian, or German, and not surprisingly he makes use of the rich proverb repertoire of these languages and cultures.

Above all, Chesterfield believes in the classical Latin proverb of "A healthy *mind* in a healthy body." This he considers one of the basic laws of life, quoting it four times in Latin only without seeing any particular need to expound on its obvious wisdom in any detail: "*Mens sana in corpore sano,* is the truest description of human happiness; I think you have them both at present; take care to keep them; it is in your power to do it," "*Mens sana in corpore sano,* is the first and greatest blessing. I would add *et pulchro* [and beautiful], to complete it. May you have that and every other!" and "You have, too, *mens sana in corpore sano,* the greatest blessing of all." He certainly is not negating these old proverbs and is far from pushing them away as vulgar expressions. It helps, of course, that they are cited in the learned language of Latin, a language that the "vulgar" would not know. But proverbs they are nevertheless!

And then there is that Spanish proverb that Chesterfield cites three times in English only. It suits him just fine since it does express very candidly how people form their opinions about others. In all three cases Chesterfield explicitly states that he is dealing with a proverb and that this wisdom is indeed true:

> There is good sense in the Spanish saying, "Tell me whom you live with, and I will tell you who you are." Make it therefore your business, wherever you are, to get into that company which everybody in the place allows to be the best company next to their own; which is the best definition that I can give you of good company.

Chesterfield is correct in calling the text in this reference from 1748 a Spanish proverb, since it does exist in that language as "Dime con quien andas, diréte quien eres. Tell me what *company* you keep, and I will tell you who you are." But when he used it for the third time as a fitting leitmotif to comment on the proper company that one should keep, he must finally have realized that this proverb was also long established since the sixteenth century in the English language as "Tell me with whom you *go,* and I'll tell you who you are." And how shocked might the good Lord have been, if he had found out that this proverb is actually of medieval Latin origin. In fact, the Latin text "Noscitur ex socio, qui non cognoscitur ex se" (One recognizes him by his companions whom one does not recognize from himself) was subsequently translated into most European languages, making it a generally accepted truism about human behavior. In any case, Lord Chesterfield approved of the content of the proverb, and there is no indication whatsoever that he considered it too "vulgar" for his educational epistles.

The situation is quite similar with a number of French proverbs cited in the letters. It must, however, be added that Chesterfield was absolutely fluent in French and that he delighted in writing French letters. In an English-language letter of 1751, he cites a French proverb, once again dealing with proper behavior in company:

> Have a watch over yourself never to say anything that either the whole company, or any one person in it, can reasonably or probably take ill, and remember the French saying, *qu'il ne faut pas parler de corde, dans la maison d'un pendu.* Good nature usually charms, even all those who have none, and it is impossible to be *amiable* without both the reality and the appearances of it.

But what is it, snobbery or actual ignorance, which kept Chesterfield from citing the English version of this proverb? After all, this folk wisdom is once again quite common in Europe and current in English since the late sixteenth century as "Never mention a *rope* in the house of a man who has been hanged." It seems that Lord Chesterfield wanted to add some linguistic prowess to his style by employing foreign-language equivalents of English proverbs. Perhaps he felt that the French language would hide the "vulgar" tone of English proverbs while maintaining their undeniable wisdom and truth, something that even Chesterfield seems not to have been able to live without in his letters.

Lord Chesterfield simply could not escape the pitfalls of folk speech in general and proverbs in particular. In a letter of June 13, 1758, he even cites merely the first half of an English and a French proverb, obviously convinced of their general currency. Speaking of marriages, he quips, "The lady has wanted a man so long, that she now compounds for half a one. Half a loaf—." And then he closes his letter with a more personal reflection concerning his health: "I have been worse since my last letter; but am now, I think, recovering; *tant va la cruche à l'eau;*—and I have been there very often." Surely his son and his contemporaries knew the sixteenth-century proverb "Half a *loaf* is better than no bread," and the obvious sexual implication in this context will have been understood as well. Regarding the truncated version of the French proverb "Tant va la cruche à l'eau, qu'à la fin elle se brise" of medieval Latin origin, he might just as well have cited its fourteenth-century English translation "The *pitcher* goes so often to the water that it is broken at last." But no matter in what language the polyglot Chesterfield cites the proverb, he is employing a particularly popular proverb with frequent appearances in literature and art during the eighteenth century (see Vinken 1958; Zick 1969).

One thing is for certain, Lord Chesterfield's letters and his Age of Enlightenment are not void of proverbs, and there is no proverbial blackout during this time of reason and rationality. In fact, Chesterfield quite literally delighted in their repeated use, and in the few occasions that he questioned their value, he is merely following normal disagreements with proverbs in particular contexts. Above all, however, his two letters of 1741 and 1749 calling for the careful avoidance of proverbs by educated and fashionable people are nothing but words spoken to the wind. In half-heartedly fighting their employment or in claiming that they disappeared during the eighteenth century from common use, both Lord Chesterfield and scholars have tilted at proverbial windmills. People then and now do have recourse to common proverbs, and they use these traditional metaphors as part of the communicative art of indirection.

"EARLY TO BED AND EARLY TO RISE": FROM PROVERB TO BENJAMIN FRANKLIN AND BACK

In a short essay entitled "The Truth and Myths about Benjamin Franklin" that appeared in the 1990 issue of *The Old Farmer's Almanac* commemorating the bicentennial of Benjamin Franklin's (1706–1790) death, David Lord repeats the often-stated claim that "Franklin coined countless catch phrases [i.e., proverbs] of morality and wisdom in his peerless *Poor Richard's Almanac.*" Yet nothing could be further from the truth, as Robert Newcomb, in particular, has shown in his seminal study *The Sources of Benjamin Franklin's Sayings of Poor Richard* (1957). Among Franklin and proverb scholars it is now generally known that this pragmatist of commonsense philosophy relied heavily on various proverb collections for the numerous proverbial texts that he included in his instructive and entertaining *Poor Richard's Almanack,* which he published for 25 years from 1733 to 1758 (see Barbour 1974). Many of these proverbs he integrated verbatim into the almanacs, but as an acute "proverb stylist" he also reformulated some of them in his own wording (see Meister 1952–1953). They became current owing to the unrivaled popularity of the almanacs, of which about 10,000 copies were sold every year. A very few of his own creations, at most 5 percent of the total of 1,044 proverbial texts that appeared in the almanacs, did become proverbs in their own right, notably "Three *removes* is (are) as bad as a fire," "*Laziness* travels so slowly, that poverty soon overtakes it" and "There will be *sleeping* enough in the grave" (see Gallacher 1949).

It is important to note that Franklin himself tried to rectify this popular error at the end of his famous preface to the almanac of 1758, which he wrote in the summer of 1757 and which became an international best-seller essay with the title "The Way to Wealth." At the end of this masterful treatise on virtue, prosperity, prudence, and above all economic and monetary common sense he openly admitted the following: "[. . .] my vanity was wonderfully delighted with it [that people quote "his" proverbs by adding the formula "as Poor Richard says"], though I was conscious that not a tenth part of the wisdom was my own, [. . .], but rather the gleanings that I made of the sense of all ages and nations." There was thus no intentional deception on Franklin's part, but in keeping with the spirit of the time he certainly didn't mind copying proverbs and maxims out of books without citing his sources and taking a bit of credit where he could.

But what is the origin and history of the proverb "Early to bed and early to rise, makes a man healthy, wealthy and wise" for which Benjamin Franklin appears to have been but an intermediate popularizer and at best an apocryphal source? The first recorded reference of this proverb in the English language is an early variant that appeared in *A Treatyse of Fysshynge wyth an Angle* dating from 1496:

> Who soo woll vse the game of anglynge: he must ryse erly. [. . .] As the olde englysshe prouverbe sayth in this wyse. Who soo woll ryse erly shall be holy helthy & zely.

This proverb does not yet talk about "going to bed early," and the triad of "holy helthy & zely" (i.e., happy, fortunate) does not yet completely agree with the proverb as it is cited later, but this variant is clearly a precursor. That the author introduces the text with the introductory formula "as the olde englysshe prouverbe sayth in this wyse" is, of course, of great importance in establishing the fact that the proverb might be considerably older than 1496, dating perhaps from the middle or even the beginning of the fifteenth century.

The second historical reference stems from *The Book of Husbandry* (1523) by Anthony Fitzherbert who states:

> At grammar-scole I lerned a verse, that is this, *Sanat, sanctificat, et ditat surgere mane.* That is to say, Erly rysyng maketh a man hole in body, holer in soule, and rycher in goodes.

Fitzherbert points out that he learned the Latin verse "Sanat, sanctificat, et ditat surgere mane" in grammar school and cites the English version as its translation. This naturally leads to the important question of what came first—the Latin or the English proverb? Realizing that Fitzherbert must have been in grammar school around 1480, this Latin text is certainly older than the English variant from the 1496 treatise on fishing. The medieval Latin proverb appears after 1576 in many Latin proverb collections throughout Europe, but not in Erasmus of Rotterdam's famous *Adagia* (1500ff.). Since it cannot be traced to any of the classical Latin proverb collections either, it appears to belong to the group of common medieval Latin proverbs that were used in European schools for language instruction. It thus is probably justified to conjecture that the English proverb "Early to bed and early to rise, makes a man healthy, wealthy and wise" has its roots in the Latin language of the Middle Ages.

By 1639, when John Clarke published his bilingual proverb collection *Paroemiologia Anglo-Latina,* the English proverb had found its final wording in print that Franklin used some 100 years later and that is still the most common form today. Under the key word "diligentia" Clarke juxtaposes the English and Latin texts: "*Earely to bed and earely to rise, makes a man healthy, wealthy, and wise* / Sanat, sanctificat, ditat quoque surgere mane." Twenty years later the proverb appears in this exact wording in James Howell's important polyglot collection *Paroimiografia. Proverbs, or, Old Sayed Savves & Adages in English (or the Saxon Toung), Italian, French and Spanish* (1659) as a bona fide English proverb: "Early to bed, and early to rise, / Makes a man healthy, wealthy and wise." And according to Robert Newcomb's careful analysis of Benjamin Franklin's sources for the proverbs in his *Poor Richard's Almanacks,* this American friend of old proverbs excerpted about 150 proverbs from Howell's collection and integrated them into his almanacs that appeared between 1733 and 1742. In fact, "for the *Almanack* of 1735, 1736 and 1737 Franklin relied almost exclusively on Howell," and he clearly found this proverb there—a fact that does not, of course, preclude the possibility that Franklin knew the proverb from oral tradition as well.

Be that as it may, Franklin's first use of the proverb in his *Poor Richard's Almanack* for the year 1735 might by itself not have been able to attach his name so lastingly to it. The credit for accomplishing this feat belongs more appropriately to Franklin's stroke of genius in preparing the manuscript of *Poor Richard's Almanack* for 1758 in the summer of 1757. For its introduction Franklin composed his famous essay "The Way to Wealth" which could be considered as the manifesto of Puritan ethics based on 105 proverbs that he excerpted from the previous 24 almanacs. Towards the beginning of this didactic and pragmatic rhetorical masterpiece, Franklin talks about the value of time and industry and concludes his ethical paragraph very appropriately with the proverb that instructs people to adhere to solid work ethics:

If Time be of all Things the most precious, wasting Time must be, as Poor Richard says, the greatest Prodigality, since, as he elsewhere tells us, Lost Time is never found again; and what we call Time enough, always proves little enough: Let us then up and be doing, and doing to the Purpose; so by Diligence shall we do more with less Perplexity. Sloth makes all Things difficult, but Industry all easy, as Poor Richard says; and He that riseth late, must trot all Day, and shall scarce overtake his Business at Night. While Laziness travels so slowly, that Poverty soon overtakes him, as we read in Poor Richard, who adds, Drive thy Business, let not that drive thee; and Early to Bed, and early to rise, makes a Man healthy, wealthy and wise.

Proverb follows proverb instructing the average Colonial American that industry and frugality will eventually lead to economic and personal independence. There is no doubt that this "proverb essay" became a sort of "national orthodoxy" whose proverbs were cited ad infinitum if not ad nauseam at every conceivable opportunity.

The fact that the proverb was indeed well known towards the end of the eighteenth century can be seen from a diary entry from January 9, 1782, by a loyalist contemporary of Benjamin Franklin, in which Samuel Curwen cites part of the proverb not so much in its economic but rather medical sense:

Doctor Jeffries called and gave me his opinion, that considering my advanced age and past state of body, I should use warming and best dry wines. Choicest flesh, roast, baked or boiled only, without butter fat or sauces, of vegetables, turnips, carrots, onions, potatoes and no other. Tea very sparingly, not to suffer stomach to be a long time empty, nor to go to bed on a full one. Early to bed, early to rise, moderate exercise.

The good doctor realized that the proverb "Early to bed, early to rise, makes a man healthy, wealthy and wise" is clearly sound advice from a medical point of view, telling people that they need a proper amount of sleep. Whether that will also translate into wealth and wisdom is not necessarily a solid guarantee. In any case, the paragraph cited reads almost like a statement out of a popular magazine article on diet and exercise, and it is quite conceivable that the proverb variation "Early to bed, early to rise, moderate exercise" might reappear any day as a ready-made slogan for yet another health program.

But the proverb contains much more than commonsense medical advice. Its main purpose is doubtlessly to get people, especially children, to adhere to rigid work ethics, as can be seen from the first stanza of Eliza Cook's didactic poem "Early to Bed and Early to Rise" (1868):

"Early to bed and early to rise."
Ay! note it down in your brain,

For it helpeth to make the foolish wise,
And uproots the weeds of pain.

This almost pious interpretation of a proverb preaching rigorous Protestant ethics deserves to be contrasted with a more liberal view. Benjamin Franklin and his proverbial wisdom had reached such heights of adoration and adherence that Mark Twain saw fit to react humorously and ironically to it several times during his life. In a sketch on "Early Rising" (1864), Twain takes Benjamin Franklin and "his" proverb to task in a wonderfully humorous way. Following the proverbial motto with Benjamin Franklin's name attached to it, Twain writes:

I have tried getting up early, and I have tried getting up late—and the latter agrees with me best. As for a man's growing any wiser, or any richer, or nay healthier, by getting up early, I know it is not so; because I have got up early [. . .] many and many a time, and got poorer and poorer [. . .] instead of richer and richer [. . .] and so far from my growing healthier on account of it, I got to looking blue, and pulpy, and swelled, like a drowned man. And as far as becoming wiser is concerned, you might put all the wisdom I acquired in these experiments in your eye, without obstructing your vision any to speak of.

About 1870 Mark Twain dealt once again with this "objectionable" proverb in a short essay with the ironic title "The Late Benjamin Franklin." Here he attacks Franklin for having "prostituted his talents to the invention of maxims and aphorisms calculated to inflict suffering upon the rising generation of all subsequent ages." Remembering his own childhood and how his father, and probably most parents, quoted "Poor Richard's" proverbs ad nauseam, Twain makes the following humorous yet telling remarks:

Nowadays a boy cannot follow out a single natural instinct without tumbling over some of those everlasting aphorisms [i.e., proverbs] and hearing from Franklin on the spot. [. . .] And that boy is hounded to death and robbed of his natural rest, because Franklin said once, in one of his inspired flights of malignity:

Early to bed and early to rise
Makes a man healthy and wealthy and wise.

As if it were any object to a boy to be healthy and wealthy and wise on such terms. The sorrow that that maxim has cost me, through my parents, experimenting on me with it, tongue cannot tell. The legitimate result is my present state of general debility, indigence, and mental aberration.

Twain makes plain here that proverbs can indeed have their negative side if they are applied as universal rules in an excessive fashion. Even a health proverb can lead to illness if adhered to too strictly. The proverb "*Moderation in all things*" obviously also applies to the use of proverbs.

Mark Twain would certainly have agreed completely with some of the following irreverent reinterpretations of master Franklin's proverb. The most famous one-liner parodies of the proverb are George Ade's "Early to bed and early to rise and you won't meet many prominent people" and "Early to bed and early to rise / Will make you miss all the regular guys" from around 1900. The basic idea of Ade's proverb parody, or anti-proverb, is marvelously present in Groucho Marx's autobiography *Groucho and Me* (1959) some 50 years later:

Take, for example, "Early to bed, early to rise, makes a you-know-what." This is a lot of hoopla. Most wealthy people I know like to sleep late. You don't see Marilyn Monroe getting up at six in the morning. I'm sure if you had your choice, you would rather watch Miss Monroe rise at three in the afternoon than watch the most efficient garbage collector in your town hop out of bed at six.

To this might be added the parodying moral of one of James Thurber's modern anti-fables from 1939: "Moral: Early to rise and early to bed makes a male healthy and wealthy and dead."

Two other texts commenting on the time change that takes place twice a year echo this obvious dislike of going to bed early and rising at an early hour. Robertson Davies wrote the following remarks concerning the Daylight Saving Time in his *Diary of Samuel Marchbanks* (1947):

At the back of the Daylight Savings scheme I detect the boney, blue-fingered hand of Puritanism, eager to push people into bed earlier, and get them up earlier, to make them healthy, wealthy and wise in spite of themselves.

This concern over time changes is still an issue today, as can be seen from an article in the *Burlington Free Press* from January 5, 1974, with the appropriate headline "Early-bird Vermonters To Rise In Darkness as DST Resumes":

Nobody was more serious about DST than Ben Franklin back in 1784 as U.S. ambassador to France [...]. His solution: a daily sunrise serenade of clanging church bells and booming cannons to "wake the slug-

gards and make them open their eyes." The French managed to survive
without adopting Franklin's early-to-bed, early-to-rise advice.

Such statements in newspapers and magazines do their share in keeping
Franklin's name attached to the proverb, as can also be seen from Robert L.
Fish's mystery novel *Rub-a-dub-dub* (1971), where a character states: "I'm
afraid that after dinner I'm scarcely at my best. Getting on, you know. Early
to bed and early to rise, has some salubrious effect on a man, if I recall my
Franklin correctly."

Mere proverb allusions run the risk of not being understood, even if they refer
to very common proverbs. Nevertheless, such lack of communication is rather
rare among native speakers, especially if the name of Franklin is mentioned as
well. A headline in the renowned *Wall Street Journal* of March 20, 1987, proves
that Franklin's apocryphal proverb is as true for today's business executives as it
was 250 years ago when Franklin preached its wisdom to his contemporaries for
their economic well-being: "Early to Bed...The motto of Ben Franklin has become the M.O. [i.e., *modus operandi*] of many a chief executive."

In this respect it is of interest that the business world already in 1898 created the following slogan from the proverb to encourage merchants to advertise their products:

TO SUCCEED

Early to bed, early to rise,
Never get tight, and—advertise.

This advertising slogan was also recorded a few years later as "Early to bed and
early to rise / Is no good unless you advertise." Decades later, on June 17,
1991, the magazine *Money* and the cereal producer General Mills joined
forces in an advertising page that included the large headline "Healthy,
wealthy and wise." Eating whole grain Total cereal and reading *Money* magazine will obviously make you healthy and wealthy, and you will also gain in
wisdom about food and prosperity. That at least must have been the thoughts
of the advertisers when they put this particular advertisement together. The
modern world would, of course, not argue that advertising is the only way to
have success in business. It would also push the computer on people, since it
facilitates accounting procedures. One might even argue that today's work
ethic is best expressed in the way a father lectures his son in a *Punch* cartoon
from 1989: "Remember this: early to bed, early to rise, work like hell and
computerise [*sic*]." The modern term "computerise" does not only end with
the same sound as the old "wise," thus clearly indicating that this is an effec-

"Remember this: early to bed, early to rise,
work like hell and computerise."

Cited from *Punch* (January 13, 1989), p. 15. Reproduced with permission of Punch Ltd.

tive adaptation of the traditional proverb, it also equates the technological computer with wisdom. One only wonders what will become of the important aspect of health in a world of stress and competition! In any case, imagine to be awakened in the morning by the chambermaid exclaiming "Early to bed and early to rise—or the boss'll promote the other guys...," which was the caption of a 1959 cartoon in *The Boston Herald*.

The frequent quotation of this proverb has led people to react with humor or satire to its solid-work-ethics ideal, and these proverb parodies, or anti-proverbs, clearly express some sort of wisdom as well:

1935   Early to bed, early to rise
        And your girl goes out with the other guys.
1942   Late to bed, late to rise,
        who in the hell wants to be wise?

1965	Early to bed, early to rise:
	dull isn't it?
1967	Late to bed and early to rise,
	—and your head will feel five times its size.
1976	Early to bed and early to rise
	makes sure you get out before her husband arrives.
1980	If you're not interested in being healthy, wealthy, and wise—how about
	early to bed?

Some of these parodies, including the last one, which served as a suggestive birthday card message, are clearly sexual and at times chauvinistic. Considering the linguistic awareness to sexism in everyday language, it should not be surprising that there is some objection to the gender-specific noun "man" in the traditional proverb. Women have reacted to the male dominance and the misogyny in proverbs in recent years, but it might come as a pleasant surprise to find the "man" replaced by "woman" as early as 1880 in a short humorous verse:

Early to bed and early to rise
Makes *woman* healthy, wealthy, and wise.

From 1969 stems the variant "Early to bed, early to rise, makes a girl healthy, wealthy and wise," yet the term "girl" is not at all acceptable to feminists at the present time. The way to go is without doubt to cite the old proverb as "Early to bed and early to rise, makes you healthy, wealthy and wise," as Stephen Vizinczey did in his book *In Praise of Older Women* (1965). Another gender-free possibility would be to replace "man" with "person," as it was recorded from an informant in 1986 in California: "Early to bed, early to rise, makes a person healthy, wealthy, and wise."

The fact that such parodies in the form of anti-proverbs exist at all is ample proof that the traditional proverb is still very much present and valid. A wonderful example of how people to this day are surrounded by this proverbial wisdom can be seen from a Häger comic strip from 1985 that presents a number of proverbs that argue for getting up early and then creates a new text in order to avoid rising that early: "'Up and at 'em, Tiger'—'The early bird gets the worm'—'Up sluggard, and waste not life'—'Early to bed and early to rise makes a man healthy, wealthy and wise'—'He who gets up early is a blooming fool'—'I knew if I tried long enough I'd find one I liked'." That last self-rationalizing invented pseudo-proverb won't do the "trick" unfortunately—everybody confronted by this comic strip knows that. There is not much or at least only a temporary chance of escaping the inevitability of proverbs. It is one thing to poke fun at proverbs, to parody them or to argue against them with biting satire, but a complete escape from or utter denunciation of the age-old wisdom expressed in them is simply not possible. Benjamin Franklin knew this only too well when he drew on the traditional proverb stock of the English language to instruct his colonial Americans with their wisdom in his many volumes of *Poor Richard's Almanack*. He invented or coined barely any proverbs, but he popularized them to such an extent that some of them, notably the proverb "Early to bed and early to rise, makes a man healthy, wealthy and wise," came to be attached to his name especially in the mind of Americans. Yet even this apocryphal identification of the proverb with Benjamin Franklin is starting to be forgotten as the general level of cultural literacy appears to be declining, and the proverb is once again becoming a piece of true folk wisdom that is attached to no individual person. Benjamin Franklin as "coiner" of the proverb was thus but a mere interlude in the history of this proverb about health, wealth, and wisdom. It was, therefore, quite appropriate that a traditional embroidery sampler of the proverb from 1977 did not attach the name of Benjamin Franklin to it but rather let the proverb speak for itself with proper anonymity:

Early to Bed,
Early to Rise,
Makes a Man
Healthy, Wealthy
and Wise.

"BEHIND THE CLOUD THE SUN IS SHINING": ABRAHAM LINCOLN'S PROVERBIAL FIGHT AGAINST SLAVERY

It is well known that Abraham Lincoln (1809–1865), like Harry S. Truman in the twentieth century, never went to college. In fact, by his own admission, he probably had little more than one year of formal schooling altogether. But he learned the basics and then developed his keen mind on his own. He became an avid reader of virtually all the printed matter he could lay his hands on. In addition to newspapers and magazines, he read, studied, and memorized Shakespeare (notably parts of *Macbeth, Hamlet,* and *King Lear*), he was acquainted with authors such as Robert Burns, Byron, Daniel Defoe, Oliver Wendell Holmes, and James Russell Lowell, and he became extremely well-versed in the Bible. His active life as a lawyer and politician prevented him from reading extensively for pleasure. His time was taken up by informing himself of the news of the day as well as with reports of all types, and if there was time for reading, Lincoln would usually stick to Shakespeare or the Bible. But this was reading not so much for pleasure as for comparing his own thoughts, problems, and challenges with those of previous ages and for finding moral and ethical values to face his own time.

For someone who "adopted at several stages of his career the practice of daily Bible reading," it became natural to cite quotations or at least paraphrased verses from the Bible with high frequency in oral as well as written statements. Lincoln scholars have not failed to comment on this preoccupation with biblical phrases, claiming that "his familiarity with and use of Biblical phraseology was remarkable even in a time when such use was more common than now." But what they have forgotten to comment about are precisely the numerous biblical phrases that long ago turned into folk proverbs and metaphors (see Mieder 2000b: 171–203). These proverbial utterances gave Lincoln the opportunity to speak and write both authoritatively and somewhat colloquially, adding much imagery and color to his arguments of persuasion in speeches and letters.

This preoccupation with biblical phraseology can take on rather overpowering proportions, as in his written reply of May 30, 1864, to a delegation of Baptists:

> I can only thank you for adding to the effective and almost unanimous support which the Christian communities are so zealously giving to the country, and to liberty. Indeed it is difficult to conceive how it could be otherwise with any one professing christianity, or even having ordinary perceptions of right and wrong. To read the Bible, as the word of God himself, that "In the sweat of *thy* face shalt thou eat bread" [Gen. 3:19], and to preach there from that, "In the sweat of *other mans* [sic] faces shalt thou eat bread," to my mind can scarcely be reconciled with honest sincerity. When brought to my final reckoning, may I have to answer for robbing no man of his goods; yet more tolerable even this, than for robbing one of himself, and all that was his. When, a year or two ago, those professedly holy men of the South, met in the semblance of prayer and devotion, and, in the Name of Him who said "As ye would all men should do unto you, do ye even so unto them" [Matt. 7:12] appeal to the christian world to aid them in doing to a whole race of men, as they would have no man do unto themselves, to my thinking they contemned and insulted God and His church, far more than did Satan when he tempted the Saviour with the Kingdoms of the earth. The devil's attempt was no more false, and far less hypocritical. But let me forbear, remembering it is also written "Judge not, lest ye be judged" [Matt. 7:1].

What a paragraph! What a rhetorical masterpiece! Without even mentioning that horrid word "slavery," Lincoln employs three biblical proverbs known to everybody, and certainly to the Baptist ministers, and ridicules countless numbers of slaveholders of the South who have earned their bread through the work of their slaves. He also points out proverbially that they have forgotten the "Golden Rule," and by quoting its proverbial wording, he shows vividly how false their behavior has been. But lest he were to elevate himself to an exaggerated self-righteousness, Lincoln closes his mini-sermon with the proverb that warns everybody against sitting in judgment over others and forgetting that all people commit sinful acts. The message is direct, clear, and authoritative, and the three biblical proverbs add a didactic and ethical persuasiveness to this masterful statement.

An additional example of such proverbial rhetoric based on the Bible can be found in Lincoln's incredibly short (a mere two pages) "Second Inaugural Address" of March 4, 1865. The president actually uses two of the previous proverbs once again to make his point that slavery is wrong but that people must be careful in their judgment of others. Lincoln in all of his condemnations of slavery is always ready and willing to find a way to bring North and South back together and to save the Union. For him, all Americans deserve to be treated alike:

> Neither party expected for the war, the magnitude, or the duration, which it has already attained. Neither anticipated that the *cause* of the conflict might cease with, or even before, the conflict itself should cease. Each looked for an easier triumph, and as a result less fundamental and astounding. Both read the Bible, and pray to the same God; and each invokes His aid against the other. It may seem strange that any men should dare to ask a just God's assistance in wringing their bread from the sweat of other men's faces; but let us judge not that we be not judged. The prayers of both could not be answered; that of neither has been answered fully. The Almighty has His own purposes. [...] Fondly do we hope—fervently do we pray—that this mighty scourge of war may speedily pass away.

One further example may serve as an illustration of how much Lincoln's speeches and writings are permeated with biblical proverbs. The following text is purposely chosen to show Lincoln from a more humorous side. After all, stories and books abound on Lincoln as humorist and raconteur. It should be noted, however, that none of them, not even those dealing with folklore and Lincoln, comment on his rich stock of proverbs and proverbial expressions. In any case, the following story was written by Lincoln for one Noah Brooks, who claimed that the president handed it to him with the comment: "Here is one speech of mine which has never been printed, and I think it worth printing. Just see what you think." Lincoln even signed the little speech and added the humorous title "The President's Last, Shortest, and Best Speech" to it. All of this probably took place on December 6, 1864, for on the next day the Washington *Daily Chronicle* published it with that title, clearly to the delight of all inhabitants in the capital:

The President's Last, Shortest, and Best Speech

On thursday of last week two ladies from Tennessee came before the President asking the release of their husbands held as prisoners of war at Johnson's Island. They were put off till friday, when they came again; and were again put off to saturday. At each of the interviews one of the ladies urged that her husband was a religious man. On saturday the President ordered the release of the prisoners, and then said to this lady "You say your husband is a religious man; tell him when you meet him, that I say I am not much of a judge of religion, but that, in my opinion, the religion that sets men to rebel and fight against the government, because, as they think, that government does not sufficiently help *some* men to eat their bread on the sweat of *other* men's faces, is not the sort of religion upon which people can get to heaven!"

A. Lincoln.

Once again Lincoln has twisted the biblical proverb "In the *sweat* of thy face shalt thou eat bread" to comment rather indirectly and with a good dose of humor on slavery and thereby ridicule both the Southern soldier and his wife, whose "religion" is based on false premises.

This little speech was by far and fortunately not Abraham Lincoln's last speech. Many more oral and written statements were to follow in which he employed biblical proverbs galore. But how about Lincoln's integration of traditional folk proverbs into his speeches and writings? These ready-made bits of folk wisdom were there to serve him at any time to communicate effectively by appealing to common sense and generational authority. He certainly integrated them on numerous occasions both in the most mundane messages and in his very best speeches and proclamations.

And yet, this fact seems to escape scholars again and again. A good case in point is the last paragraph in Lincoln's famous Cooper Union speech given on February 27, 1860, in New York City. In this speech Lincoln outlined in very clear and logical terms his solid commitment to maintaining the Union and

Postcard (ca. 1900), purchased at an antique shop in December 1977 at Detroit, Michigan.

to keeping slavery from spreading. As he moved towards the final two paragraphs of his speech, the president rose to an oratorical height that must have moved his audience then just as it does readers today. One can sense here the tension and anxiety in yet one more pitch to prevent the country from entering a devastating civil war:

> Wrong as we think slavery is, we can yet afford to let it alone where it is, because that much is due to the necessity arising from its actual presence in the nation; but can we, while our votes will prevent it, allow it to spread into the National Territories, and to overrun us here in these Free States? If our sense of duty forbids this, then let us stand by our duty, fearlessly and effectively. Let us be diverted by none of those sophistical contrivances wherewith we are so industriously plied and belabored—contrivances such as groping for some middle ground between the right and the wrong [...].

Neither let us be slandered from our duty by false accusations against us, nor frightened from it by menaces of destruction to the Government nor of dungeons to ourselves. *Let us have faith that right makes might, and in that faith, let us, to the end, dare to do our duty as we understand it.*

In an otherwise superb essay on "Lincoln's Development as a Writer," Roy P. Basler, one of the most knowledgeable Lincoln scholars, introduces his quotation of the last short paragraph of this speech with the observation that Lincoln's "peroration is one of his most effective and memorable conclusions." But his readers would want to know why this is the case. This is also true for the comments of two authors who state that these words are "a fitting climax to Lincoln's efforts. Rational principle develops into moral conviction, and the resulting emotional intensity emerges from and synthesizes all that has gone before. Yet the intensity is controlled. Speaker and audience are resolute and principled, but at the same time, they are poised and logical." What these authors have said is, of course, true and correct, but might it not have helped for a better understanding of Lincoln's rhetorical power to point out that by claiming that "*Right* makes might" he is employing a proverb that dates back at least to the fourteenth century? And, to be sure, its antipode "*Might* makes right" is just as old. Surely it must be agreed by all interpreters of the very last sentence of this significant speech that it is the wisdom of the proverb "Right makes might" that adds authority and conviction to Lincoln's argument. It summarizes everything that he had just argued about, namely that the preservation of the Union and the control of slavery are just and "right" goals. This being the case, people believing in these principles will have the "might" to keep matters under control.

Lincoln definitely had a predilection to quote proverbs, as can be seen from his fondness for the proverb "Broken *eggs* cannot be mended" in two of his letters. On July 31, 1862, Lincoln wrote the following thoughts about the political situation in Louisiana to August Belmont:

Broken eggs cannot be mended; but Louisiana has nothing to do now but to take her place in the Union as it was, barring the already broken eggs. The sooner she does so, the smaller will be the amount of that which will be past mending. This government cannot much longer play a game in which it stakes all, and its enemies stake nothing. Those enemies must understand that they cannot experiment for ten years trying to destroy the government, and if they fail still come back into the Union unhurt. If they expect in any contingency to ever have the Union as it was, I join with the writer [Lincoln had been shown a letter calling for action on his part] in saying, "Now is the time."

It must be noted that Lincoln does not merely cite the proverb, but he expands on it and makes it part of his entire rhetorical argument why Louisiana must fish or cut bait. About half a year later, in a letter of January 8, 1863, to Major General John A. McClernand, Lincoln picks up his message about maintaining the Union and employs the proverb once again as a persuasive metaphor:

> I never did ask more, nor ever was willing to accept less, than for all the States, and the people thereof, to take and hold their places, and their rights, in the Union under the Constitution of the United States. For this alone have I felt authorized to struggle; and I seek neither more nor less now. Still, to use a coarse, but an expressive figure, broken eggs can not be mended. I have issued the emancipation proclamation, and I can not retract it.

This is indeed a powerful use of a proverb (strange that Lincoln does not call it such), and it is by far not merely integrated at this place to add a bit of colorful folk language. This coarse or simple piece of wisdom becomes the ultimate point of the entire statement, namely that there is no way of retracting his courageous, laudable, and absolutely humane emancipation of the slaves.

Of course, Lincoln did not win the war with his metaphors or proverbs, but as in the case of that other great wartime orator and rhetorician Winston S. Churchill, his metaphorical prowess helped to stir people into action. Without doubt his use of proverbs gave his speeches, memoranda, proclamations, and letters a remarkable element of common sense and thus persuasive ethical power. In order to underscore this claim, a few additional contextualized examples of actual proverbs in Lincoln's published works will be presented. Here is a paragraph from the "Temperance Address" that Lincoln delivered on February 22, 1842, at the Second Presbyterian Church in Springfield, Illinois. It should be noted that while he first cites the proverb in its usual wording, he then elaborates on it in most vivid terms to bring his point across:

> When the conduct of men is designed to be influenced, *persuasion,* kind, unassuming persuasion, should ever be adopted. It is an old and a true maxim, that a "drop of honey catches more flies than a gallon of gall." So with men. If you would win a man to your cause, *first* convince him that you are his sincere friend. Therein is a drop of honey that catches his heart, which, say what you will, is the great high road to his reason, and which, when once gained, you will find but little trouble in

convincing his judgment of the justice of your cause, if indeed that cause really be a just one. On the contrary, assume to dictate to his judgment, or to command his action, or to mark him as one to be shunned and despised, and he will retreat within himself, close all the avenues to his head and his heart; and do tho' your cause be naked truth itself, transformed to the heaviest lance, harder than steel, and sharper than steel can be made, and tho' you throw it with more than Herculean force and precision, you shall no more be able to pierce him, than to penetrate the hard shell of a tortoise with a rye straw.

This is indeed a fine example of his use of metaphor and imagery, but the fact that he starts the paragraph with "an old and a true maxim" (i.e., a proverb) gives his explanations and arguments that power of proverbial persuasion. It is fascinating to observe here Lincoln's skill in positive and ethical persuasion, a rhetorical and moral approach that he used throughout his political life.

Lincoln can also give very straightforward advice by quoting a non-metaphorical proverb, as is the case in his fragmentary "Notes for a Law Lecture" of July 1, 1850. Here he is very matter of fact in his explanations, and not necessarily at the height of his oratorical abilities:

I am not an accomplished lawyer. I find quite as much material for a lecture in those points wherein I have failed, as in those wherein I have been moderately successful. The leading rule for the lawyer, as for the man of every other calling, is diligence. Leave nothing for to-morrow, which can be done to-day. Never let your correspondence fall behind. Whatever piece of business you have in hand, before stopping, do all the labor pertaining to it which then can be done.

Of special interest is, however, Lincoln's metaphorical statement of October 4, 1854, in yet another speech at Springfield, where he tried to explain the dangers of having slavery spill over into new areas. His figurative analysis appears to be a paraphrase of the proverb "The *grass* is always greener on the other side of the fence":

It is said that there are more slaves in that extreme north-west portion of Missouri, jutting broadside against Kansas and Nebraska than in any other equal area in Missouri! Will it not go, then, into Kansas and Nebraska, if permitted? Why not? What will hinder? Do cattle nibble a pasture right up to a division fence, crop all close under the fence, and even put their necks through and gather what they can reach, over the line, and still refuse to pass over into that next green pasture, even if the fence shall be thrown down?

There is a great deal of irony in these questions, and Lincoln is indeed drawing on the colorful folk speech that he heard and learned as a young country boy. But he is *not* alluding to the proverb mentioned above! I have shown in a detailed study that the proverb "The *grass* is always greener on the other side of the fence (pasture)" has its origin in an American song entitled *The Grass Is Always Greener (In the Other Fellow's Yard)*, of which Raymond B. Egan wrote the lyrics and Richard A. Whiting composed the music only in 1924 (Mieder 1993b)! Lincoln is then merely being figurative in his statement and not yet proverbial. Thus are the pitfalls of proverb scholarship that is not based on historical analyses of individual texts.

Proverbs also appear in some of his short letters, with Lincoln feeling bad that he does not have the time to compose longer epistles: "You will readily understand and appreciate why I write only very short letters," he informs Schuyler Colfax on May 31, 1860. But precisely to add at least some poignancy to such letters and drive home a point in the shortest possible way, Lincoln incorporates traditional proverbs without any other comment. In a response to John M. Pomeroy of August 31, 1860, regarding regional quarrels among some Pennsylvania Republicans, Lincoln simply states: "I am slow to listen to criminations among friends, and never expose [*sic*] their quarrels on either side. My sincere wish is that both sides will allow by-gones to be by-gones, and look to the present & future only." Lincoln was also quite capable of giving the shortest possible oral remarks rather than speeches that could last more than three hours! For example, when he left Springfield on February 11, 1861, on his way to Washington to assume the presidency, he also stopped at Tolono, Illinois, on the way, and here is what this humble and clearly moved man had to say:

> I am leaving you on an errand of national importance, attended, as you are aware, with considerable difficulties. Let us believe, as some poet has expressed it: "Behind the cloud the sun is still shining." I bid you an affectionate farewell.

Today he might have used the proverb "Every *cloud* has a silver lining," but the people who had come to the train to wish him well certainly knew the variant "Behind the *cloud*(s) the sun is shining" and understood well what their new president meant with this hopeful proverb in those bitter times. Short as this impromptu statement might be, it is revealing about Lincoln's character.

There is no doubt that Lincoln was able to cut through a lot of verbiage and red tape by employing proverbs in such short messages, in each case hitting the proverbial nail on the head, as it were. One last contextualized proverb reference might serve as the conclusion to these comments. It is part of a speech that President Lincoln gave on April 18, 1864, at the Sanitary Fair in Baltimore, Maryland, almost exactly one year before his assassination. As was to be expected, he commented on the war and slavery:

> When the war began, three years ago, neither party, nor any man, expected it would last till now. Each looked for the end, in some way, long ere to-day. Neither did any anticipate that domestic slavery would be much affected by the war. But here we are; the war has not ended, and slavery has been much affected—how much needs not now to be recounted. So true is it that man proposes, and God disposes. But we can see the past, though we may not claim to have directed it; and seeing it, in this case, we feel more hopeful and confident for the future.

Once again this tall and yet humble president stands in front of the people and calmly tries to project a positive image for the future. He can indeed claim some progress with the Emancipation Proclamation and the Civil War perhaps nearing its end. But there is no celebration, and there is no hubris, there is only humility and perhaps a shutter within Lincoln and the people listening to him as everybody is wondering how all of this will finally come to a conclusion. It is at this moment that Abraham Lincoln returns to his stock of biblical proverbs, putting the fate of the nation into God's hands, for "*Man proposes, and God disposes*" (see Prov. 16:9).

"CONVENTIONAL PHRASES ARE A SORT OF FIREWORKS": CHARLES DICKENS'S PROVERBIAL LANGUAGE

The vast scholarship on Charles Dickens (1812–1870) has rather tangentially dealt with his rich proverbial language. While a few scholars have commented in passing on Dickens's predilection for the use of metaphorical language, George B. Bryan and I have finally presented a detailed study on *The Proverbial Charles Dickens: An Index to Proverbs in the Works of Charles Dickens* (1997) that registers and interprets the contextual function of the numerous proverbs, proverbial expressions, proverbial comparisons, and wellerisms in his voluminous works. Dickens certainly used proverbial language in all of his writings, reflecting its general use in nineteenth-century England among people of all social classes.

It should be noted that Charles Dickens makes frequent use of proverbial language in his numerous letters, which he described to his wife Catherine Hogarth on November 9, 1835, as having "brevity and matter-of-fact style." But even in the shortest of them, he includes proverbs or proverbial phrases at strategic locations in order to add some expressiveness and colloquial color to his often rather mundane epistles occupied with everyday problems and frustrations. This becomes quite obvious in the following short excerpts:

To Samuel Rogers, 14 November 1839:

Did you ever "move"? We have taken a house near the Regents Park, intending to occupy it between this [date of the letter] and Christmas, and the consequent trials have already begun. There is an old proverb that three removes are as bad as a fire. I don't know how that may be, but I know that one is worse.

To Mrs. Gore, 7 September 1852:

So you want a godchild. May I never have the opportunity of giving you one! But *if* I have—if my cup (I mean my quiver) be not yet full—then shall you hear again from the undersigned Camel that his back is broken by the addition of the last overbalancing straw.

Quite revealing are also those proverbial passages from Dickens's letters, in which the author comments on his busy life as a serial writer working under extreme time pressure:

To Lady Kay-Shuttleworth, 4 July 1850:

But my work (which is particularly hard just now) obliges me to avoid all public meetings, and almost all other interruptions of my attention, except long country walks and fresh air. If I were to permit anything to interfere with these relaxations just now, I fear the old spelling-book would "come true", and Jack would be but a dull boy.

There are also several very short letters in the form of a note of few lines that employ a proverb or two in a didactic or humorous fashion. They indicate how much Dickens liked to play with language and how freely he manipulated so-called fixed expressions. To him they were ready-made linguistic wares that could be adapted in any way or shape that he saw fit:

To Peter Cunningham, 12 September 1855:

We must put our shoulders to the wheel and come forward...throwing ourselves into the tide, and a going with the stream.

To George Dolby, 28 September 1856:

I don't care much for the weather and am off to the Foundling [Hospital], and (unless it should rain Tiger cats and Newfoundland dogs), to Hampstead afterwards.

Such short epistolary notes are true gems by a master proverbialist, who never tired of citing complete and traditional proverbs or of alluding to them in a playful manner that added much humor and irony to his concise statements. When one proverbial phrase is not enough, a second metaphor quickly comes to mind, and it is this amassment of folk expressions that can also be observed in his novels and speeches.

Turning next to how Dickens made use of proverbial rhetoric in his speeches, it will become apparent that he expended quite a bit of rhetorical energy in elaborating on proverbs. In a speech delivered on October 5, 1843, in Manchester, Dickens argued convincingly for the support of schools and education by disagreeing with the wisdom of a well-known proverb. This splendidly innovative rhetorical procedure must have attracted the attention of the audience:

How often have we heard from a large class of men wise in their generation, who would really seem to be born and bred for no other purpose than to pass into currency counterfeit and mischievous scraps of wisdom, as it is the sole pursuit of some other criminals to utter base coin—how often have we heard from them, as an all-convincing argument, that "a little learning is a dangerous thing"? Why, a little hanging was considered a very dangerous thing, according to the same authorities, with this difference, that, because a little hanging was dangerous, we had a great deal of it; and, because a little learning was dangerous, we were to have none at all. Why, when I hear such cruel absurdities gravely reiterated, I do sometimes begin to doubt whether the parrots of society are not more pernicious to its interests than its birds of prey.

But what sounds as an enjoyable pun at the beginning of the speech is in fact only the introduction to yet another plea for more interest in good schools. Dickens, the social realist and reform-minded activist, does not do small talk, not even with proverbs. His speeches always have a goal and purpose in mind, and their proverbial rhetoric is subservient to these social commitments.

In some of the essays that Charles Dickens wrote for his journal *Household Words,* he continued his preoccupation with proverbs in a wonderfully humorous paragraph in the essay "First Fruits," which Dickens published together with George Augustus Sala on May 15, 1852. While they translate the French proverb, they also delight in alluding playfully to the proverb "A *bird* in the hand is worth two in the bush":

> That it is *"le premier pas qui coûte"*—that the first step is the great point—is as much a household word to us, and is as familiar to our mouths as that the descent of Avernus is unaccompanied by difficulty, or that one member of the feathered creation held in the hand is worth two of the same species in the bush. And, if we might be permitted to add to the first quoted morsel of proverbial philosophy a humble rider of our own, we would say that we *never* forget the first step, the first ascent, the first stumble, the first fall.

Clearly Dickens wants his readers to notice that he is playing with "proverbial philosophy," and he insists rather often in his novels in particular on identifying proverbs as such by means of an introductory formula. Such emphasis sets the proverbial utterance apart from the rest of the narration or dialogue, making it a particularly noteworthy statement couched in metaphorical and traditional language:

> [...] for your popular rumour, unlike the rolling stone of the proverb, is one which gathers a deal of moss in its wanderings up and down, [...]. (*The Old Curiosity Shop*)

> [...] others had been desperate from the beginning, and comforted themselves with the homely proverb, that, being hanged at all, they might as well be hanged for a sheep as a lamb. (*Barnaby Rudge*)

By drawing attention to the fact that he is using a proverb, Dickens thought that he did not necessarily have to cite the proverb completely. He certainly felt that he could break the rigid structure of the traditional proverb in order to integrate it more effectively into his narrative flow. However, there are many examples of proverbs cited in their entirety and without any introductory formulas. In this case the reader will usually have no difficulty in recognizing the traditional proverb as a piece of folk wisdom:

"Where's the good of putting things off? Strike while the iron's hot; that's what I say." (*Barnaby Rudge*)

"You and me know what we know, don't we? Let sleeping dogs lie—who wants to rouse 'em? I don't." (*David Copperfield*)

Quite often Charles Dickens cites proverbs in their traditional wording and then adds a rather humorous comment to them. This practice undermines the didactic aspect of the proverbs and serves as proof that Dickens knows very well that the folk does not always use proverbs as a moral statement. The mere fact that they are cited so often invites this type of ironic opposition to their underlying wisdom, and it is to be assumed that Dickens's readers enjoyed these rhetorical twists then and still do today:

"He will talk about business, and won't give away his time for nothing. He's very right. Time is money, time is money."
   "He was one of us who made that saying. I should think," said Ralph. "Time is money, and very good money too, to those who reckon interest by it. Time *is* money! Yes, and time costs money; it's rather an expensive article to some people we could name, or I forget my trade." (*Nicholas Nickleby*)

"Half a loaf's better than no bread, and the same remark holds good with crumbs. There's a few." (*Dombey and Son*)

It should be noted at this place that there exists a folk tradition of adding humorous comments to proverbs and proverbial expressions in a typically triadic structural pattern, as for example in "'Everyone to his own *taste*,' as the farmer said, when he kissed the cow" or "'*Like* will to like,' as the devil said to the collier." Normally these sayings consist of three parts: a statement (quite often a proverb, proverbial expression, quotation, exclamation, etc.), a speaker who makes the remark, and a phrase or clause that places the utterance in a new light or an incompatible setting. Charles Dickens made much use of these traditional structures, and he placed many of them in the mouth of his character Samuel Weller in *The Posthumous Papers of the Pickwick Club* (1837). In fact, scholars have decided to name these unique sayings "wellerisms" in direct association with Sam Weller's frequent use of them. After Dickens had popularized such humorous, ironic, and satirical sayings as elements of a literary work, there followed a wave of imitations both in Great Britain and the United States. The wellerisms in the novels give Charles Dickens as social critic an opportunity to make ironic, detached, and entertaining comments on sociopolitical issues and conflicts of the day:

> "That's the pint," interposed Sam; "out vith it, as the father said to the child, wen he swallowed a farden." (*Pickwick Papers*)

> "He wants you particklar; and no one else'll do, as the Devil's private secretary said ven he fetched avay Doctor Faustus," replied Mr. Weller. (*Pickwick Papers*)

> "Vell, sir," rejoined Sam, after a short pause, "I think I see your drift; and if I do see your drift, it's my 'pinion that you're a comin' it a great deal too strong, as the mail-coachman said to the snow-storm, ven it overtook him." (*Pickwick Papers*)

It is exactly in his use of "language as play" that Sam Weller, a most prolific employer of at times humorous, grotesque, and also macabre wellerisms, is such a memorable character.

But there are also plenty of additional proverbs and proverbial expressions in the *Pickwick Papers*, which has made this novel a special challenge for translators. A particularly vexing problem would be the following paragraph from that novel with its amassment of proverbs, proverbial expressions, and idioms:

> "Come along, then," said he of the green coat, lugging Mr. Pickwick after him by main force, and talking the whole way. "Here, No. 924, take your fare, and take yourself off—respectable gentleman,—know him well—none of your nonsense—this way, sir,—where's your friends?—all a mistake, I see—never mind—accidents will happen—best regulated families—never say die—down upon your luck—pull him up—put that in his pipe—like the flavour—damned rascals." And with a lengthened string of similar broken sentences, delivered with extraordinary volubility, the stranger led the way to the travellers' waiting-room, whither he was closely followed by Mr. Pickwick and his disciples. (*Pickwick Papers*)

Similar amassments can be found especially in those cases where Dickens strings several proverbial comparisons together to create a vivid if not grotesque imagery. His works are replete with comparisons and metaphors, of which the following example might serve as a representative illustration:

"He is uncommonly improving to look at, and I am not at all so. He is as sweet as honey, and I am as dull as ditch-water. He provides the pitch, and I handle it, and it sticks to me." (*Little Dorrit*)

Of course, Dickens will also string two common proverbs together for a double didactic effect, as for example in the statement "'My advice is, never do to-morrow what you can do to-day. Procrastination is the thief of time'" (*David Copperfield*).

Yet such direct citations of traditional proverbs are well balanced with Dickens's intentional variations of these fixed phrases. His purpose of employing proverbs is only at times didactic and moralistic. He actually seems to prefer to play with the wording and the structure of standard proverbs, always creating innovative variations and allusions, and thereby entertaining his readers with his humorous or satirical puns. He is indeed a "liberated" proverbialist, who uses them with utmost linguistic freedom to add metaphorical language to his own narrative and colorful spice to the language of his characters. Most readers will be able to recognize the underlying proverbs without too much difficulty, and the juxtaposition of traditional proverb and authorial innovation results in a stylistic peculiarity that makes Dickens's prose so rich in metaphorical language. By overcoming the direct didacticism of many proverbs, Dickens is able to communicate his social criticism and his desire to improve the lot of his fellow citizens in a language that is not tiring in its social message but rather refreshingly colorful and often humorous. It is this "proverbial realism" that makes some of the following passages so appealing to readers of Dickens's novels still today:

"Roving stones gather no moss, Joe," said Gabriel.
    "Nor mile-stones much," replied Joe. "I'm little better than one here, and see as much of the world." (*Barnaby Rudge*)

I did not allow my resolution, with respect to the Parliamentary Debates, to cool. It was one of the irons I began to beat immediately, and one of the irons I kept hot, and hammered at, with perseverance I may honestly admire. (*David Copperfield*)

At times Dickens takes his game with proverbs a bit too far, and the modern reader in particular might not be able to reconstruct the traditional saying alluded to in the passage. Note, for example, the beginning of Dickens's letter of September 23, 1854, to Thomas Beard: "Catherine is at last persuaded that October really *is* the finest month in the year at the seaside—though she is

Cited from Grace Frank and Dorothy Miner,
*Proverbes en Rimes: Text and Illustrations of the
Fifteenth Century from a French Manuscript in
the Walters Art Gallery, Baltimore.* Baltimore,
MD: Johns Hopkins Press, 1937, plate 109.
Reprinted with permission of the Walters Art
Museum. Baltimore.

not yet quite converted to that other axiom concerning the salutary effects of
going to bed at 8 o'Clock." It takes a considerable jolt of the "proverbial"
mind to realize that the axiom mentioned here alludes to the proverb "Early
to *bed* and early to rise, makes a man healthy, wealthy, and wise." In a second
"play" with this proverb, Dickens is a bit more obvious with his allusion, thus
enabling most of his readers to recall the traditional saying: "At length it became high time to remember the first clause of that great discovery made by
the ancient philosopher, for securing health, riches, and wisdom; the infalli-
bility of which has been for generations verified by the enormous fortunes

constantly amassed by chimney-sweepers and other persons who get up early and go to bed betimes" (*Martin Chuzzlewit*). What a wonderfully ironic reaction to an early medical proverb dating back to 1496 which, under the craftsmanship of Dickens, becomes a social criticism against the unfair distribution of wealth.

The final point in these remarks on Charles Dickens's repeated use of proverbial rhetoric relates to his often commented upon inclination towards repetition in general. He attached certain "habitual phrases" to particular characters, and such statements become "the 'signature tune' by which a character may be recognized." As was explained earlier, in the case of Sam Weller, these habitual phrases become a whole series of wellerisms. Since the *Pickwick Papers* appeared in installments, readers were literally waiting for the wellerisms of the next issue. But Dickens can also delight in cramming a proverbial expression repeatedly into one short paragraph. This last example is a telling one and centers around the proverbial expression "To have a *skeleton* in the cupboard (closet)" in the meaning of a secret source of shame or pain to a family or person. In the following passage, Dickens succeeds in personifying the proverbial phrase and has it partake as a third party in the marriage quarrel between Mr. and Mrs. Alfred Lammle. The repetitive use of the "phrasal person" adds much to the humor of the situation and the authorial wisdom expressed in this short dialogue at the breakfast table:

"It seems to me," said Mrs. Lammle, "that you have had no money at all ever since we have been married."

"What seems to you," said Mr. Lammle, "to have been the case, may possibly have been the case. It doesn't matter."

Was it the specialty of Mr. and Mrs. Lammle, or does it ever obtain with other loving couples? In these matrimonial dialogues they never addressed each other, but always some invisible presence that appeared to take station about midway between them. Perhaps the skeleton in the cupboard comes out to be talked to, on such domestic occasions?

"I have never seen any money in the house," said Mrs. Lammle to the skeleton, "except my own annuity. That I swear."

"You needn't take the trouble of swearing," said Mr. Lammle to the skeleton; "once more, it doesn't matter. You never turned your annuity to so good an account."

"Good an account! In what way?" asked Mrs. Lammle.

"In the way of getting credit, and living well," said Mr. Lammle.

Perhaps the skeleton laughed scornfully on being intrusted with this question and this answer; certainly Mrs. Lammle did, and Mr. Lammle did.

"And what is to happen next?" asked Mrs. Lammle of the skeleton.

"Smash is to happen next," said Mr. Lammle to the same authority.

After this, Mrs. Lammle looked disdainfully at the skeleton—but without carrying the look on to Mr. Lammle—and drooped her eyes. After that, Mr. Lammle did exactly the same thing, and drooped *his* eyes. A servant then entering with toast, the skeleton retired into the closet, and shut itself up. (*Mutual Friend*)

One thing is for certain though, Charles Dickens as the author of this passage and of volumes of letters, essays, speeches, and novels (also a few plays and poems) does not need to hide in a closet when it comes to judging his ability to integrate proverbial language into his texts. He is doubtlessly a master craftsman in the traditional and innovative use of proverbial rhetoric. For an author with a commitment to the realistic depiction of social and political problems of the nineteenth century, proverbs and proverbial expressions as fixed phrases of human behavior had to enter his prose by necessity. These elements of folk speech do not only add metaphorical color to the prose but rather they function as intrinsic parts of the entire meaning and message of the novels. Charles Dickens knew this only too well, and in 1850, in the middle of his remarkable career as one of the greatest British writers, he quite appropriately stated that "conventional phrases are a sort of fireworks, easily let off, and liable to take a great variety of shapes and colours not at all suggested by their original form" (*David Copperfield*). These proverbial fireworks, as expressions of wit and wisdom, are indeed a major part of the language and message of an author who cared deeply about the human comedy and tragedy of his time.

"MAKE HELL WHILE THE SUN SHINES": PROVERBIAL WAR RHETORIC OF WINSTON S. CHURCHILL

Systematic investigations of public figures of the twentieth century (or earlier times) are necessary to ascertain the permeating presence of proverbs in political rhetoric. Speeches, essays, letters, diaries, memoranda, autobiographies, and so on need to be studied to gain a complete picture of the role that folk speech plays in the verbal communication on the highest political level. A unique person who fits this bill is without doubt Winston S. Churchill (1874–1965), whose long life as a distinguished public servant has been treated in perhaps more volumes than any other individual of the twentieth century. Churchill's stormy political career reached its summit when in 1940 he became prime minister and minister of defence, two pivotal posts that he held until 1945 and that enabled him to mobilize Britain and the rest of the free world against the Fascist forces in Europe and Japan. For a period of five years this man of words and deeds was indeed at the proverbial top of his political power and prominence, rallying the British people, those of the British Empire, the United States, and numerous other nationalities to fight the menace of Hitlerism.

Fortunately most of what Churchill uttered and wrote during those eventful five years of World War II has survived and has been published. Clearly, all of these materials and more in the form of memoranda and notes were all available to Churchill when he set out to write his celebrated six-volume personal and yet historical account of *The Second World War* (1948–1954). Manfred Weidhorn in a chapter on Churchill's style entitled "An Affair of Sentences" speaks of Churchill's "comprehensive, flexible, and perceptive use of imagery from the institutions of society and the disciplines of man—from Scripture, marriage, commerce, science, medicine, sports, games, painting, and, especially, the theater." He also refers to the fact that "while some of his metaphors and similes are predictable or pedestrian, others are effectively, even pithily, used, adeptly moving [...] from the literal to the figurative." Next Weidhorn mentions that "Churchill enjoys racy colloquialisms no less than formal Latinisms," and he also refers to Churchill's inclination towards "epigrammatic statements." Churchill himself was well aware of the importance of imagery, metaphor, pithiness, idiom, colloquialism, antithesis, and epigram in his speaking and writing. At the age of 21 he wrote a revealing yet never published short essay on "The Scaffolding of Rhetoric" (November 2, 1897), touching on the importance of correctness of diction, rhythm, accumulation of argument, and analogy in political oratory. Especially important are his observations that "all the speeches of great English rhetoricians display an uniform preference for short, homely words of common usage."

The six volumes of *The Second World War* contain 410 proverbial texts on a total of 4,405 pages, which yields a ratio of one proverbial phrase for every 10.7 pages. It might be interesting to note here, however, that Churchill's major enemy Adolf Hitler used about 500 proverbial phrases on a total of 792 pages of his *Mein Kampf* (*My Struggle,* 1925/26), making this aggressive, polemic, and propagandistic bible of National Socialism and anti-Semitism much more "proverbial" and by extension manipulatively authoritarian. Where Churchill himself becomes more aggressive and emotional in his speeches and writings, he appears to be more inclined to underscore his rhetoric with proverbial wisdom to strengthen his points and arguments. A short proverb or fitting proverbial phrase enables him to hit the nail on the head, as it were, also realizing very well that everybody would understand these proverbial colloquialisms when they were juxtaposed to the normal and factual rhetoric of organizing the war effort.

One senses a certain feeling of fatalism not only in many incidents in which Churchill employs proverbial language but also throughout many of these over four thousand pages of war history. Once the free democracies of the world permitted Hitler to gain ultimate power, Churchill resigned himself to the fact that this foe had to be fought on his terms, that is, through the resolve of the British people and the strongest military alliance that could possibly be assembled. There was no way to escape the fate of a major war, and a number of proverbial leitmotifs underscore this determined viewpoint in these volumes. The proverb that by its nature expresses the inescapable course of events that would occur once all attempts at preventing it had been exhausted is the classical "The *die* is cast," used by Julius Caesar on crossing the Rubicon after coming from Gaul and advancing into Italy against Pompey (49 B.C.). Churchill in a similar vein plunged himself into desperate and daring action when he accepted the position of prime minister during the Second World War. Being a man of action and deeds who worked best in crisis situations, he made use of this fatalistic proverb 10 times in short and decisive statements before the war. Two of them deserve closer scrutiny since they relate on the one hand to Churchill personally and on the other to one of the most crucial decisions of World War II. In his letter of January 12, 1942, to Lord Privy Seal one finds a contextualized reference showing Churchill's tribulations about flying home to Britain after meeting President Roosevelt in Washington:

> I must confess that I felt rather frightened. I thought of the ocean spaces, and that we should never be within a thousand miles of land until we approached the British Isles. I had always regarded an Atlantic flight with awe. But the die was cast. Still I must admit that if at breakfast, or even before luncheon, they had come to me to report that the weather had changed and we must go by sea I should have easily reconciled myself to a voyage by ship.

The second reference deals with the final decision as to the day the long awaited invasion of mainland Europe to liberate France and other countries and to give Hitler's Germany its final blow would take place:

> The hours dragged slowly by until, at 9:15 p.m. on the evening of June 4 [1944], a fateful conference opened at Eisenhower's battle headquarters. Conditions were bad, typical of December rather than June, but

the weather experts gave some promise of a temporary improvement on the morning of the 6th. After this they predicted a return of rough weather for an indefinite period. Faced with desperate alternatives of accepting the immediate risks or of postponing the attack for at least a fortnight, General Eisenhower boldly chose to go ahead with the operation. At 4 a.m. on June 5 the die was irrevocably cast: the invasion would be launched on June 6.

Churchill, who had proudly served as the first lord of the admiralty, very much felt at home on the high seas, and it should not be surprising that he enjoyed the rich proverbial metaphors of the English language that relate to the sea and seafaring. Of particular interest is the use of a proverbial expression at a time of an earth-shaking historical event. In the chapter on "Pearl Harbor," Churchill reports that he received a telephone call from President Roosevelt in which the latter stated that "'They [the Japanese] have attacked us at Pearl Harbor. We are all in the same boat now'." Two days later, on December 9, 1941, Churchill began a letter to Roosevelt by repeating this maritime expression that so aptly expresses the fact that the United States and Britain were now in the same position of fighting Japan and Germany:

> Now that we are, as you say, "in the same boat", would it not be wise for us to have another conference? We could review the whole war plan in the light of reality and new facts, as well as the problems of production and distribution.

It is doubtful that either Roosevelt or Churchill knew that they were employing the classical Latin proverbial expression "in eadem es navi" (to be in the same *boat*) that has been traced back to a letter by Cicero from 53 B.C. Yet in the same boat they certainly were now, for just as Britain, "the United States was in the war, up to the neck and in to the death," as Churchill put it proverbially in the same letter.

Suffering and fighting were, of course, the driving forces behind Churchill's famous and by now proverbial statement made in a speech to the House of Commons on May 13, 1940, his first after having become prime minister three days earlier:

> In this crisis I hope I may be pardoned if I do not address the House at any length to-day. [. . .] I would say to the House, as I said to those who have joined this Government: "I have nothing to offer but blood, toil, tears and sweat."

With this statement Churchill electrified not only members of the House of Commons but also the entire British nation and free peoples throughout the world who heard it broadcast on the radio waves. The novelty of the famous phrase, however, rests only in the fact that Churchill made a quadratic and rhythmic structure out of the triad of "*blood,* sweat, and tears" which he himself had used in *The World Crisis* (1931) to describe the valiant struggle of the Russian armed forces during World War I: "These pages [...] record the toils, perils, sufferings and passions of millions of men. Their sweat, their tears, their blood bedewed the endless plain." The order of the three nouns is reversed here, but the preceding sentences mention the "toils" that were to be added about nine years later. It must also be noted that the British author John Donne already in 1611 speaks of "tears, or sweat, or blood," and Lord Byron in 1823 has the rhyming couplet "Year after year they voted cent per cent, / Blood, sweat, and tear-wrung millions—why? for rent?" Churchill might have known these earlier references, but there is also the chance that he might have remembered the classical twin formula of "*sanguis et sudor*" (blood and sweat) which was very popular with Cicero and many other Latin authors. Be that as it may, there is *no* instance in classical Latin literature or anywhere else in English literature for that matter of the rhetorical group of four nouns corresponding to the sweeping "blood, toil, tears, and sweat."

It happens rather frequently in Churchill's narrative that he uses proverbial language in a personal manner. It must not be forgotten that *The Second World War* and his other historical volumes were not written in an objective scholarly style. Churchill himself is the persona in the center, and sentences with the "I" pronoun abound, including those that include folk speech:

I fear this may be another example of the adage "A stitch in time saves nine."

I thought it my duty to break the ice.

I found it very hard to make head or tail of the bundle of drafts.

I am completely at the end of my tether.

I said we must face the facts.

"Facing the facts" was yet another proverbial leitmotif that Churchill used to convince his allies and opponents to follow his war strategies. To add rhetorical strength to his verbal arguments, he would quite often shift from the subjective "I" to the more collective "we," thus arguing for a united front. A few convincing examples of this shrewd and at times manipulative procedure can be seen in the following list:

We will let bygones go and work with anyone who convinces us of his resolution
to defeat the common enemy.

We had to make the best of it, and that is never worth doing by halves.

Everything we had touched had turned to gold, and during the last seven weeks
there had been an unbroken run of military success.

The last reference refers to Churchill's remarks during a meeting with President Roosevelt and numerous other high officials on September 13, 1944, at Washington, D.C. Like Midas in the classical myth, the war efforts of the Allies were bearing gilded fruit if not turning literally to pure gold. Much of this was due to the deep friendship and absolute trust between Churchill and Roosevelt. Churchill once described the British and American relationship during the entire war with the proverb: "A *friend* in need is a friend indeed."

The feeling of gratitude led Churchill in a speech to the House of Commons on August 20, 1940, to formulate one of his most memorable utterances, which by now has taken on a proverbial status of sorts. Expressing his appreciation of the British pilots who in the summer of 1940 fended off the German air attacks, he said:

The gratitude of every home in our Island, in our Empire, and indeed throughout the world, except in the abodes of the guilty, goes out to the British airmen who, undaunted by odds, unwearied in their constant challenge and mortal danger, are turning the tide of the World War by their prowess and by their devotion. Never in the field of human conflict was so much owed by so many to so few.

Churchill was well aware of the special and memorable formulation of this phrase. In calling Churchill a "phrase forger," Manfred Weidhorn is correct in observing that Churchill "made his rhetoric memorable by these simple, proverb-like utterances."

Yet Churchill's own inclination towards coining "proverb-like" phrases did not prevent him from making use of traditional proverbs whenever they suited his rhetorical purposes. If, on the other hand, a traditional proverb did not quite express what the moment called for, Churchill had no problems in changing the wording to fit his needs. At times such innovative proverb manipulations actually resulted in powerful statements the messages of which appear to carry the authority of traditional wisdom. It should surprise no one that Churchill delighted in using the proverb "*Deeds,* not words" as a leitmotif 15 times throughout his long life. Not that words or rhetoric were not important to the great orator, but the following random citations from his speeches clearly show that they were only a means to the more important end of precipitating action:

> One of the ways to bring this war to a speedy end is to convince the enemy, not by words, but by deeds, that we have the will. (1940)

> In wartime there is a lot to be said for the motto: "Deeds, not words." (1941)

> We hope to be judged by deeds, and not by words, and by performance rather than by promises. (1953)

One wonders, of course, what Churchill's political opponents might have thought of this last statement, when everybody in Britain knew about his love of words. It must also not be forgotten that Churchill was a man of action, that no assignment ever appeared too much for him, and that he worked untiringly for His Majesty's Government and its people. As Victor Albjerg in his chapter on "The Essence of the Man" has put it so aptly, "Churchill enjoyed work. To him it was not drudgery, but purposeful creativity."

In his countless memoranda to various ministers and generals, Churchill again and again cited proverbs to support his arguments. They acted as folkloric strategies to add emphasis to what would otherwise be rather bureaucratic messages. An example of this is his short memorandum of May 27, 1944, to the Minister of Aircraft Production in which he expresses his perturbation about the minister's proposal "to centralise jet-propulsion development in [a] new Government company. There is a great deal to be said for encouraging overlapping in research and development rather than putting all the eggs in one basket." In another memorandum of November 16, 1944, Churchill informed General Ismay of about twenty 18-inch howitzers that he could make available to him for the direct attack of Germany: "Every dog has his day, and I have kept these [very heavy guns] for a quarter of a century in the hope that they would have their chance." There appears to be no detail that escaped Churchill. One gets the feeling that he thought of everything, as can be seen from yet another memorandum of April 4, 1945, to Sir Edward Bridges. The war was not even over yet, but Churchill as the shrewd politician and proponent of the British Commonwealth was already planning to transfer some ships to Canada and Australia as a goodwill gesture for their contributions to the war:

> No financial considerations should be adduced. We owe too much to Canada in money alone, and the effect of gestures like this upon both Dominions concerned will be achieved far better than by arguments about trading off the value of the ships against certain financial consider-

ations. This is not a moment for a "penny-wise, pound-foolish" policy. Now is the time to make the presentation in the most friendly form. Cast your bread upon the waters; it will return to you in not so many days.

Notice how Churchill supplements the wisdom of the folk proverb in this situation with the authority of the biblical proverb (Eccles. 11:1), even though he does not quite remember the original second part as "for you shall find it after many days." Or is he, in fact, altering the proverb on purpose in order to indicate that this benevolent gesture will bear its fruit in return sooner than people might think?

Churchill the masterful proverbial strategist can also be seen in the effective use of two proverbs in his reflection on the fateful signing of the Non-Aggression Pact between the Soviet Union and Germany on August 22, 1939. The proverbs serve as moralizing tools by Churchill, who had worked hard to keep Stalin from siding with Hitler:

A moral may be drawn from all this, which is of homely simplicity. "Honesty is the best policy." Only twenty-two months were to pass before Stalin and the Russian nation and its scores of millions were to pay a frightful forfeit. If a Government has no moral scruples, it often seems to gain great advantages and liberties of action, but "All comes out even at the end of the day, and all will come out yet more even when all the days are ended."

In addition to their moralizing purpose, the proverbs in the narrative of this first volume of *The Second World War* also serve as prophetic statements of "homely simplicity" that dishonesty and treachery will lead to doom.

Other proverbs show Churchill's pragmatism in his dual role as prime minister and minister of defence. In one of his typical memoranda, he raises the question about much-needed war supplies and then gives a bit of pithy advice that action should be taken immediately:

What is being done about getting our twenty motor torpedo-boats, the one hundred and fifty to two hundred aircraft, and the two hundred and fifty thousand rifles? I consider we were promised all the above, and more too. Not an hour should be lost in raising these questions. "Beg while the iron is hot."

What an ingenious way to vary a standard proverb in order to express the definite need of getting these war supplies! Churchill clearly was a master of this

Make Hay while the Sun shines.

In Summer heat, when brightly shines the sun,
To make your hay, the proper time is come :
Spread round the new mown grass, and do it right,
Work while the sky is clear, and sun is bright.

Cited from John W. Barber, *The Handbook of Illustrated Proverbs*. New York: George F. Tuttle, 1856, p. 135.

type of proverb manipulation, his best creation perhaps being the following anti-proverb based on the well-known English proverb "Make *hay* while the sun shines." In a memorandum of June 23, 1941, to General Ismay, Churchill wrote pointedly, "Now [that] the enemy [Germany] is busy in Russia is the time to 'Make hell while the sun shines'" in gaining air domination over the Channel and France. In its metaphorical simplicity this statement can be seen as a proverbial *modus operandi* not only of warfare as Churchill envisioned it but also of his political life in general. Take advantage of every possible situation and give the enemy "hell" while you can.

Toward the end of his long life, the honorary citizenship of the United States was bestowed upon Churchill on April 9, 1963. On that occasion President John F. Kennedy summarized Winston S. Churchill's rhetorical grandeur with the statement that "In the dark days and darker nights when England stood alone—and most men save Englishmen despaired of England's life—he mobilized the English language and sent it into battle." It is doubtful that either Kennedy or Churchill thought of the importance that proverbial speech played in this mobilization. Yet a good 20 years earlier, in a long speech on the war situation to the House of Commons on January 27, 1942, Churchill had expressed his thoughts on the rhetorical significance of proverbial folk speech:

> There is no objection to anything being said in plain English, or even plainer, and the Government will do their utmost to conform to any standard which may be set in the course of the debate. But no one need be mealy-mouthed in debate, and no one should be chicken-hearted in voting.

Despite his erudition and vast knowledge that could lead Churchill to very sophisticated heights of the English language (he received the Nobel Prize for Literature in 1953!), he was always ready "to speak in plain English" and to voice his opinion without fear of the consequences. Speaking plainly and proverbially certainly helped in arousing the peoples of the free world against the tyranny of dictators. There definitely is proverbial truth in the claim that Winston S. Churchill "mobilized the English language and sent it into battle."

"MAN IS A WOLF TO MAN": PROVERBIAL DIALECTICS IN BERTOLT BRECHT

In January 1956, six months before his death, Bertolt Brecht (1898–1956) spoke to the IVth German Writers Convention in Berlin about the construction of a new world, in which the socialist and realist style of writing had to participate "through the study of material dialectic and the wisdom of the people." Already in the late thirties he had pointed out in reference to his "non-Aristotelian drama," that "not everything that comes from the people and goes to the people [is] popular. Those are truisms, but there are also falsisms, which cannot be opposed." This seemingly simple remark by Brecht is also applicable to proverbial folk wisdom that is particularly marked by contradictions. After all, it is well known that an anti-proverb can be found for every proverb, because this type of wisdom only stems from experience and does not contain a logical system. As early as 1920 Brecht declared in his notebooks his "enjoyment of dialectics," and in his essay "Looking At My First Plays" (1954) he refers to his general "spirit of opposition." Brecht characterized his contradictory work style proverbially by saying that "it was not just [...] 'swimming against the stream' from a formal perspective [...], but also always the attempt to show interaction between people as contradictory, tumultuous, violent."

With another proverbial statement Brecht reduces all this to a common denominator in his play *Caucasian Chalk Circle* (1945): "It may be wrong to mix different wines, but old and new wisdom blend very well."

Brecht's preoccupation with proverbial language begins at the age of 15, when he uses his first proverb in a letter written in verse to the Reitter family in July of 1913, which exemplifies his linguistically playful humor:

> We really did find an apartment right away
> Mama did not like it all THAT much
> but we could not get any other.
> But when in need, even if that is too bad,
> beggars can't be choosers.

About 20 years later, Brecht combines in another letter of January 1934 to Kurt Kläber as many as three proverbs into an innovative statement. Reacting to news that friends from Germany would follow him into Danish exile, he writes with linguistic playfulness and yet meaningfully: "Help yourselves, pioneers, still the best pastures are here for the taking, gold mines lie directly underground, the land awaits your initiative. He who comes first, grinds terribly small and the dogs devour the hindermost." The first part of the proverbial statement combines the first half of the proverb "First *come,* first served" with the second part of the proverb "The *mills* of God grind slowly, yet they grind exceedingly small," and the word "exceedingly" has been replaced by "terribly." In the additional proverb "The *dogs* bite the hindermost" the change of verb to "devour" considerably coarsens the metaphorical implications. Taking into account Hitler's takeover of power and Brecht's flight into exile, this manipulation of proverbs can be interpreted as Brecht's warning for the friends of the lurking danger in Nazi Germany. Only too quickly does such language play turn serious, as is also evident in the proverbial alienations of his literary works.

In spite of their literal or alluded citing, proverbs in Brecht's works are constantly subject to change, so that interesting parallel contradictions can be observed in the oeuvre. In *The Caucasian Chalk Circle,* for example, Azdak asks a doctor whether he can name a mitigating cause for his crime. The doctor replies: "At the most that to err is human." In the fragment *Downfall of the Egoist Johann Fatzer* (1930), the chorus changes the proverb considerably:

> Injustice is human,
> but more human it is
> to fight against it!

But even here, spare
man, leave him unharmed.
The dead cannot be
taught!

Repeatedly Brecht deals with proverbs by adding aphoristically to them. In the short play *He Who Said No* (1930), intended for schoolchildren, a boy reacts to the proverb "Whoever says '*a*', must also say 'b'" by adding a contradiction: "Whoever says '*a*', doesn't have to say 'b'. You can also recognize that '*a*' was wrong." At the same time Brecht uses the identical proverb in its original meaning in an essay "On the Necessity of Art in Our Time" (1930) to argue that the price of art cannot keep rising while children go hungry all over the world: "Art should not be regarded as the 'expression of great and unique personalities in the sense of exceptional manifestations.' In that case, we have said 'A' and must then say 'B'. Then exceptional personalities dictate their prices to the world, prices so high that there can be no more thought of feeding numerous insignificant children." Here it becomes obvious that Brecht knew how to make use of the multiple functionality of proverbs, although it has to be said that alienation and literal quotation do not have to be a contradiction.

In the play *Life of Galileo* (1939), the metaphorical proverb "No *rose* without a thorn" is rephrased by way of a structurally identical addition to comment on Galileo's realistic conflict: "What good would it do to have as much free time for research as you like, if any uneducated monk of the inquisition could simply forbid your thoughts? No rose without a thorn, no nobleman without a monk, Master Galileo." However, it should be pointed out that such additions are also not uncommon in colloquial language, as for example in "No *rose* without a thorn, no love without a competitor." Such double expressions, of course, show Brecht's interest in contradictory phrases. The following two instances illuminate this interest further: "It is bitter that children turn into people, but still bitterer that people can turn into children!" and "There is not much knowledge that provides power, but there is a lot of knowledge that is provided by power." Beginning with a proverb, Brecht in each case forms an opposing expression which lets a bit of folk wisdom appear in a completely different light.

It is often enough to change one single word to give a proverb an entirely new meaning. The following examples can be understood without context, but it must be remembered that alienations may well be intended as humor or joke. Not every alienation is necessarily designed to uncover social wrongs dialectically, although bitter satire often plays a part: "War [Christmas] comes but once a year," "Sweaty feet [misfortunes] never come singly," "Laziness [idleness] is the root of all evil," "Diligence is the mother of knockout [good luck]," and "Hunger is a bad [the best] sauce."

Brecht, as a Marxist, of course also presents the reversal of the proverb "*Money* doesn't stink" into "Money stinks," but that is only uttered by Puntila in a drunken stupor in the play *Mr. Puntila and His Man Matti* (1940). The strongest statement by Brecht against profiteering capitalism and in favor of the poor can be found in the four-line epigram "Ach, des Armen Morgenstund (O, the Poor Man's Morning Hour)" (1932). In this context, he varies what has been proven to be the most popular German proverb "*Morgenstunde* hat Gold im Munde" (the closest English equivalent would be "The early *bird* catches the worm") and adds as a doubled accusation an alienation of the biblical proverb "He that will not *work* shall not eat" (2 Thess. 3:10):

O, the poor man's morning hour
gold for the rich man has in its mouth
One thing almost I had forgotten:
He who works shall not eat, either.

Almost 20 years later, Brecht returns to the morning hour variation in his fragment *The Salzburg Dance of Death* (1950). The short bridge-building scene starts with a conversation between three carpenters and Death who appears as a foreman:

Death:	Up with the beam, get moving, you!
First Carpenter:	It's heavy enough for three, foreman!
Death:	Time is money, move, move!
First Carpenter:	Not for us, dear man.
Death:	No jokes! Do it with a little singing
	and you'll succeed before you know it!
First Carpenter (sings):	O, the poor man's morning hour, heave-ho!
	gold for the rich man has in its mouth, heave-ho!
Death:	Men, such songs give me a tear,
	they are an annoyance to me.

Here again the topic is exploitation, and the pecuniary proverb "*Time* is money" acts as an additional verbal whip.

Occasionally, Brecht goes so far in his alienations that the original proverb can only be recognized with difficulty. Surely the following statement is rooted in the proverb "The *unexpected* always happens," and it even gives a reasonable explanation for this bit of folk wisdom: "To be sure: Unexpected / often comes expectedly, often we expect / something unexpected, that's life." But for the most part, things aren't as complicated as that, as is pointed out in Brecht's adaptation of Molière's *Don Juan* (1953). There, Don Juan's servant Sganarelle resorts to six proverbs to argue ironically against his master's ridiculous death wish. He and Brecht succeed mainly through the purposeful parody of folk wisdom: "And honesty is the worst policy and lies have long legs and he laughs best who laughs first and last come, first served, and rotten fish, good fish, and forgive us our innocence and the camel goes through the eye of the needle" (Matt. 19:24). This alienated proverbial tirade shows with great clarity how much "proverbial humor" Brecht employed in his proverbial dialectics.

Often, proverbs are directly taken from the Bible, but their wisdom and applicability in modern times is questioned. In the *Conversations Among Exiles* (1941) there is the following comment about Hitler's war plans: "To retaliate, the enemy will also throw its population into our territory, because war stands and falls with the phrase 'An eye for an eye and a tooth for a tooth' [Exod. 21:24; Matt. 5:38]. One thing is for sure: if the total war is not supposed to remain an idea of the future, a solution has to be found. The question is simply: either the population is done away with, or war becomes impossible. Sometime, and soon, a decision has to be made." Justifiably, Brecht argues against the proverb of retaliation from the Old Testament, particularly because he knew that this proverb was used for war propaganda and the persecution of the Jews. A horrifying example of such usage can be found in Hitler's speech of January 30, 1942, in which the biblical proverb "An *eye* for an eye and a tooth for a tooth" is perverted into the colloquial justification of the real elimination of the European Jews: "We are aware that the war can only end in two ways: either, the Aryan people are exterminated or Judaism disappears from Europe. [...], the result of this war [will] be the annihilation of Judaism. For the first time, the real ancient Jewish law will be applied: Eye for eye and tooth for tooth!"

The most drastic description of human misery, however, can be found in the *Threepenny Opera* (1928) in the form of the alienated biblical proverb "*Man* does not live by bread alone" (Deut. 8:3; Matt. 4:4), used in the second finale with the title "What does man live by?" About six years later, Brecht used the chorus of that song also as a motto for the third chapter of the *Threepenny Novel* (1934):

What does man live by? He lives by hourly
Tormenting, stripping, attacking, strangling and devouring others.

This Funny World®

"Thanks, lady, but man does not live by bread alone."

Brattleboro [Vermont] *Reformer* (November 25, 1978), p. 13.

Man only lives by thoroughly forgetting
That indeed he is still human.
Chorus: Gentlemen, no more illusions:
Man lives by misdeed alone!

While the biblical proverb wants to express that people besides nutrition need spiritual values to survive, this pessimistic anti-proverb claims that they are primarily bad. And still, at the end of the great novel, Peachum, ever the businessman, expresses precisely the opposite in his speech to the newlywed couple Macheath and Polly, even if it is just with an eye on commercial success:

I would like to start with a practical suggestion. You, gentlemen, and you, my dear son-in-law, sell razor blades and watches, and household goods and who knows what else, but man does not live by that alone. It is not enough that he is clean shaven and knows what time it is. You have to go further. You have to sell him education, too. I mean books and I am thinking of cheap novels which don't paint life in shades of gray, but in lighter colors which give the everyday person an idea of higher worlds [...]. I am not talking about the business opportunities in this—which might be significant—, I am talking of the service offered to mankind.

But this speech to mankind is again full of ironies, because the mankind it talks about and for which it pretends to look out can be bought. People here are classified as consumers of goods and one is strongly reminded of one of the songs in *Mother Courage and Her Children* (1939), where people turn into commodities for the war machinery:

From Ulm to Metz, from Metz to Moravia!
Mother Courage is coming along!
War will provide for all
It only needs powder and lead.
It cannot live by lead alone,
nor by powder, It needs people!

In these lines Brecht plays with two proverbs. Hidden beneath the sentence "War will provide for all" lies the proverb "The *land* provides for all," and a convincing contrast is established between the devastation of war and the harvesting of the land. Of course, the sentence "It [war] cannot live by lead alone" contains another variation of the biblical proverb "*Man* does not live by bread alone." In this stanza, man turns into food for war, which means that war devours people as its innocent victims. Clearly the alienating language play turns deadly serious in this case.

And so in the end one is left with the question about the purpose of life and human existence. Does the moralist Brecht have an answer for that? Is it even possible, in addition to the proverbial motto: "First comes the *grub*, then morality" used but once in the *Threepenny Opera*, to find a specific proverb that appears in the collected works and represents Brecht's essential wisdom? In the scale of life, which part of Brecht's philosophy carries more weight—the "grub" or morality, the animalistic or the human?

Hans Mayer has tried to find an answer to this question in a 1964 lecture with the provocative title "Brecht and Humanity." In the introduction he says: "Brecht and humanity: a questionable combination. How can this author who, throughout his work, and perhaps most notably in the parable play about the *Good Person of Szechwan*, has derided any sayings about humanity and the general condition of man, be mentioned in connection with the problem of humanity?" The answer is simply that Brecht, in spite of his derision, is always writing about human fate. In his well-known "Playwright's Song" (1935) he says programmatically in the first stanza:

> I am a playwright. I show
> What I have seen. On the people-markets
> I saw how people are traded. That
> I show, I, the playwright.

In a variation of the proverb "Every *man* has his price" one finds the same human theme as early as 1930 in the "Song of the Wares" that is part of the didactic play *The Measure Taken:*

> What, after all, is man?
> Do I know what man is?
> Do I know who knows it?
> I don't know what man is
> I only know his price.

Resigning before the seemingly predestined invariability of the human condition, the early Brecht resorts to tautological proverbs such as "Human is human" in *Baal* (1919) and "Man is man" in the "Man-is-man-Song" (1925) as well as in the title of the comedy *Man Equals Man* (1926).

As was mentioned earlier, the proverbial alienation "Man lives by misdeed alone" symbolizes human misery per se, in which man, as in the animal world, struggles against others for the survival of the fittest. Helmut Koopmann has argued convincingly that "Brecht inevitably [resorted] to a counter-world: The animal side of man—hence, not what distinguished man from animal, but rather, what they had in common, only that one was aware of what the other lived unconsciously." Franz Norbert Mennemeier talks even more directly of a "wolf society," which Brecht uses as metaphor for his "negative didactics." To picture this inhuman existence, Brecht has indeed used exceedingly drastic animal symbols, many of which center upon the notorious wolf of proverbs and proverbial expressions. Proverbial instances such as "He is just a lamb between two wolves," "We are holding an old wolf by the ear / who, if he escapes, will attack us both," and "Killing wolf in a sheep skin" illustrate this very clearly. With five occurrences, the most frequently employed leitmotif for Brecht became the internationally known classical proverb "Homo homini lupus" (*Man is a wolf to man*), which is a traditional proverb in most European languages. Brecht had expressed this already in 1932 in his discussion of the question "Is communism exclusive?" as part of his "Comments about the [play] *Mother.*"

There, Brecht summarizes his thoughts with a proverbial formula that simply declares exploitative people to be wolves: "Our enemies are the enemies of humankind. [...] Those who are a wolf to man aren't human, but wolves." And the short poem "On a Japanese Drawing of a Puppet Show Played for Children by Children" (1934) begins by making the alarming statement of how fragile the establishment of a world is in which people act like wild animals:

Woe!
The immature stand on the tables.
In their play
They show what they have seen
How man treated man and was a wolf to him.

But then, in the first stanza of the poem "The Active Discontented" (1943), Brecht, in the middle of World War II, achieved a positive alienation of the proverb by adding just a single letter (from "ein" [a] to "kein" [no]):

The active discontented, your big teachers
Invented the construction of a community
In which man is no wolf to man.
And discovered the delight of man to eat his fill
    and live in a dry place.
And his wish to be in charge of his own affairs.

This human wish itself has found expression in Brecht's most humane proverbial alienation, written in the fateful year of 1938 at the end of his well-known poem "To Posterity," in which he defines the purpose of his own writing as the fight to turn human wolves into helpful people:

But you, when at last it comes to pass
That man is a helper to man
Think of us
With mercy.

With this vision of the future, Brecht's spirit of opposition would, of course, disintegrate. But since he found himself only in a transition period toward humanitarianism, he had to and could only portray what is happening among people. Nevertheless, Brecht has anthropomorphized the proverb in this statement in a hopeful manner, because in a new world of humanity, the wolf in man would have to reform himself to a noble person.

BENJAMIN FRANKLIN'S "THE WAY TO WEALTH"

For 25 years, from 1733 to 1758, the printer, publisher, inventor, scientist, businessman, and diplomat Benjamin Franklin (1706–1790) published his successful *Poor Richard's Almanack* for his fellow colonists. He sold about 10,000 copies each year, filling the small booklets of 24 to 36 pages with weather and planting information as well as various short instructional and entertaining tidbits. Next to the Bible, these almanacs were perhaps the most widely read materials in the colonies. In fact, while preachers were quoting Bible passages, the citizens of the day enjoyed citing the wisdom of the almanacs, which to a large degree was expressed in common proverbs.

Franklin was well aware of the success of his best-seller almanacs, and he also knew, of course, that most of the proverbs listed in them he had in fact taken from such well-known British proverb collections as George Herbert's *Outlandish Proverbs* (1640), James Howell's *Paroimiografia* (1659), and Thomas Fuller's *Gnomologia* (1732). Nevertheless, he enjoyed hearing people refer to them as proverbs of Poor Richard or even of Benjamin Franklin, admitting rather indirectly that he had "lifted" them from "the wisdom of many ages and nations." In 1788 he made the following comments, albeit without explicitly revealing his sources (see Newcomb 1957):

In 1732 I first published my Almanac [for the year 1733] under the name of *Richard Saunders;* it was continued by me about twenty-five years, and commonly called *Poor Richard's Almanack.* I endeavoured to make it both entertaining and useful, and it accordingly came to be in such demand, that I reaped considerable profit from it, vending annually near ten thousand. And observing that it was generally read, (scarce any neighbourhood in the province being without it,) I considered it as a proper vehicle for conveying instruction among the common people, who bought scarcely any other books. I therefore filled all the little spaces, that occurred between the remarkable days in the Calendar, with proverbial sentences, chiefly such as inculcated industry and frugality, as the means of procuring wealth, and thereby securing virtue; it being more difficult for a man in want to act always honestly, as (to use here one of those proverbs) *"It is hard for an empty sack to stand upright."* These proverbs, which contained the wisdom of many ages and nations, I assembled and formed into a connected discourse, prefixed to the Almanac of 1758, as the harangue of a wise old man to the people attending an auction. The bringing all these scattered counsels thus into a focus, enabled them to make greater impression. The piece, being universally approved, was copied in all the newspapers of the American Continent, reprinted in Britain on a large sheet of paper to be stuck up in houses; two translations were made of it in France, and great numbers bought by the clergy and gentry, to distribute gratis among their poor parishioners and tenants.

(cited from *The Works of Benjamin Franklin,* ed. by Jared Sparks. Philadelphia, Pennsylvania: Childs & Peterson, 1840, vol. 2, p. 92)

Altogether Franklin included 1,044 proverbs (about 40 each year) in his almanacs (see Barbour 1974), of which he chose 105 to be part of his celebrated essay "The Way to Wealth" (1758). As Stuart A. Gallacher has shown, only the following five proverbs in this essay were actually coined by Franklin: "Three *removes* is (are) as bad as a fire," "*Laziness* travels so slowly, that poverty soon overtakes him," "*Sloth* makes all things difficult, but industry all easy," "*Industry* pays debts, while despair increases them," and "There will be *sleeping* enough in the grave" (Gallacher 1949). But while these texts actually took on a proverbial status during Franklin's time and beyond, they are not

"Not so fast, pal. How do I know Benjamin Franklin really said everything you say he did?"

New Yorker (November 15, 1976), p. 47.

particularly current any longer, except perhaps for "Three removes is as bad as a fire" and "There will be sleeping enough in the grave" (one of my personal favorites).

In any case, as Franklin himself stated in 1788, his essay on "The Way to Wealth" was a hit among his compatriots, instructing them and later generations about virtue, prosperity, prudence, and above all economic common sense. The essay contained the so-called Puritan ethics expressed in proverbs that helped to shape the worldview of the young American nation. But there was much influence also in Europe as the essay was translated into several languages. The masterful treatise thus became a secular Bible of sorts, spreading social wisdom in the form of folk wisdom to thousands of eager followers. There is no doubt then that "The Way to Wealth" is one of the truly significant documents in the history of proverbs, even if, as Franklin admitted already in 1758 at the end of his essay, "not a tenth part of the wisdom was my own."

The Way to Wealth (1758)

Courteous Reader, I have heard, that nothing gives an author so great pleasure as to find his works respectfully quoted by others. Judge, then, how much I must have been gratified by an incident I am going to relate to you. I stopped my horse lately, where a great number of people were collected at an auction of merchants' goods. The hour of the sale not being come, they were conversing on the badness of the times; and one of the company called to a plain, clean, old man, with white locks, "Pray, Father Abraham, what think you of the times? Will not these heavy taxes quite ruin the country? How shall we ever be able to pay them? What would you advise us to?" Father Abraham stood up, and replied, "If you would have my advice, I will give it you in short; for *A word to the wise is enough,* as Poor Richard says." They joined in desiring him to speak his mind, and gathering round him, he proceeded as follows.

"Friends," said he, "the taxes are indeed very heavy, and, if those laid on by the government were the only ones we had to pay, we might more easily discharge them; but we have many others, and much more grievous to some of us. We are taxed twice as much by our idleness, three times as much by our pride, and four times as much by our folly; and from these taxes the commissioners cannot ease or deliver us, by allowing an abatement. However, let us hearken to good advice, and something may be done for us; *God helps them that help themselves,* as Poor Richard says.

"I. It would be thought a hard government, that should tax its people one-tenth part of their time, to be employed in its service; but idleness taxes many of us much more; sloth, by bringing on diseases, absolutely shortens life. *Sloth, like rust, consumes faster than labor wears, while the used key is always bright,* as Poor Richard says. *But dost thou love life, then do not squander time, for that is the stuff life is made of,* as Poor Richard says. How much more than is necessary do we spend in sleep, forgetting, that *The sleeping fox catches no poultry,* and that *There will be sleeping enough in the grave,* as Poor Richard says.

"*If time be of all things the most precious, wasting time must be,* as Poor Richard says, *the greatest prodigality;* since, as he elsewhere tells us, *Lost time is never found again; and what we call time enough, always proves little enough.* Let us then up and be doing, and doing to the purpose; so by diligence shall we do more with less perplexity. *Sloth makes all things difficult, but industry all easy,* and *He that riseth late must trot all day, and shall scarce overtake his business at night;* while *Laziness travels so slowly, that Poverty soon overtakes him. Drive thy business, let not that drive thee,* and *Early to bed, and early to rise, makes a man healthy, wealthy, and wise,* as Poor Richard says.

"So what signifies wishing and hoping for better times? We may make these times better, if we bestir ourselves. *Industry need not wish, and he that lives upon hopes will die fasting. There are no gains without pains, then help, hands, for I have no lands;* or, if I have, they are smartly taxed. *He that hath a trade hath an estate; and he that hath a calling, hath an office of profit and honor,* as Poor Richard says; but then the trade must be worked at, and the calling followed, or neither the estate nor the office will enable us to pay our taxes. If we are industrious, we shall never starve; for, *At the working man's house hunger looks in, but dares not enter.* Nor will the bailiff or the constable enter, for *Industry pays debts, while despair increaseth them.* What though you have found no treasure, nor has any rich relation left you a legacy, *Diligence is the mother of good luck, and God gives all things to industry. Then plough deep while sluggards sleep, and you shall have corn to sell and to keep.* Work while it is called today, for you know not how much you may be hindered to-morrow. *One to-day is worth two to-morrows,* as Poor Richard says; and further, *Never leave that till to-morrow, which you can do to-day.* If you were a servant, would you not be ashamed that a good master should catch you idle? Are you then your own master? Be ashamed to catch yourself idle, when there is so much to be done for yourself, your family, your country, and your king. Handle your tools without mittens; remember, that *The cat in gloves catches no mice,* as Poor Richard says. It is true there is much to be done, and perhaps you are weak-handed; but stick to it steadily, and you will see great effects; for *Constant dropping wears away stones;* and *By diligence and patience the mouse ate in two the cable;* and *Little strokes fell great oaks.*

"Methinks I hear some of you say, 'Must a man afford himself no leisure?' I will tell thee, my friend, what Poor Richard says, *Employ thy time well, if thou meanest to gain leisure; and, since thou art not sure of a minute, throw not away an hour.* Leisure is time for doing something useful; this leisure the diligent man will obtain, but the lazy man never; for *A life of leisure and a life of laziness are two things. Many, without labor, would live by their wits only, but they break for want of stock;* whereas industry gives comfort, and plenty, and respect. *Fly pleasures, and they will follow you. The diligent spinner has a large shift; and now I have a sheep and a cow, everybody bids me good morrow.*

"II. But with our industry we must likewise be steady, settled, and careful, and oversee our own affairs with our own eyes, and not trust too much to others; for, as Poor Richard says,

I never saw an oft-removed tree,
Nor yet an oft-removed family,
That throve so well as those that settled be.

And again, Three removes are as bad as a fire; and again, Keep thy shop, and thy shop will keep thee; and again, If you would have your business done, go; if not, send. And again,

He that by the plough would thrive,
Himself must either hold or drive.

And again, The eye of a master will do more work than both his hands; and again, Want of care does us more damage than want of knowledge; and again, Not to oversee workmen, is to leave them your purse open. Trusting too much to others' care is the ruin of many; for In the affairs of this world men are saved, not by faith, but by the want of it; but a man's own care is profitable; for, If you would have a faithful servant, and one that you like, serve yourself. A little neglect may breed great mischief; for want of a nail the shoe was lost; for want of a shoe the horse was lost; and for want of a horse the rider was lost, being overtaken and slain by the enemy; all for want of a little care about a horse-shoe nail.

"III. So much for industry, my friends, and attention to one's own business; but to these we must add frugality, if we would make our industry more certainly successful. A man may, if he knows not how to save as he gets, keep his nose all his life to the grindstone, and die not worth a groat at last. *A fat kitchen makes a lean will;* and

> *Many estates are spent in the getting,*
> *Since women for tea forsook spinning and knitting,*
> *And men for punch forsook hewing and splitting.*

If you would be wealthy, think of saving as well as of getting. The Indies have not made Spain rich, because her outgoes are greater than her incomes.

"Away then with your expensive follies, and you will not then have so much cause to complain of hard times, heavy taxes, and chargeable families; for

> *Women and wine, game and deceit,*
> *Make the wealth small and the want great.*

And further, *What maintains one vice would bring up two children.* You may think, perhaps, that a little tea, or a little punch now and then, diet a little more costly, clothes a little finer, and a little entertainment now and then, can be no great matter; but remember, *Many a little makes a mickle.* Beware of little expenses: *A small leak will sink a great ship,* as Poor Richard says; and again, *Who dainties love, shall beggars prove;* and moreover, *Fools make feasts, and wise men eat them.*

"Here you are all got together at this sale of fineries and knick-knacks. You call them *goods;* but, if you do not take care, they will prove *evils* to some of you. You expect they will be sold cheap, and perhaps they may for less than they cost; but, if you have no occasion for them, they must be dear to you. Remember what Poor Richard says; *Buy what thou hast no need of, and ere long thou shall sell thy necessaries.* And again, *At a great pennyworth pause a while.* He means, that perhaps the cheapness is apparent only, and not real; or the bargain, by straitening thee in thy business, may do thee more harm than good. For in another place he says, *Many have been ruined by buying good pennyworths.* Again, *It is foolish to lay out money in a purchase of repentance;* and yet this folly is practised every day at auctions, for want of minding the Almanac. Many a one, for the sake of finery on the back, have gone with a hungry belly and half-starved their families. *Silks and satins, scarlet and velvets, put out the kitchen fire,* as Poor Richard says.

"These are not the necessaries of life; they can scarcely be called the conveniences; and yet, only because they look pretty, how many want to have them! By these, and other extravagances, the genteel are reduced to poverty, and forced to borrow of those whom they formerly despised, but who, through industry and frugality, have maintained their standing; in which case it appears plainly, that *A ploughman on his legs is higher than a gentleman on his knees,* as Poor Richard says. Perhaps they have had a small estate left them, which they knew not the getting of; they think, *It is day, and will never be night;* that a little to be spent out of so much is not worth minding; but *Always taking out of the meal-tub, and never putting in, soon comes to the bottom,* as Poor Richard says; and then, *When the well is dry, they know the worth of water.* But this they might have known before, if they had taken his advice. *If you would know the value of money, go and try to borrow some; for he that goes a borrowing goes a sorrowing,* as Poor Richard says; and indeed so does he that lends to such people, when he goes to get it in again. Poor Dick further advises, and says,

> *Fond pride of dress is sure a very curse;*
> *Ere fancy you consult, consult your purse.*

And again, *Pride is as loud a beggar as Want, and a great deal more saucy.* When you have bought one fine thing, you must buy ten more, that your appearance may be all of a piece; but Poor Dick says, *It is easier to suppress the first desire, than to satisfy all that follow it.* And it is as truly folly for the poor to ape the rich, as for the frog to swell in order to equal the ox.

> *Vessels large may venture more,*
> *But little boats should keep near shore.*

It is, however, a folly soon punished; for, as Poor Richard says, *Pride that dines on vanity, sups on contempt. Pride breakfasted with Plenty, dined with Poverty, and supped with Infamy.* And, after all, of what use is this pride of appearance, for which so much is risked, so much is suffered? It cannot promote health, nor ease pain; it makes no increase of merit in the person; it creates envy; it hastens misfortune.

"But what madness must it be to *run in debt* for these superfluities? We are offered by the terms of this sale, six months' credit, and that, perhaps, has induced some of us to attend it, because we cannot spare the ready money, and hope now to be fine without it. But, ah! think what you do when you run in debt; you give to another power over your liberty. If you cannot pay at the time, you will be ashamed to see your creditor; you will be in fear when you speak to him; you will make poor, pitiful, sneaking excuses, and, by degrees, come to lose your veracity, and sink into base, downright lying; for *The second vice is lying, the first is running in debt,* as Poor Richard says; and again, to the same purpose, *Lying rides upon Debt's back;* whereas a free-born Englishman ought not to be ashamed nor afraid to see or speak to any man living. But poverty often deprives a man of all spirit and virtue. *It is hard for an empty bag to stand upright.*

"What would you think of that prince, or of that government, who should issue an edict forbidding you to dress like a gentleman or gentlewoman, on pain of imprisonment or servitude? Would you not say that you were free, have a right to dress as you please, and that such an edict would be a breach of your privileges, and such a government tyrannical? And yet you are about to put yourself under such tyranny, when you run in debt for such dress! Your creditor has authority, at his pleasure, to deprive you of your liberty, by confining you in gaol till you shall be able to pay him. When you have got your bargain, you may, perhaps, think little of payment; but, as Poor Richard says, *Creditors have better memories than debtors; creditors are a superstitious sect, great observers of set days and times.* The day comes round before you are aware, and the demand is made before you are prepared to satisfy it; or, if you bear your debt in mind, the term, which at first seemed so long, will, as it lessens, appear extremely short. Time will seem to have added wings to his heels as well as his shoulders. *Those have a short Lent, who owe money to be paid at Easter.* At present, perhaps, you may think yourselves in thriving circumstances, and that you can bear a little extravagance without injury; but

> For age and want save while you may;
> No morning sun lasts a whole day.

Gain may be temporary and uncertain, but ever, while you live, expense is constant and certain; and *It is easier to build two chimneys, than to keep one in fuel,* as Poor Richard says; so, *Rather go to bed supperless, than rise in debt.*

> Get what you can, and what you get hold;
> 'Tis the stone that will turn all your lead into gold.

And, when you have got the Philosopher's stone, sure you will no longer complain of bad times, or the difficulty of paying taxes.

"IV. This doctrine, my friends, is reason and wisdom; but, after all, do not depend too much upon your own industry, and frugality, and prudence, though excellent things; for they may all be blasted, without the blessing of Heaven; and, therefore, ask that blessing humbly, and be not uncharitable to those that at present seem to want it, but comfort and help them. Remember, Job suffered, and was afterwards prosperous.

"And now, to conclude, *Experience keeps a dear school, but fools will learn in no other,* as Poor Richard says, and scarce in that; for, it is true, *We may give advice, but we cannot give conduct.* However, remember this, *They that will not be counselled, cannot be helped;* and further, that, *If you will not hear Reason, she will surely rap your knuckles,* as Poor Richard says."

Thus the old gentleman ended his harangue. The people heard it, and approved the doctrine; and immediately practised the contrary, just as if it had been a common sermon; for the auction opened, and they began to buy extravagantly. I found the good man had thoroughly studied my Almanacs, and digested all I had dropped on these topics during the course of twenty-five years. The frequent mention he made of me must have tired any one else; but my vanity was wonderfully delighted with it, though I was conscious that not a tenth part of the wisdom was my own, which he ascribed to me, but rather the gleanings that I had made of the sense of all ages and nations. However, I resolved to be the better for the echo of it; and, though I had at first determined to buy stuff for a new coat, I went away resolved to wear my old one a little longer. Reader, if thou wilt do the same, thy profit will be as great as mine. I am, as ever, thine to serve thee,

RICHARD SAUNDERS.

(cited from *The Works of Benjamin Franklin,* ed.
by Jared Sparks. Philadelphia, Pennsylvania: Childs &
Peterson, 1840, vol. 2, pp. 94–103; italics in original)

PROVERB POEMS AND POPULAR SONGS

Proverbs do not only appear in prose and dramatic literature. They also play a considerable role in lyric poetry and in the lyrics of songs. Some poetical texts simply exemplify but one proverb in a didactic or critical fashion, employing the proverb as the title and citing it within the poetic text, as for example in Arthur Gillespie's song "*Absence* Makes the Heart Grow Fonder" (1900) or Susan Fromberg Schaeffer's poem "The Burnt *Child* Dreads the Fire" (1972). But there are also poems and songs of several stanzas in which the proverb title is repeated at the beginning and/or end of each stanza as a leitmotif. This is the case with such poems and songs as Alice Cary's "Hoe Your Own *Row*" (1849), Harry Clifton's "Paddle Your Own *Canoe*" (1866), and Vincent Godfrey Burns's "*Man* Doth not Live by Bread Alone" (1952). Some lines from popular songs have in fact become proverbs over time (see Barbour 1963), as for example the proverb "The *grass* is always greener on the other side of the fence" that originated with Raymond B. Egan's and Richard A. Whiting's humorous song "The *Grass* Is Always Greener in the Other Fellow's Yard" (1924; see Mieder 1993b).

While the proverb is usually cited in its standard form when used as a leitmotif, there is also W.H. Auden's poem "Leap Before You Look" (1940) that twists the wisdom of the traditional proverb "*Look* before you leap" around and encourages people to take the "leap" into absurdity (see Mieder 1989: 189–190). And Bob Dylan definitely has the proverb "A rolling *stone* gathers no moss" in mind in the lyrics of his song "Like a Rolling Stone" (1965), whose title alludes to the proverb and is repeated at the end of each stanza (see Mieder 1989: 211–213). And yet, such proverb allusions are nothing new, as can be seen from Emily Dickinson's short poem "Which Is Best?" (1865) with its play on the proverb "A *bird* in the hand is worth two in the bush" (see Barnes 1979).

In addition to these poems and songs that interpret but one proverb, texts can also be found in which several proverbs or proverbial expressions are combined into a meaningful message. One of the finest examples is the eleventh section of Carl Sandburg's epic poem "Good Morning, America" (1928), where Sandburg presents dozens of proverbs and proverbial expressions to characterize the United States as a country of immigrants by means of folk speech (see Mieder 1971). An even greater tour de force poem that consists of nothing but proverbial language is Arthur Guiterman's "Proverbial Tragedy" (1915). As this American poet twists and changes standard English proverbs into a proverbial montage, he succeeds in presenting a negative view of the world at the beginning of the First World War. Eighty years later, the modern poet Paul Muldoon once again assembled numerous fractured proverbs in his "sonnet" with the title "Symposium" (1995) to express in a (non)sensical fashion the contradictory views expressed at an intellectual gathering.

There is no need to mention every poem and song reproduced here, but these 11 chronologically arranged texts are ample proof that poets and songwriters delight in using proverbs (for additional texts see Mieder 1989: 171–221). In fact, proverb poetry and proverb songs go back to the Middle Ages, showing once again that the traditional or innovative use of proverbs is truly ubiquitous (see Doyle 1975; Mieder 1980 and 1988). And how could it be any different? After all, proverbs contain the wisdom of humankind and as such they add much metaphorical expressiveness to the indirect language of poetry and song.

Hoe Your Own Row (1849)

Alice Cary (1820–1871)

 I think there are some maxims
 Under the sun,
 Scarce worth preservation;
 But here, boys, is one
 So sound and so simple
 'Tis worth while to know;
 And all in the single line,
 "Hoe your own row!"

 If you want to have riches,
 And want to have friends,
 Don't trample the means down
 And look for the ends;
 But always remember
 Wherever you go,
 The wisdom of practicing
 "Hoe your own row!"

 Don't just sit and pray
 For increase of your store,
 But work; who will help himself,
 Heaven helps more.
 The weeds while you're sleeping,
 Will come up and grow,
 But if you would have the
 Full ear, you must hoe!

 Nor will it do only
 To hoe out the weeds,
 You must make your ground mellow
 And put in the seeds;
 Any when the young blade
 Pushes through, you must know
 There is nothing will strengthen
 Its growth like the hoe!

There's no use of saying
What will be, will be;
Once try it, my lack-brain,
And see what you'll see!
Why, just small potatoes,
And few in a row;
You'd better take hold then,
And honestly hoe!

A good many workers
I've known in my time—
Some builders of houses,
Some builders of rhyme;
And they that were prospered,
Were prospered, I know,
By the intent and meaning of
"Hoe your own row!"

I've known too, a good many
Idlers, who said,
"I've right to my living,
The world owes me bread!"
A *right!* lazy lubber!
A thousand times No!
'Tis his, and his only
Who hoes his own row.

(cited from Alice and Phoebe Cary, *Ballads for Little Folks*.
Boston: Houghton Mifflin, 1873, pp. 81–83)

Which Is Best? (1865)

Emily Dickinson (1830–1886)

Which is best? Heaven—
Or only Heaven to come
With that old Codicil of Doubt?
I cannot help esteem

The "Bird within the Hand"
Superior to the one
The "Bush" may yield me

Or may not
Too late to choose again.

(cited from *The Poems by Emily Dickinson*,
ed. by Thomas H. Johnson. Cambridge,
Massachusetts: Harvard University Press,
1951, 1955, 1963, 1979, vol. 2, p. 726)

Paddle Your Own Canoe (1865)

Harry Clifton (1832–1872), author

Martin Hobson (1833–1880), composer

> I've traveled about a bit in my time
> And of troubles I've seen a few,
> But I found it better in every clime
> To paddle my own canoe.
> My wants are small; I care not at all
> If my debts are paid when due;
> I drive away strife in the ocean of life
> While I paddle my own canoe.
>
> *Chorus:*
> Then love your neighbor as yourself,
> As the world you travel through.
> And never sit down with a tear or frown,
> But paddle your own canoe.
>
> I have no wife to bother my life,
> No lover to prove untrue;
> But the whole day long, with a laugh and a song,
> I paddle my own canoe.
>
> I rise with the lark, and from daylight till dark
> I do what I have to do;
> I'm careless of wealth if I've only the health
> To paddle my own canoe.
>
> It's all very well to depend on a friend,
> That is, if you've proved him true;
> But you'll find it better by far in the end
> To paddle your own canoe.

To borrow is dearer by far than to buy,
A maxim, though old, still true;
You never will sigh if you only will try
To paddle your own canoe.

If a hurricane rise in the mid-day skies
And the sun is lost to view,
Move steadily by, with a steadfast eye,
And paddle your own canoe.

The daisies that grow in the bright green fields
Are blooming so sweet for you;
So never sit down with a tear or a frown,
But paddle your own canoe.

> (cited from the sheet music of the song
> *Paddle Your Own Canoe,* lyrics by Harry Clifton,
> music by Martin Hobson. Philadelphia,
> Pennsylvania: W.R. Smith, 1865)

Absence Makes the Heart Grow Fonder (1900)

Arthur Gillespie (1868–1914)

Sweetheart I have grown so lonely,
Living thus away from you,
For I love you and you only;
Still I wonder if you're true.
I regret the harsh words spoken,
That I know have caused you pain,
And my heart is nearly broken,
Say you love me once again.

Chorus:
Absence makes the heart grow fonder,
That is why I long for you;
Lonely thro' the nights I ponder,
Wond'ring darling, if you're true.
Distance only lends enchantment,
Tho' the ocean waves divide,
Absence makes the heart grow fonder,
Longing to be near your side.

Has the love that once was dearer
Than all else to me grown cold?

Or has absence drawn us nearer,
To each other as of old?
Promise then you will not sever,
From the ties that bind us two.
Say you will be mine forever,
Tell me that you still are true.

(cited from 500 Songs that Made the All-Time Hit Parade,
ed. by Lyle Kenyon Engel. New York:
Bantam Books, 1964, p. 135)

A Proverbial Tragedy (1915)

Arthur Guiterman (1871–1943)

The Rolling Stone and the Turning Worm
And the Cat that Looked at a King
Set forth on the Road that Leads to Rome—
For Youth will have its Fling,
The Goose will lay the Golden Eggs,
The Dog must have his Day,
And Nobody locks the Stable Door
Till the Horse is stol'n away.

But the Rolling Stone, that was never known
To Look before the Leap
Plunged down the hill to the Waters Still
That run so dark, so deep;
And the leaves were stirred by the Early Bird
Who sought his breakfast where
He marked the squirm of the Turning Worm—
And the Cat was Killed by Care!

(cited from Arthur Guiterman, The Laughing Muse.
New York: Harper & Brothers, 1915, p. 16)

The Grass Is Always Greener in the Other Fellow's Yard (1924)

Raymond B. Egan (1890–1952), author

Richard A. Whiting (1891–1938), composer

Why do you wash your windows said Misses Haggerty
So I can watch the neighbors said Misses Hennessy

Cover illustration of sheet music publication of the song (1924).

They have a new piano She has a hat I like
Lots better things than I have so I took it up with Mike
The language that he used might seem amiss
Translated from profane it goes like this

1st Verse Chorus

Sure the Grass is always greener in the other fellow's yard
And the little row we have to hoe Seems mighty hard
You loved our little roadster Till O'Day's got their sedan
And now you call our roadster just an old tomato can
I can see where Pat is lucky as I look across the fence

And as like as not he thinks I've got more luck than sense
If we all could wear green glasses then it wouldn't be so hard
Just to see how green the grass is in our own back yard
The Grass is always greener in the other fellow's yard
And the little row we have to hoe Seems mighty hard
You always see the fine clothes Maggie's hangin' on her back
And never see the mortgage that is hangin' on their shack
Mike is buying fancy bonnets just to decorate her dome
But he hasn't got a single drop of rye at home
Get the home brew and some glasses than it wouldn't be so hard
Just to see how green the grass is in our own back yard.
Maggie and Mike are married that may be why they fight
They dearly love to battle they're at it day and night
He's always praising some girl Who married someone else
Surely a lot of trouble started with their wedding bells
But there's one comeback that she loves to spring
And he shuts up each time she starts to sing

2nd Verse Chorus

Sure the Grass is always greener in the other fellow's yard
And the little row you have to hoe Seems mighty hard
You're mighty fond of Pat's wife Just because she isn't yours
And I tho't Pat was handsome till I found that he snores
While you love to knock my cooking and to praise each girl you see
Does it dawn on you there's husbands who rave over me
If you'd only wear green glasses then it wouldn't be so hard
Just to see how green the grass is in our own back yard
The Grass is always greener in the other fellow's yard
And the little row you have to hoe Seems mighty hard
You criticize my dresses 'Cause I made each one I've worn
If I wore what you bought me I could shock September Morn
When you stagger home some evening and you don't know who I am
And you start to sing that you are king of old Siam
After I remove your glasses explanations won't be hard
And you'll see how green the grass is in your own back yard.

(cited from the sheet music of the song *The Grass Is Always Greener
[In The Other Fellow's Yard]*, lyrics by Raymond B. Egan, music by
Richard A. Whiting. New York: Jerome H. Remick, 1924)

Takes Two to Tango (1952)

Al Hoffman (1902–1960), author

Dick Manning (born 1912), composer

Pearl Bailey (1918–1990), singer

> Takes two to tango, two to tango,
> Two to really get the feeling of romance.
> Let's do the tango, do the tango,
> Do the dance of love.
>
> You can sail in a ship by yourself,
> Take a nap or a nip by yourself.
> You can get into debt on your own.
> There are lots of things that you can do alone.
> (But it)
> Takes two to tango (etc.)
>
> You can croon to the moon by yourself.
> You can laugh like a loon by yourself.
> Spend the lot, go to pot on your own.
> There are lots of things that you can do alone.
>
> (But it)
> Takes two to tango (etc.)

> (cited from the sheet music of the song *Takes Two to Tango*,
> lyrics by Al Hoffman, music by Dick Manning.
> New York: Harman Music, 1952)

Man Doth not Live by Bread Alone (1952)

Vincent Godfrey Burns (1893–1979)

> Man doth not live by bread alone
> But by each elevating thought
> By which his ship of life is wrought;
> Each harbor light however dim
> That makes life's broad sea plain to him
> Is like a searchlight from the throne—
> Man doth not live by bread alone.

Man doth not live by bread alone
But by those truths which greatly feed
His hungering soul's deep spirit-need,
By inward music sweet and clear
That tunes with joy his inner ear;
Give man the food of soul, not stone—
He doth not live by bread alone.

Man doth not live by bread alone,
He hath a hunger of the heart
And cannot walk from man apart;
No living human long can stand
Without the grasp of friendly hand,
The touch, the fellowship, the voice
That make the lonely heart rejoice;
Love all our sorrows can atone—
Man doth not live by bread alone.

(cited from Vincent Godfrey Burns, *Redwood and Other Poems.*
Washington, D.C.: New World Books, 1952, p. 114)

The Burnt Child Dreads the Fire (1972)

Susan Fromberg Schaeffer (born 1941)

The burnt child dreads the fire.
So does the toast, and the match.
The burnt match dreads the child.
Those miserable creatures,

They can cremate a whole box at a time.
It is a great conflagration,
Little flames waving their victory flags.
Doesn't anyone worry about them?

Not to mention the little burning
Stomachs of Edison ovens,
What they suffer every day,
And the heart-burn

Under the hoods of the cars.
And the candles, the beautiful candles,

The lovely manicured fingers
On altars, melting themselves down

In prayer.
I tell you, *everything* dreads the fire.
And I will cry over spilt milk
As if I were spilt milk

Until they all are put out
And I tell you
You don't have the slightest idea
Of what it all means.

> (cited from Susan Fromberg Schaeffer, "Proverbs," *Poetry*, 120, no. 1
> [April 1972], pp. 6–11 [this poem on pp. 10–11])

Symposium (1995)

Paul Muldoon (born 1951)

> You can bring a horse to water but you can't make it hold
> its nose to the grindstone and hunt with the hounds.
> Every dog has a stitch in time. Two heads? You've been sold
> one good turn. One good turn deserves a bird in the hand.
>
> A bird in the hand is better than no bread.
> To have your cake is to pay Paul.
> Make hay while you can still hit the nail on the head.
> For want of a nail the sky might fall.
>
> People in glass houses can't see the wood
> for the new broom. Rome wasn't built between two stools.
> Empty vessels wait for no man.
>
> A hair of the dog is a friend indeed.
> There's no fool like the fool
> who's shot his bolt. There's no smoke after the horse is gone.

> (cited from Paul Muldoon, *Hay*. New York: Farrar,
> Straus and Giroux, 1998, p. 27)

Exception (2001)

David R. Slavitt (born 1935)

But, in the land of the blind,
where the one-eyed man is king,
when he wears the emperor's new clothes,
he can get away with it.

(cited from David R. Slavitt, *Falling from Silence. Poems.*
Baton Rouge, Louisiana: Louisiana State
University Press, 2001, p. 11)

PROVERBS IN CARICATURES, CARTOONS, AND COMICS

The pictorialization of proverbs began during the Middle Ages, when metaphorical proverbs were illustrated in woodcuts and misericords. But proverbs were also depicted in engravings and emblems, with Pieter Bruegel the Elder's oil painting *Netherlandish Proverbs* (1559) and its more than 100 individual proverb scenes representing the ultimate achievement in this long iconographic tradition (see the numerous studies in Mieder and Sobieski 1999). Even the use of proverbs as satirical caricatures or humorous cartoons goes back at least to the seventeenth century, and certainly by the beginning of the nineteenth century sequences of framed images based on proverbs foreshadow the comic strips of today.

This tradition of illustrating proverbs for the purpose of humorous, ironical, or satirical commentaries on the sociopolitical life has been maintained by modern artists (see Mieder 1989: 277–292). They too delight in depicting common proverbs like "Strike while the *iron* is hot," "The early *bird* gets the worm," or "Too many *cooks* spoil the broth." For some proverbs there exists an iconographic history from medieval to modern times that comprises dozens of woodcuts, misericords, emblems, paintings, caricatures, cartoons, and comic strips, including also various types of illustrated greeting cards. Usually the modern illustrations have captions to assure meaningful communication, but there are also proverb depictions that merely allude to the proverb or that exclude any caption whatsoever. In the latter case the cartoonist expects viewers to understand the proverbial message from the picture alone, something that is perfectly possible if the proverb is in fact well known.

Even though the proverbs in the captions are at times cited traditionally, their texts are for the most part slightly changed in order to create the humor or satire that is underscored by their depiction in the caricature or cartoon (see Bryant 1951). But be that as it may, it certainly is not difficult to find such proverb depictions in magazines and newspapers, commenting as it were with image and text on literally all social issues. While caricatures in newspapers usually refer to social and political problems, proverb illustrations in the comics section stress the humorous side of life. Single-frame series like *Family Circus, Dennis, the Menace,* and *The Far Side* abound with proverbs (see Winick 1998: 217–283), and comic strips like *Peanuts, Hi and Lois,* and *Beetle Bailey* are frequently based on more than one proverb. It would certainly be erroneous to assume that proverb illustrations find their way primarily into conservative publications owing to the didactic and sapient nature of proverbs. Nothing could be further from the truth, for sophisticated magazines or newspapers like the *New Yorker* and the *New York Times* abound with proverbial caricatures and cartoons. The same is true for *Playboy,* for example, where such proverb depictions are employed for sexual humor. I have been able to collect many references from various languages and cultures over the years, with my international proverb archive containing about 7,500 proverb illustrations of various types. Here are at least a few chronologically arranged representative examples, showing that metaphorical proverbs are in fact verbalized pictures that lend themselves well as humorous or serious commentaries on the human condition in an ever-changing world.

"*Good morning.*"

Proverb: "The early *bird* gets the worm." *New Yorker* (May 3, 1958), p. 43.

"A bird in the hand, Julius. . . ."

Proverb: "A *bird* in the hand is worth two in the bush." *Playboy* (May 1969), p. 245.

Proverb: "An *apple* a day keeps the doctor away." Hallmark Contemporary Cards (purchased in December 1977, Burlington, VT). Peanuts © United Feature Syndicate, Inc.

"*We do things a little differently around here, Haskell. If at first you don't succeed, you're fired.*"

Proverb: "If at first you don't *succeed*, try, try, again." *New Yorker* (April 17, 1978), p. 34.

"*Where there's a will there's a loophole!*"

Proverb: "Where there is a *will*, there is a way." Cited in *Punch* (June 14, 1978), p. 1017. Reproduced with permission of Punch Ltd.

Proverb: "The love of *money* is the root of all evil." Cited in *Brattleboro* [Vermont] *Reformer* (February 28, 1981), p. 14. Reprinted with special permission of King Features Syndicate.

"Be careful and look out for curiosity!"

Proverb: "*Curiosity* killed the cat." Cited in *Brattleboro* [Vermont] *Reformer* (November 8, 1988), p. 9. Reprinted with special permission of King Features Syndicate.

"Opportunity keeps knocking at my door . . . but by the time I
unlock the dead bolt and two keylocks, unlatch the chain,
and shut off the burglar alarm, it's gone."

Proverb: "*Opportunity* knocks but once." *Better Homes and Gardens*
(September 1981), p. 184.

Proverb: "A *dog* is man's best friend." *New Yorker* (February 22, 1988),
p. 96.

"Garbage in, garbage out!"

Proverb: "*Garbage* in, garbage out." *New Yorker* (August 23, 1993), p. 60.

Proverb: "If you can't stand the *heat*, get out of the kitchen." Cited in *Burlington* [Vermont] *Free Press* (April 4, 1994), p. 6A. Reprinted with special permission of King Features Syndicate.

HI AND LOIS

Proverb: "April *showers* bring May flowers." Cited in *Burlington* [Vermont] *Free Press* (April 28, 1999), p. 4C. Reprinted with special permission of King Features Syndicate.

FAMILY CIRCUS

"If I ever get a gift horse, I promise not to look in its mouth."

Proverb: "Don't look a *gift horse* in the mouth." Cited in *Burlington* [Vermont] *Free Press* (September 22, 2000), p. 5C. Reprinted with special permission of King Features Syndicate.

PROVERBS AND THE WORLD OF ADVERTISING

Proverbs have been an intricate part of the persuasive if not manipulative tactics of advertisements for a long time. Copywriters noted decades ago that the authority and truth inherent in proverbs could easily be exploited as advertising headlines. In order to add even more convincing power to such proverbial slogans, they often use biblical proverbs, thus putting an almost sacrosanct claim of high value on the advertised product. While such traditional use of proverbs continues in advertisements to the present day, the modern proverbial slogans tend to be based on different strategies. Proverbs are more often than not twisted into innovative formulations based on puns that act as attention-getters. An eye-catching picture and relatively little precise information do the rest to push the reader and viewer into a purchasing decision (Mieder 1989: 293–315; Winick 1998: 163–216).

Another reason for the frequent use of proverbs or proverbial structures as advertising slogans lies in the fact that their messages need to be communicated in clear and short sentences. Proverbs certainly satisfy the demand for conciseness and simplicity, but even more importantly, they inspire trustworthiness in the advertised product by awakening positive traditional feelings in the consumer. After all, proverbs contain apparent truths and merchants supposedly want to tell the truth about their products. The authority of generations speaks through proverbs, and they are thus perfectly suited to be employed as large headlines. It is a known fact that the headline or slogan is the most important single element of an advertisement, for usually five times as many people read the headline as read the explanatory text. Little wonder, then, that most advertisements consist of a large headline and an illustration rather than detailed verbal descriptions.

While many advertisements contain traditional or twisted proverbs as headlines, copywriters have also attempted to create proverb-like slogans that will be memorable and recognizable. For this reason their slogans are based on the same markers as proverbs, to wit alliteration, parallelism, rhyme, ellipsis, and so on (Powers 1933). The difference between the slogan and the proverb lies therefore not so much in form but rather in the intended message. The slogan is a more narrow statement of a particular advertising theme, whereas the proverb expresses a generalized truth (Mieder and Mieder 1977). This is especially the case when the name of a product appears in the proverbial slogan, as is the case with the following Coca-Cola slogans based on proverbs: "All *roads* lead by Coca-Cola signs" (1929), "Thirst *come*—thirst served" (1932), "Where there's Coca-Cola, there's hospitality" (1935), and "Coca-Cola: A chore's best friend" (1936). But there are also such slogans as "It's the real thing" (1942) and "Things go better with Coke" (1963), that were not based on proverbs and their structures but that certainly have taken on a proverbial character.

In a culture where the mass media have a constant presence, advertisements play an incredible communicative role. They certainly represent a fertile ground for the traditional and innovative use of proverbs and are ample proof that proverbs and twisted anti-proverbs are part of modern communication. But advertisements are not only tradition bearers of proverbial wisdom, they also help to create new proverbs, to wit "A *picture* is worth a thousand words" that was coined by Fred Barnard in 1921 as a slogan to argue for the need of eye-catching pictures in good advertisements. By now the slogan has become a proverb that expresses a basic truth about modern societies with their stress on visual communication (see Mieder 1990). There are many other examples of this process from advertising slogans to new proverbs (see Barrick 1986), and the wide and fast dissemination of these messages via the mass media helps to establish them as bona fide proverbs of the modern age.

Proverb: "One man's *meat* is another man's poison." *Gourmet* (September 1974), p. 69.

Different Volks for different folks.

VW Super Beetle

While most prices have gone up, up, up, the Beetle's has stayed the same, same, sam only $2825* fully equipped.

412 Sedan

Simply can't do without plush wall-to-wall carpeting, fuel injection, or an automatic tran mission? Fret not. They're all standard on the luxurious 412. And our Special End-of-Ye prices†make it even more affordable.

Dasher

Granted $4,000 is $4,000.* But it's also a small price to pay for what POPULAR MECHANI calls "...a perfect combination of styling and engineering."

The "Thing"

The cost of every "Thing" has just gone down from $3150 to $2775.* And it seems ev less expensive when you compare it to the price of a Jeep, Land Rover or Land Cruiser.

When inflation hits you, folks, you can't do better than a Volks.

*Suggested Retail Prices P.O.E. Super Beetle $2825, Dasher 2-dr sedan $3975, 181 "Thing" $2775 (West Coast prices slightly higher for r models) Local taxes and any other dealer delivery charges additional.
†Available at participating dealers.

Proverb: "Different *strokes* for different folks." Cited in *Time* (December 16, 1974), p. 31. Reprinted with permission of Volkswagen of America.

MAN DOES NOT LIVE BY TOAST ALONE.

Feast your eyes on the new GE Ultra Oven Broiler.
It not only toasts your daily bread but can cook up most anything you can dream up.
Tall orders like hamburgers, chicken or steaks are easy as pie to make because of its roomy (10"x13"x4") interior. Short orders like grilled cheese or bacon are done in a jiffy, too.

The Ultra Oven defrosts frozen foods and features a unique cake-bake setting.
It even has a slide-back top to keep muffins, buns and dinner rolls warm.
So if it takes more than toast to tickle your fancy, start cooking with the new General Electric Ultra Oven Broiler. After all, variety is the spice of life.

WE BRING GOOD THINGS TO LIFE.

Proverb: "*Man* does not live by bread alone." Cited in *Women's Day* (December 13, 1983), p. 51. Reprinted with permission of General Electric.

Two dips are better than one.

Brach's Chocolate Covered Peanuts and Peanut Clusters are America's number one favorites. Partly because we individually inspect each and every peanut.

And then, fresh roast only the very best to perfection.

But the clincher is that each peanut gets dipped not once, but twice in Brach's own rich, real creamy milk chocolate.

So for double-delicious chocolate covered peanuts, treat yourself to number one.

Nobody treats America like Brach's.

Proverb: "Two *heads* are better than one." Cited in *Women's Day* (December 13, 1983), p. 184.

The pen is mightier than the sword.

Proverb: "The *pen* is mightier than the sword." Cited in *Los Angeles Times* (December 13, 1987), p. 32.

A pfennig saved is a pfennig earned.

Fox Trying to economize? Who isn't. Trouble is, if you buy cheap, you usually get cheap.
The other side of the coin? If you buy smart, you get a Volkswagen.
The car that lends panache to practicality. And loads of fun to frugality. Take our Fox.

It has the stuff Volkswagens are made of.
Front disc brakes, 4-wheel independent suspension and a 1.8-liter fuel-injected engine.
So besides being a car you can afford to drive, it's one you'd actually want to.
No wonder Car and Driver advised those shopping for a

car for under $10,000 to put the Fox on their short list.
Of course, you could always get a car for a little less. But then you'd run the risk of getting less of a car.
And wouldn't that be pfennig wise and pound foolish?
German engineering. The Volkswagen way.

Proverb: "A *penny* saved is a penny earned." Cited in *New Yorker* (May 22, 1989), back cover. Reprinted with permission of Volkswagen of America.

Proverb: "*Absence* makes the heart grow fonder." Cited in *New Yorker* (February 14, 1994), back cover.

NOT ONLY ABSENCE MAKES THE HEART GROW FONDER.

Sometimes all it takes is a little something sublimely delicious and rapturously wrapped to bring out the passion in a certain someone's soul. Stop in or call 1-800-643-1579

GODIVA
Chocolatier

Proverb: "*Waste* not, want not." Cited in *Parade Magazine* (April 17, 1994), p. 10.

Proverb: "*Been* there, done that." Cited in *Playboy* (September 1998), p. 42.

PROVERBS AS HEADLINES AND SLOGANS

Journalists have long ago discovered the usefulness and effectiveness of proverbial headlines. Placed at the beginning of an article in large and bold print, they summarize the content of a newspaper or magazine article into an interpretive and emotionalized image. As with advertising slogans, traditional proverbs or their innovative variations serve as attention-getters to get readers to stop and actually read the following article. While the proverb of the headline does not deal with specifics, the subtitle usually zeroes in on the actual topic. For example, the headline might simply read "A new *broom* sweeps clean," while the subtitle states "New president makes major structural changes," with the article discussing the details of the innovations. The subject matter of the articles does not appear to be of any consequence in this matter. Journalists simply delight in citing traditional proverbs that are short enough to fit into a one-line headline. If they exceed the limited space, they are quickly shortened into mere allusions that will be understood by most readers. But above all, journalists enjoy "playing" with proverbs, creating revealing anti-proverbs that will get the attention of the readers, who then want to read the entire article (Alexander 1986; McKenna 1996; Mieder 1993: 58–97). Such proverbial headlines can be found in all sections of newspapers and magazines, from politics and economics to sports and entertainment. This play with proverbial language can go so far that up to three headlines based on proverbs and proverbial expressions can be found on just one page, including sophisticated newspapers like the *New York Times* and the *Wall Street Journal.*

It should also be noted that journalists and freelance writers like writing popular essays on various aspects of proverbs. There are numerous essays that deal with the origin, meaning, and value of proverbs. Usually such essays question the wisdom of proverbs, pointing to such contradictory pairs as "You're never too old to *learn*" and "You can't teach an old *dog* new tricks." And yet, these essays in the mass media show that people continue to be fascinated by the ubiquitous proverbs, realizing very well that they are part and parcel of everyday communication (Mieder 1993: 18–40). And besides, who would not be interested in knowing, for example, that the splendid slogan "When it *rains,* it pours" first appeared in 1914 to advertise the fact that the Morton Salt Company had developed a salt that would pour out of a package even in humid weather. The slogan was based on the eighteenth-century proverb "It never *rains* but it pours," but today the advertising slogan has basically pushed the proverb aside. While packages of Morton's Salt still exhibit the slogan together with the little umbrella girl and her salt container in the rain, the slogan-turned-proverb has taken on a life of its own. Most speakers today are not necessarily identifying its message and wisdom with the original advertisement any longer when they comment on situations that have nothing to do with pouring salt but rather with problems or inconveniences that appear to be making a bad situation even worse.

Mention should also be made that proverbs and their structures are used in graffiti, on bumper stickers, and of course also on that ubiquitous T-shirt with its proverbial slogans. Many of them contain political and socioeconomic messages, while maintaining the structure and some of the basic wording of the original proverb. There is much satire, irony, humor, wordplay, and at times nonsense in these modern anti-proverbs. Some of them also exhibit aggressive, scatological, obscene, sexual, and defiant messages (see Dundes 1966; Nierenberg 1983; Williams 1991; Tóthné Litovkina 1999). In fact, proverbial graffiti on the Berlin Wall, bridge abutments, walls, subway cars, or bathrooms are a revolt of sorts against the rationality, conformity, and moral standards of the traditional proverbial rules and the social mores that they represent. The parodies of proverbs scrawled on walls can also be purchased as innovative bumper stickers and T-shirts, which are popular in many parts of the world (Oledzki 1979; Mato 1994). All of these modern anti-proverbs are clear indications that proverbs contain impressive regenerational powers, with some of these innovative formulations reaching proverbial status in due time.

Proverb: "*Hope* springs eternal." Cited in *Time* (April 26, 1976), front cover.

Proverb: "*Blood* is thicker than water." Graffiti on the Berlin Wall (1980s). Terry Tillman, *The Writings on the Wall. Peace at the Berlin Wall.* Santa Monica, CA: 22/7 Publishing Co., 1990, p. 31.

ACTIONS SPEAK LOUDER THAN BUMPERSTICKERS

Proverb: "*Actions* speak louder than words." *Northern Sun Company* (purchased in July 2001 at Burlington, Vermont).

Proverb: "When it *rains* it pours." Cited from Brad Herzog, "They're Gr-r-reat! From Fast Food to Fast Shoes, Icons are Everything." *US Airways Attaché* (August 1999), p. 57 (entire article on pp. 54–59).

SELECTED BIBLIOGRAPHY

Book-length studies are listed in the major bibliography at the end of this book. Cross-references at the ends of entries correspond to collections listed in the bibliography.

Alexander, Richard. 1986. "Article Headlines in *The Economist*. An Analysis of Puns, Allusions and [Proverbial] Metaphors." *Arbeiten aus Anglistik und Amerikanistik* 11: 159–187.

Barbour, Frances M. 1963. "Some Uncommon Sources of Proverbs." *Midwest Folklore* 13: 97–100.

Barnes, Daniel R. 1979. "Telling It Slant: Emily Dickinson and the Proverb." *Genre* 12: 219–241; also in Mieder 1994: 439–465.

Barrick, Mac E. 1986. "'Where's the Beef'?" *Midwestern Journal of Language and Folklore* 12: 43–46.

Bryant, Margaret M. 1951. "Proverbial Lore in American Life and Speech." *Western Folklore* 10: 134–142.

Doyle, Charles C. 1975. "On Some Proverbial Verses." *Proverbium,* no. 25: 979–982.

Dundes, Alan. 1966. "Here I Sit—A Study of American Latrinalia." *The Kroeber Anthropological Society Papers,* no. 34: 91–105.

Gallacher, Stuart A. 1949. "Franklin's *Way to Wealth:* A Florilegium of Proverbs and Wise Sayings." *Journal of English and Germanic Philology* 48: 229–251.

Mato, Daniel. 1994. "Clothed in Symbols: Wearing Proverbs." *Passages: A Chronicle of the Humanities* 7: 4–5, 9, 11–12.

McKenna, Kevin J. 1996. "Proverbs and *Perestroika:* An Analysis of *Pravda* Headlines, 1988–1991." *Proverbium* 13: 215–233.

Meister, Charles W. 1952–1953. "Franklin as a Proverb Stylist." *American Literature* 24: 157–166.

Mieder, Barbara and Wolfgang. 1977. "Tradition and Innovation: Proverbs in Advertising." *Journal of Popular Culture* 11: 308–319; also in Mieder and Dundes 1981 (1994): 309–322.

Mieder, Wolfgang. 1971. "'Behold the Proverbs of a People': A Florilegium of Proverbs in Carl Sandburg's Poem *Good Morning, America.*" *Southern Folklore Quarterly* 35: 160–168.

———. 1980. "A Sampler of Anglo-American Proverb Poetry." *Folklore Forum* 13: 39–53.

———. 1988. "Proverbs in American Popular Songs." *Proverbium* 5: 85–101.

———. 1990. "'A Picture is Worth a Thousand Words': From Advertising Slogan to American Proverb." *Southern Folklore* 40: 207–225; also in Mieder 1993: 135–151.

———. 1993a. "'Early to Bed and Early to Rise': From Proverb to Benjamin Franklin and Back." In *Proverbs Are Never Out of Season: Popular Wisdom in the Modern Age,* by W. Mieder, 98–134. New York: Oxford University Press; also in Mieder 2000b: 69–108.

———. 1993b. "'The Grass Is Always Greener on the Other Side of the Fence': An American Proverb of Discontent." *Proverbium* 10: 151–184, also in Mieder 1994: 515–542.

———. 1995. "'Make Hell While the Sun Shines': Proverbial Rhetoric in Winston Churchill's *The Second World War.*" *Folklore* (London) 106: 57–69; also in Mieder 1997: 39–66 and 200–206 (notes).

———. 1998. "'Conventional Phrases Are a Sort of Fireworks': Charles Dickens's Proverbial Language." *Proverbium* 15: 179–199; also considerably longer in Mieder 2000b: 145–170.

———. 1999. "'Man Is a Wolf to Man': Proverbial Dialectics in the Works of Bertolt Brecht." *Proverbium* 16: 247–277; also in Mieder 2000b: 237–264.

———. 2000a. "'A Man of Fashion Never Has Recourse to Proverbs': Lord Chesterfield's Tilting at Proverbial Windmills." *Folklore* 111: 23–42; also in Mieder 2000b: 35–68.

———. 2000b. "'Behind the Clouds the Sun Is Shining': Abraham Lincoln's Proverbial Fight Against Slavery." In *A voz popular: Estudos de ethnolinguística,* ed. by Gabriele Funk, 123–137. Cascais, Portugal: Patrimónia.

Nierenberg, Jess. 1983. "Proverbs in Graffiti: Taunting Traditional Wisdom." *Maledicta* 7: 41–58; also in Mieder 1994: 543–561.

Oledzki, Jacek. 1979. "On Some Maxims [Proverbs] on African Cars." *Africana Bulletin* 28: 29–35.

Powers, Marsh K. 1933. "Proverbs as Copy-Patterns." *Printers' Ink* 164 (August 17): 24–26.

Tóthné Litovkina, Anna. 1999. "If You Are not Interested in Being Healthy, Wealthy and Wise—How about Early to Bed? Sexual Proverb Transformations." *Semiotische Berichte* 23: 387–412.

Vinken, P.J. 1958. "Some Observations on the Symbolism of 'The Broken Pot' in Art and Literature." *American Imago* 15: 149–174.

Williams, Fionnuala. 1991. "'To Kill Two Birds with One Stone': Variants in a War of Words." *Proverbium* 8: 199–201.

Zick, Gisela. 1969. "Der zerbrochene Krug als Bildmotiv des 18. Jahrhunderts." *Wallraf-Richartz Jahrbuch* 31: 149–204.

Bibliography

This bibliography is divided into seven sections on major book-length studies and comprehensive collections that have appeared for the most part in the English language. Included are sections on Bibliographies, Proverb Journals, Major Proverb Studies, Multilingual Proverb Collections, Bilingual Proverb Collections [with English as the target language], Anglo-American Proverb Collections, and Regional and Thematic Proverb Collections. Additional bibliographical references from journal articles or essay volumes are cited at the end of the four major sections of this book. For the vast international proverb scholarship in numerous languages see above all Wolfgang Mieder, *International Proverb Scholarship: An Annotated Bibliography*, 4 vols. (New York: Garland Publishing, 1982, 1990, 1993; and New York: Peter Lang, 2001).

BIBLIOGRAPHIES

Bernstein, Ignace. 1900 (2003). *Catalogue des livres parémiologiques.* 2 vols. Varsovie, Poland: W. Drugulin; repr. ed. by Wolfgang Mieder. Hildesheim, Germany: Georg Olms.

Bonser, Wilfrid. 1930 (1967). *Proverb Literature: A Bibliography of Works Relating to Proverbs.* London: William Glaisher; repr. Nendeln/Liechtenstein: Kraus.

Bushui, Anatolii. 1978–1980. *Paremiologiia Uzbekistana.* 2 vols. Samarkand, Uzbekistan: Samarkandskii gosudarstvennyi pedagogicheskii institut.

De Caro, Francis A., and William K. McNeil. 1971. *American Proverb Literature: A Bibliography.* Bloomington: Folklore Forum, Indiana University.

Gratet-Duplessis, Pierre-Alexandre. 1847 (1969). *Bibliographie parémiologique.* Paris: Potier; repr. Nieuwkoop, Netherlands: B. de Graaf.

Jaime Goméz, José de, and José María Jaime Lorén. 1992. *Catalogo de bibliografia paremiologica española.* València, Spain: E.C.V.S.A.

Lengert, Joachim. 1999. *Romanische Phraseologie und Parömiologie: Eine teilkommentierte Bibliographie. (Von den Anfängen bis 1997)*. 2 vols. Tübingen, Germany: Gunter Narr.

Mieder, Wolfgang. 1977. *International Bibliography of Explanatory Essays on Individual Proverbs and Proverbial Expressions*. Bern: Peter Lang.

————. 1982–2001. *International Proverb Scholarship: An Annotated Bibliography*. 4 vols. New York: Garland Publishing, and New York: Peter Lang (vol. 4).

————. 1984. *Investigations of Proverbs, Proverbial Expressions, Quotations and Clichés: A Bibliography of Explanatory Essays Which Appeared in "Notes and Queries" (1849–1983)*. Bern: Peter Lang.

————. 1984–present. "International Bibliography of New and Reprinted Proverb Collections." Annual Bibliography in: *Proverbium: Yearbook of International Proverb Scholarship*.

————. 1984–present. "International Proverb Scholarship: An Updated Bibliography." Annual bibliography in: *Proverbium: Yearbook of International Proverb Scholarship*.

————. 1994. *African Proverb Scholarship: An Annotated Bibliography*. Colorado Springs, Colo.: African Proverbs Project.

Mieder, Wolfgang, and George B. Bryan. 1996. *Proverbs in World Literature: A Bibliography*. New York: Peter Lang.

Mieder, Wolfgang, and Janet Sobieski. 1998. *Proverb Iconography: An International Bibliography*. New York: Peter Lang.

————. 2003. *Proverbs and the Social Sciences: An Annotated International Bibliography*. Baltmannsweiler, Germany: Schneider Verlag Hohengehren.

Moll, Otto. 1958. *Sprichwörterbibliographie*. Frankfurt am Main: Vittorio Klostermann.

Urdang, Laurence, and Frank R. Abate. 1983. *Idioms and Phrases Index*. 3 vols. Detroit, Mich.: Gale Research Company.

PROVERB JOURNALS

Flonta, Teodor, et al., eds. 1995–2000. *De Proverbio: An Electronic Journal of International Proverb Studies,* 1–6. http://info.utas.edu.au/docs/flonta/.

Kuusi, Matti, et al., ed. 1965–1975. *Proverbium: Bulletin d'information sur les recherches parémiologiques,* nos. 1–25: 1–1008. Repr. ed. by Wolfgang Mieder. 2 vols. Bern: Peter Lang, 1987.

Mieder, Wolfgang, et al., ed. 1984–. *Proverbium: Yearbook of International Proverb Scholarship*.

Sevilla Muñoz, Julia, et al., eds. 1993–. *Paremia: Boletín de Investigaciones Paremiológicas*.

Voigt, Vilmos, et al., ed. 1980–1989. *Proverbium Paratum: Bulletin d'information sur les recherches parémiologiques,* nos. 1–4: 1–460.

MAJOR PROVERB STUDIES

Adéékó, Adélékè. 1998. *Proverbs, Textuality, and Nativism in African Literature.* Gainesville: University Press of Florida.

Alster, Bendt. 1997. *Proverbs of Ancient Sumer: The World's Earliest Proverb Collections.* 2 vols. Bethesda, Md.: CDL Press.

Anido, Naiade, ed. 1983. *Des proverbes...à l'affut.* Paris: Publications Langues'O.

Anscombre, Jean-Claude. 2000. *La parole proverbiale.* Paris: Larousse.

Barakat, Robert A. 1980. *A Contextual Study of Arabic Proverbs.* Helsinki: Suomalainen Tiedeakatemia.

Baur, Rupprecht S., and Christoph Chlosta, eds. 1995. *Von der Einwortmetapher zur Satzmetapher.* Bochum, Germany: Norbert Brockmeyer.

Baur, Rupprecht S., Christoph Chlosta, and Elisabeth Piirainen, eds. 1999. *Wörter in Bildern—Bilder in Wörtern: Beiträge zur Phraseologie und Sprichwortforschung.* Baltmannsweiler, Germany: Schneider Verlag Hohengehren.

Bluhm, Lothar, and Heinz Rölleke. 1997. *"Redensarten des Volkes, auf die ich immer horche": Märchen, Sprichwort, Redensart. Zur volkspoetischen Ausgestaltung der "Kinder- und Hausmärchen" durch die Brüder Grimm.* Stuttgart: S. Hirzel.

Brown, Warren S., ed. 2000. *Understanding Wisdom: Sources, Science, and Society.* Philadelphia: Templeton Foundation Press.

Bryan, George B. 1993. *Black Sheep, Red Herrings, and Blue Murder: The Proverbial Agatha Christie.* Bern: Peter Lang.

Bryan, George B., and Wolfgang Mieder. 1994. *The Proverbial Bernard Shaw: An Index to Proverbs in the Works of George Bernard Shaw.* Westport, Conn.: Greenwood Press.

———. 1995. *The Proverbial Eugene O'Neill: An Index to Proverbs in the Works of Eugene Gladstone O'Neill.* Westport, Conn.: Greenwood Press.

———. 1997. *The Proverbial Charles Dickens: An Index to Proverbs in the Works of Charles Dickens.* New York: Peter Lang.

Bryant, Margaret M. 1945. *Proverbs and How to Collect Them.* Greensboro, N.C.: American Dialect Society.

Burger, Harald, Annelies Häcki Buhofer, and Gertrud Gréciano, eds. 2003. *Flut von Texten – Vielfalt von Kulturen. Ascona 2001 zur Methodologie und Kulturspezifik der Phraseologie.* Baltmannsweiler, Germany: Schneider Verlag Hohengehren.

Burger, Harald, Annelies [Häcki] Buhofer, and Ambros Sialm, eds. 1982. *Handbuch der Phraseologie.* Berlin: Walter de Gruyter.

Burrell, Brian. 1997. *The Words We Live By: The Creeds, Mottoes, and Pledges that Have Shaped America.* New York: The Free Press.

Cacciari, Cristina, and Patrizia Tabossi, eds. 1993. *Idioms: Processing, Structure, and Interpretation.* Hillsdale, N.J.: Lawrence Erlbaum Associates.

Calvez, Daniel. 1989. *Le langage proverbial de Voltaire dans sa correspondance (1704–1769).* New York: Peter Lang.

Carnes, Pack, ed. 1988. *Proverbia in Fabula: Essays on the Relationship of the Fable and the Proverb.* Bern: Peter Lang.

Cauvin, Jean. 1981. *Comprendre: Les proverbes.* Issy les Moulineaux, France: Les Classiques Africains.

Chlosta, Christoph, Peter Grzybek, and Elisabeth Piirainen, eds. 1994. *Sprachbilder zwischen Theorie und Praxis.* Bochum, Germany: Norbert Brockmeyer.

Colombi, Maria Cecilia. 1989. *Los refranes en el "Quijote": Texto y contexto.* Potomac, Md.: Scripta Humanistica.

Combet, Louis. 1971. *Recherches sur le "refranero" castillan.* Paris: Société d'édition "Les Belles Lettres."

Conca, Maria. 1987. *Paremiologia.* València, Spain: Universitat de València.

Cornette, James C. 1942 (1997). *Proverbs and Proverbial Expressions in the German Works of Martin Luther.* Diss. University of North Carolina at Chapel Hill. Posthumously ed. by Wolfgang Mieder and Dorothee Racette. Bern: Peter Lang.

Corpas Pastor, Gloria, ed. 2000. *Las lenguas de Europa: Estudios de fraseología, fraseografía y traducción.* Albolote, Spain: Comares.

Cowie, A.P., ed. 1998. *Phraseology: Theory, Analysis, and Applications.* Oxford: Clarendon Press.

Deskis, Susan E. 1996. *"Beowulf" and the Medieval Proverb Tradition.* Tempe: Arizona State University.

Dobrovol'skij, Dmitrij. 1988. *Phraseologie als Objekt der Universalienlinguistik.* Leipzig, Germany: Verlag Enzyklopädie.

Donker, Marjorie. 1992. *Shakespeare's Proverbial Themes: A Rhetorical Context for the "Sententia" as "Res."* Westport, Conn.: Greenwood Press.

Dundes, Alan. 1984 (1989). *Life Is Like a Chicken Coop Ladder: A Portrait of German Culture Through Folklore.* New York: Columbia University Press; repr. Detroit, Mich.: Wayne State University Press.

Dundes, Alan, and Claudia A. Stibbe. 1981. *The Art of Mixing Metaphors: A Folkloristic Interpretation of the "Netherlandish Proverbs" by Pieter Bruegel the Elder.* Helsinki: Suomalainen Tiedeakatemia.

Ďurčo, Peter, ed. 1998. *Europhras 97: Phraseology and Paremiology.* Bratislava, Czech Republic: Akadémia PZ.

Eismann, Wolfgang, ed. 1998. *Europhras 95: Europäische Phraseologie im Vergleich: Gemeinsames Erbe und kulturelle Vielfalt.* Bochum, Germany: Norbert Brockmeyer.

Everaert, Martin, Erik-Jan van der Linden, André Shenk, and Rob Schreuder, eds. 1995. *Idioms: Structural and Psychological Perspectives.* Hillsdale, N.J.: Lawrence Erlbaum Associates.

Fabian, Johannes. 1990. *Power and Performance: Ethnographic Explorations through Proverbial Wisdom and Theater in Shaba, Zaire.* Madison: University of Wisconsin Press.

Fleischer, Wolfgang. 1997. *Phraseologie der deutschen Gegenwartssprache.* Tübingen, Germany: Max Niemeyer.

Földes, Csaba. 1996. *Deutsche Phraseologie kontrastiv: Intra- und interlinguale Zugänge.* Heidelberg: Julius Groos.

Fontaine, Carole R. 1982. *Traditional Sayings in the Old Testament: A Contextual Study.* Sheffield: Almond Press.

Frank, Grace, and Dorothy Miner. 1937. *Proverbes en Rimes: Text and Illustrations of the Fifteenth Century from a French Manuscript in the Walters Art Gallery, Baltimore.* Baltimore: Johns Hopkins Press.

Gläser, Rosemarie. 1986. *Phraseologie der englischen Sprache.* Leipzig, Germany: Verlag Enzyklopädie.

Glucksberg, Sam. 2001. *Understanding Figurative Language: From Metaphors to Idioms.* Oxford: Oxford University Press.

González Rey, Isabel. 2002. *La phraséologie du français.* Toulouse, France: Presses Universitaires du Mirail.

Grauls, Jan. 1957. *Volkstaal en volksleven in het werk van Pieter Bruegel.* Antwerpen, Belgium: N.V. Standaard-Boekhandel.

Gréciano, Gertrud. 1983. *Signification et dénotation en allemand: La sémantique des expressions idiomatiques.* Paris: Librairie Klincksieck.

Gréciano, Gertrud, ed. 1989. *Europhras 88: Phraséologie contrastive.* Strasbourg: Université des Sciences Humaines.

Grzybek, Peter, ed. 2000. *Die Grammatik der sprichwörtlichen Weisheit von G.L. Permjakov.* Baltmannsweiler, Germany: Schneider Verlag Hohengehren.

Grzybek, Peter, and Wolfgang Eismann, eds. 1984. *Semiotische Studien zum Sprichwort. Simple Forms Reconsidered I.* Tübingen, Germany: Gunter Narr.

Häcki Buhofer, Annelies, Harald Burger, and Laurent Gautier, eds. 2001. *Phraseologiae Amor: Aspekte europäischer Phraseologie. Festschrift für Gertrud Gréciano.* Baltmannsweiler, Germany: Schneider Verlag Hohengehren.

Hain, Mathilde. 1951. *Sprichwort und Volkssprache: Eine volkskundlich-soziologische Dorfuntersuchung.* Gießen, Germany: Wilhelm Schmitz.

Hartmann, Dietrich, and Jan Wirrer, eds. 2002. *"Wer A sägt, muss auch B sägen": Beiträge zur Phraseologie und Sprichwortforschung.* Baltmannsweiler, Germany: Schneider Verlag Hohengehren.

Hasan-Rokem, Galit. 1982. *Proverbs in Israeli Folk Narratives: A Structural Semantic Analysis.* Helsinki: Suomalainen Tiedeakatemia.

Honeck, Richard P. 1997. *A Proverb in Mind: The Cognitive Science of Proverbial Wit and Wisdom.* Mahwah, N.J.: Lawrence Erlbaum Associates.

Hood, Edwin Paxton. 1885. *The World of Proverb and Parable.* London: Hodder & Stoughton.

Hulme, F. Edward. 1902 (1968). *Proverb Lore: Being a Historical Study of the Similarities, Contrasts, Topics, Meanings, and Other Facets of Proverbs, Truisms, and Pithy Sayings, as Expressed by the Peoples of Many Lands and Times.* London: Elliot Stock; repr. Detroit, Mich.: Gale Research Company.

Jolles, André. 1930 (1965). *Einfache Formen.* Tübingen, Germany: Max Niemeyer; repr. Tübingen, Germany: Max Niemeyer.

Kanyó, Zoltán. 1981. *Sprichwörter—Analyse einer Einfachen Form: Ein Beitrag zur generativen Poetik.* The Hague: Mouton.

Katz, Albert N., Cristina Cacciari, Raymond W. Gibbs, and Mark Turner. 1998. *Figurative Language and Thought*. New York: Oxford University Press.

Kerschen, Lois. 1998. *American Proverbs about Women: A Reference Guide*. Westport, Conn.: Greenwood Press.

Koch, Walter A., ed. 1994. *Simple Forms: An Encyclopaedia of Simple Text-Types in Lore and Literature*. Bochum, Germany: Norbert Brockmeyer.

Koller, Werner. 1977. *Redensarten: Linguistische Aspekte, Vorkommensanlysen, Sprachspiel*. Tübingen, Germany: Max Niemeyer.

Korhonen, Jarmo, ed. 1987. *Beiträge zur allgemeinen und germanistischen Phraseologieforschung*. Oulu, Finland: Oulun Yliopisto.

Krikmann, Arvo. 1974a (1984). *On Denotative Indefiniteness of Proverbs*. Tallinn, Estonia: Academy of Sciences of the Estonian SSR, Institute of Language and Literature; repr. in *Proverbium* 1: 47–91.

———. 1974b (1985). *Some Additional Aspects of Semantic Indefiniteness of Proverbs*. Tallinn, Estonia: Academy of Sciences of the Estonian SSR, Institute of Language and Literature; repr. in *Proverbium* 2: 58–85.

Kuusi, Matti. 1957a. *Parömiologische Betrachtungen*. Helsinki: Suomalainen Tiedeakatemia.

———. 1957b. *Regen bei Sonnenschein: Zur Weltgeschichte einer Redensart*. Helsinki: Suomalainen Tiedeakatemia.

———. 1972 (1972). *Towards an International Type-System of Proverbs*. Helsinki: Suomalainen Tiedeakatemia; also in *Proverbium* no. 19: 699–736.

Lakoff, George, and Mark Johnson. 1980. *Metaphors We Live By*. Chicago: University of Chicago Press.

Lauhakangas, Outi. 2001. *The Matti Kuusi International Type System of Proverbs*. Helsinki: Suomalainen Tiedeakatemia.

McKenna, Kevin J., ed. 1998. *Proverbs in Russian Literature: From Catherine the Great to Alexander Solzhenitsyn*. Burlington: The University of Vermont.

McKenzie, Alyce M. 1996. *Preaching Proverbs: Wisdom for the Pulpit*. Louisville, Ky.: Westminster John Knox Press.

Meadow, Mark. 2002. *Pieter Bruegel the Elder's "Netherlandish Proverbs" and the Practice of Rhetoric: Studies in Netherlandish Art and Cultural History*. Zwolle, Netherlands: Waanders Publications.

Mieder, Wolfgang. 1983. *Deutsche Sprichwörter in Literatur, Politik, Presse und Werbung*. Hamburg: Helmut Buske.

———. 1985. *Sprichwort, Redensart, Zitat: Tradierte Formelsprache in der Moderne*. Bern: Peter Lang.

———. 1987. *Tradition and Innovation in Folk Literature*. Hanover, N.H.: University Press of New England.

———. 1989. *American Proverbs: A Study of Texts and Contexts*. Bern: Peter Lang.

———. 1992. *Sprichwort—Wahrwort!? Studien zur Geschichte, Bedeutung und Funktion deutscher Sprichwörter*. Frankfurt am Main: Peter Lang.

———. 1993. *Proverbs Are Never Out of Season: Popular Wisdom in the Modern Age.* New York: Oxford University Press.

———. 1995a. *Deutsche Redensarten, Sprichwörter und Zitate: Studien zu ihrer Herkunft, Überlieferung und Verwendung.* Wien, Austria: Edition Praesens.

———. 1995b. *Sprichwörtliches und Geflügeltes: Sprachstudien von Martin Luther bis Karl Marx.* Bochum, Germany: Norbert Brockmeyer.

———. 1997. *The Politics of Proverbs: From Traditional Wisdom to Proverbial Stereotypes.* Madison: University of Wisconsin Press.

———. 2000a. *Aphorismen, Sprichwörter, Zitate: Von Goethe und Schiller bis Victor Klemperer.* Bern: Peter Lang.

———. 2000b. *Strategies of Wisdom: Anglo-American and German Proverb Studies.* Baltmannsweiler, Germany: Schneider Verlag Hohengehren.

———. 2000c. *The Proverbial Abraham Lincoln: An Index to Proverbs in the Works of Abraham Lincoln.* New York: Peter Lang.

———. 2001. *"No Struggle, No Progress": Frederick Douglass and His Proverbial Rhetoric for Civil Rights.* New York: Peter Lang.

———. 2002. *"Call a Spade a Spade": From Classical Phrase to Racial Slur.* New York: Peter Lang.

Mieder, Wolfgang, ed. 1978. *Ergebnisse der Sprichwörterforschung.* Bern: Peter Lang.

———. 1994. *Wise Words: Essays on the Proverb.* New York: Garland Publishing.

———. 2003. *Cognition, Comprehension, and Communication. A Decade of North American Proverb Studies (1990–2000).* Baltmannsweiler, Germany: Schneider Verlag Hohengehren.

Mieder, Wolfgang, and Alan Dundes, eds. 1981 (1994). *The Wisdom of Many: Essays on the Proverb.* New York: Garland Publishing; repr. Madison: University of Wisconsin Press.

Mieder, Wolfgang, and Deborah Holmes. 2000. *"Children and Proverbs Speak the Truth": Teaching Proverbial Wisdom to Fourth Graders.* Burlington: The University of Vermont.

Mieder, Wolfgang, and George B. Bryan. 1995. *The Proverbial Winston S. Churchill: An Index to Proverbs in the Works of Sir Winston Churchill.* Westport, Conn.: Greenwood Press.

———. 1997. *The Proverbial Harry S. Truman: An Index to Proverbs in the Works of Harry S. Truman.* New York: Peter Lang.

Naciscione, Anita. 2001. *Phraseological Units in Discourse: Towards Applied Stylistics.* Riga: Latvian Academy of Culture.

Newcomb, Robert. 1957. "The Sources of Benjamin Franklin's Sayings of Poor Richard." Diss. University of Maryland.

Norrick, Neal R. 1985. *How Proverbs Mean: Semantic Studies in English Proverbs.* Amsterdam: Mouton.

Nzambi, Philippe D. 1992. *Proverbes bibliques et proverbes kongo: Étude comparative de "Proverbia 25–29" et de quelques proverbes kongo.* Frankfurt am Main: Peter Lang.

O'Connor, Kathleen M. 1993. *The Wisdom Literature.* Collegeville, Minn.: The Liturgical Press.

Palm, Christine, ed. 1991. *Europhras 90: Akten der internationalen Tagung zur germanistischen Phraseologieforschung Aske/Schweden.* Uppsala: Acta Universitatis Upsaliensis.

Panofsky, Dora and Erwin Panofsky. 1956 (1978). *Pandora's Box: The Changing Aspects of a Mythical Symbol.* New York: Pantheon Books; repr. Princeton, N.J.: Princeton University Press.

Penfield, Joyce. 1983. *Communicating with Quotes [Proverbs]: The Igbo Case.* Westport, Conn.: Greenwood Press.

Permiakov, Gregorii L'vovich. 1970 (1979). *Ot pogovorki do skazki: Zametki po obshchei teorii klishe.* Moskva, Russia: Nauka. English translation by Y.N. Filippov as *From Proverb to Folk-Tale: Notes on the General Theory of Cliché.* Moscow: Nauka.

Permiakov, Grigorii L'vovich, ed. 1984 (1988). *Paremiologicheskie issledovaniia: Sbornik statei.* Moskva, Russia: Nauka. French translation by Victor Rosenzweig and Annette Taraillon as *Tel grain tel pain: Poétique de la sagesse populaire.* Moscou: Éditions de Progrès.

Perry, T.A. 1993. *Wisdom Literature and the Structure of Proverbs.* University Park: Pennsylvania State University Press.

Peukes, Gerhard. 1977. *Untersuchungen zum Sprichwort im Deutschen: Semantik, Syntax, Typen.* Berlin: Erich Schmidt.

Pfeffer J. Alan. 1948. *The Proverb in Goethe.* New York: King's Crown Press.

Pfeffer, Wendy. 1997. *Proverbs in Medieval Occitan Literature.* Gainesville: University Press of Florida.

Phillips, Margaret Mann. 1964. *The "Adages" of Erasmus: A Study with Translations.* Cambridge: Cambridge University Press.

Piirainen, Elisabeth and Ilpo Piirainen, eds. 2002. *Phraseologie in Raum und Zeit.* Baltmannsweiler, Germany: Schneider Verlag Hohengehren.

Pilz, Klaus Dieter. 1978. *Phraseologie: Versuch einer interdisziplinären Abgrenzung, Begriffsbestimmung und Systematisierung unter besonderer Berücksichtigung der deutschen Gegenwartssprache.* 2 vols. Göppingen, Germany: Alfred Kümmerle.

Pineaux, Jacques. 1956. *Proverbes et dictons français.* Paris: Presses Universitaires de France.

Plopper, Clifford Henry. 1926 (1969). *Chinese Religion Seen Through the Proverb.* Shanghai: China Press; repr. New York: Paragon Book Reprint Corp.

Prahlad, Sw. Anand. 1996. *African-American Proverbs in Context.* Jackson: University Press of Mississippi.

———. 2001. *Reggae Wisdom: Proverbs in Jamaican Music.* Jackson: University Press of Mississippi.

Profantová, Zuzana. 1997. *"Little Fish Are Sweet": Selected Writings on Proverbs.* Bratislava, Czech Republic: Ustav Etnológie SAV.

Rittersbacher, Christa. 2002. *Frau und Mann im Sprichwort: Einblicke in die sprichwörtliche Weltanschauung Großbritanniens und Amerikas.* Heidelberg: Das Wunderhorn.

Röhrich, Lutz, and Wolfgang Mieder. 1977. *Sprichwort.* Stuttgart: Metzler.

Ruef, Hans. 1995. *Sprichwort und Sprache: Am Beispiel des Sprichworts im Schweiz-erdeutschen.* Berlin: Walter de Gruyter.

Saayman, Willem, ed. 1997. *Embracing the Baobab Tree: The African Proverb in the 21st Century.* Pretoria: University of South Africa.

Sabban, Annette, ed. 1999. *Phraseologie und Übersetzen.* Bielefeld, Germany: Aisthesis.

Sabban, Annette, and Jan Wirrer, eds. 1991. *Sprichwörter und Redensarten im interkulturellen Vergleich.* Opladen, Germany: Westdeutscher Verlag.

Salvador, Vicent, and Adolf Piquer, eds. 2000. *El discurs prefabricat: Estudis de fraseologia teòrica i aplicada.* Castelló de la Plana, Spain: Publicacions de la Universitat Jaume.

Schulze-Busacker, Elisabeth. 1985. *Proverbes et expressions proverbiales dans la littérature narrative du moyen âge français: Recueil et analyse.* Paris: Honoré Champion.

Seiler, Friedrich. 1922 (1967). *Deutsche Sprichwörterkunde.* München: C.H. Beck; repr. München: C.H. Beck.

Sevilla Muñoz, Julia. 1988. *Hacia una aproximación conceptual de las paremias francesas y españolas.* Madrid: Editorial Complutense.

Suard, François, and Claude Buridant, eds. 1984. *Richesse du proverbe.* 2 vols. Lille, France: Université de Lille.

Szemerkényi, Agnes. 1994. *"Közmondás nem hazug szólas" A proverbiumok használatának lehetöségei.* Budapest: Akadémiai kiadó.

Tabercea, Cezar. 1982. *Poetica proverbului.* Bucuresti: Minerva.

Takeda, Katsuaki. 1992. *Kotowaza no Retorikku.* Tokyo: Kaimeisha.

Taylor, Archer. 1931 (1962, 1985). *The Proverb.* Cambridge, Mass.: Harvard University Press; repr. as *The Proverb and An Index to "The Proverb."* Hatboro, Pa.: Folklore Associates; repr. again with an introduction and bibliography by Wolfgang Mieder. Bern: Peter Lang.

———. 1972. *Comparative Studies in Folklore: Asia–Europe–America.* Taipei: The Orient Cultural Service.

———. 1975. *Selected Writings on Proverbs.* Ed. by Wolfgang Mieder. Helsinki: Suomalainen Tiedeakatemia.

Templeton, John Marks. 1997. *Worldwide Laws of Life.* Philadelphia: Templeton Foundation Press.

Thompson, John Mark. 1974. *The Form and Function of Proverbs in Ancient Israel.* The Hague: Mouton.

Tóthné Litovkina, Anna. 2000. *A Proverb a Day Keeps Boredom Away.* Pécs-Szekszárd, Hungary: IPF-Könyvek.

Trench, Richard Chenevix. 1853 (2003). *Proverbs and Their Lessons.* London: Parker; repr. ed. by Wolfgang Mieder. Burlington: University of Vermont.

Trovato, Salvatore C., ed. 1999. *Proverbi locuzioni modi di dire nel dominio linguistico italiano.* Rome: Editrice Calamo.

Vallini, Cristina, ed. 1989. *La pratica e la grammatica: Viaggio nella linguistica del proverbio.* Napoli: Istituto Universitario Orientale.

Wander, Karl Friedrich Wilhelm. 1836 (1983). *Das Sprichwort, betrachtet nach Form und Wesen, für Schule und Leben, als Einleitung zu einem volksthümlichen Sprichwörterschatz.* Hirschberg, Germany: Zimmer; repr. ed. by Wolfgang Mieder. Bern: Peter Lang.

Wanjohi, Gerald Joseph. 1997. *The Wisdom and the Philosophy of the Gikuyu Proverbs.* Nairobi: Paulines Publications Africa.

Westermann, Claus. 1995. *Roots of Wisdom: The Oldest Proverbs of Israel and Other Peoples.* Louisville, Ky.: Westminster John Knox Press.

Westermarck, Edward. 1930. *Wit and Wisdom in Morocco: A Study of Native Proverbs.* London: George Routledge.

Whiting, Bartlett Jere. 1934 (1973). *Chaucer's Use of Proverbs.* Cambridge, Mass.: Harvard University Press; repr. New York: AMS Press.

———. 1994. *"When Evensong and Morrowsong Accord": Three Essays on the Proverb.* Ed. by Joseph Harris and Wolfgang Mieder. Cambridge, Mass.: Department of English and American Literature and Language, Harvard University.

Winick, Stephen D. 1998. "The Proverb Process: Intertextuality and Proverbial Innovation in Popular Culture." Diss. University of Pennsylvania.

Winton, Alan P. 1990. *The Proverbs of Jesus: Issues of History and Rhetoric.* Sheffield: Sheffield Academic Press.

Yankah, Kwesi. 1989. *The Proverb in the Context of Akan Rhetoric: A Theory of Proverb Praxis.* Bern: Peter Lang.

MULTILINGUAL PROVERB COLLECTIONS

Abrishami, Ahmad. 1996. *A Comparative Dictionary of 920 Persian Proverbs & Dictums with English, French, German & Spanish Equivalents.* Tehran: Homa Tej.

Arthaber, Augusto. 1929 (1986). *Dizionario comparato di proverbi e modi proverbiali italiani, latini, francesi, spagnoli, tedeschi, inglesi e greci antichi con relativi indici sistematico-alfabetici.* Milano: Ulrico Hoepli; repr. Milano: Ulrico Hoepli.

Bartlett, John. 1855 (2002). *Familiar Quotations: A Collection of Passages, Phrases and Proverbs Traced to Their Sources in Ancient and Modern Literature.* Boston: Little, Brown & Company (17th ed.).

Berman, Louis A. 1997. *Proverb, Wit & Wisdom: A Treasury of Proverbs, Parodies, Quips, Quotes, Clichés, Catchwords, Epigrams and Aphorisms.* New York: Perigee Books.

Bilgrav, Jens Aage Stabell. 1985. *20,000 Proverbs and Their Equivalents in German, French, Swedish, Danish.* Copenhagen: Hans Heide.

Bohn, Henry G. 1857 (1968). *A Polyglot of Foreign Proverbs, Comprising French, Italian, German, Dutch, Spanish, Portuguese, and Danish, with English Translations and a General Index.* London: Henry G. Bohn; repr. Detroit, Mich.: Gale Research Company.

Champion, Selwyn Gurney. 1938 (1963). *Racial Proverbs: A Selection of the World's Proverbs Arranged Linguistically with Authoritative Introductions to the Proverbs of 27 Countries and Races.* London: George Routledge; repr. London: Routledge & Kegan.

————. 1945. *The Eleven Religions and Their Proverbial Lore.* New York: E.P. Dutton.

Christy, Robert. 1887 (1977). *Proverbs, Maxims and Phrases of All Ages.* New York: G.P. Putnam's Sons; repr. Norwood, Pa.: Norwood Editions.

Cohen, Israel. 1961. *Dictionary of Parallel Proverbs in English, German and Hebrew.* Tel Aviv: Machbarot Lesifrut Publishers.

Conklin, George W. 1906. *The World's Best Proverbs.* Philadelphia: Mackay.

Cordry, Harold V. 1997. *The Multicultural Dictionary of Proverbs.* Jefferson, N.C.: McFarland.

Cox, Henryk L. 2000. *Spreekwoordenboek: Nederlands, Fries, Afrikaans, Engels, Duits, Frans, Spaans, Latijn.* Utrecht, Netherlands: Van Dale Lexicografie.

Davidoff, Henry. 1946. *A World Treasury of Proverbs from Twenty-Five Languages.* New York: Random House.

Donato, Elena, and Gianni Palitta. 1998. *Il grande libro dei proverbi.* Roma: Newton & Compton.

Düringsfeld, Ida von, and Otto von Reinsberg-Düringsfeld. 1872–1875 (1973). *Sprichwörter der germanischen und romanischen Sprachen.* 2 vols. Leipzig, Germany: Hermann Fries; repr. Hildesheim, Germany: Georg Olms.

Fergusson, Rosalind. 1983. *The Facts on File Dictionary of Proverbs.* New York: Facts on File; also with the title *The Penguin Dictionary of Proverbs.* New York: Penguin Books.

Finbert, Elian-J. 1965. *Dictionnaire des proverbes du monde.* Paris: Robert Laffont.

Flonta, Teodor. 2001. *A Dictionary of English and Romance Languages Equivalent Proverbs.* Tasmania, Australia: DeProverbio.com.

Ghitescu, Micaela. 1997. *Novo dicionário de provérbios: Português, espanhol, francês, italiano, romeno.* Lisboa, Portugal: Fim de Século Edições.

Gleason, Norma. 1992. *Proverbs from Around the World.* New York: Citadel Press.

Gluski, Jerzy. 1971. *Proverbs: A Comparative Book of English, French, German, Italian, Spanish and Russian Proverbs with a Latin Appendix.* New York: Elsevier Publishing.

Griffin, Albert Kirby. 1991. *Religious Proverbs: Over 1600 Adages from 18 Faiths Worldwide.* Jefferson, N.C.: McFarland.

Grigas, Kazys. 2000. *Lietuviu patarlés ir priežodžiai.* 5 vols. [planned]. Vilnius, Lithuania: Lietuviu literaturos ir tautosakos institutas.

Herg, E. 1933. *Deutsche Sprichwörter im Spiegel fremder Sprachen unter Berücksichtigung des Englischen, Französischen, Italienischen, Lateinischen und Spanischen.* Berlin: Walter de Gruyter.

Iscla, Luis. 1995. *English Proverbs and Their Near Equivalents in Spanish, French, Italian and Latin.* New York: Peter Lang.

Karagiorgos, Panos. 2000. *Greek Maxims and Proverbs with Their Counterparts in 5 Languages: English, French, German, Italian, Spanish.* Corfu, Greece: Apostrofos.

Kelly, Walter K. 1859 (1972, 2003). *A Collection of the Proverbs of All Nations. Compared, Explained, and Illustrated.* London: W. Kent; repr. Darby, Pa.: Folcroft Library Editions; repr. ed. by Wolfgang Mieder. Burlington: The University of Vermont.

Krikmann, Arvo, and Ingrid Sarv. 1980–1988. *Eesti vanasõnad.* 5 vols. Tallinn, Estonia: Eesti Raamat.

Krzyzanowski, Julian, and Stanisław Swirko. 1969–1978. *Nowa ksiega przysłów pols-kich i wyrazen przysłowiowych polskich*. 4 vols. Warszawa: Panstwowy Instytut Wydawniczy.

Kuusi, Matti. 1970. *Ovambo Proverbs with African Parallels*. Helsinki: Suomalainen Tiedeakatemia.

Kuusi, Matti et al. 1985. *Proverbia septentrionalia: 900 Balto-Finnic Proverb Types with Russian, Baltic, German and Scandinavian Parallels*. Helsinki: Suomalainen Tiedeakatemia.

Lawson, James Gilchrist. 1926. *The World's Best Proverbs and Maxims*. New York: Grosset & Dunlap.

Ley, Gerd de. 1998. *International Dictionary of Proverbs*. New York: Hippocrene Books.

Mair, James Allan. 1873. *A Handbook of Proverbs: English, Scottisch, Irish, American, Shakespearean and Scriptural*. London: George Routledge.

Marvin, Dwight Edwards. 1916 (1980). *Curiosities in Proverbs: A Collection of Un-usual Adages, Maxims, Aphorisms, Phrases and Other Popular Dicta from Many Lands*. New York: G.P. Putnam's Sons; repr. Darby, Pa.: Folcroft Library Editions.

———. 1922. *The Antiquity of Proverbs: Fifty Familiar Proverbs and Folk Sayings with Annotations and Lists of Connected Forms, Found in All Parts of the World*. New York: G.P. Putnam's Sons.

Mawr, E.B. 1885. *Analogous Proverbs in Ten Languages*. London: Elliot Stock.

Middlemore, James. 1889. *Proverbs, Sayings and Comparisons in Various Languages*. London: Isbister.

Mieder, Wolfgang. 1986. *Encyclopedia of World Proverbs*. Englewood Cliffs, N.J.: Prentice-Hall.

———. 1990. *Not by Bread Alone: Proverbs of the Bible*. Shelburne, Vt.: New England Press.

Pachocinski, Ryszard. 1996. *Proverbs of Africa: 2600 Proverbs from 64 Peoples*. St. Paul, Minn.: Professors World Peace Academy.

Paczolay, Gyula. 1997. *European Proverbs in 55 Languages with Equivalents in Arabic, Persian, Sanskrit, Chinese and Japanese*. Veszprém, Hungary: Veszprémi Nyomda.

Reinsberg-Düringsfeld, Otto von. 1863 (1992). *Internationale Titulaturen*. 2 vols. Leipzig, Germany: Hermann Fries; repr. ed. by Wolfgang Mieder. Hildesheim, Germany: Georg Olms.

Roback, Abraham Aaron. 1944 (1979). *A Dictionary of International Slurs*. Cambridge, Mass.: Sci-Art Publishers; repr. Waukesha, Wis.: Maledicta Press.

Röhrich, Lutz. 1991–1992. *Das große Lexikon der sprichwörtlichen Redensarten*, 3 vols. Freiburg, Germany: Herder.

Singer, Samuel, and Ricarda Liver et al. 1995–2002. *Thesaurus proverbiorum medii aevi. Lexikon der Sprichwörter des romanisch-germanischen Mittelalters*. 13 vols. Berlin: Walter de Gruyter.

Stevenson, Burton. 1948. *The Macmillan (Home) Book of Proverbs, Maxims and Familiar Phrases*. New York: Macmillan.

Strauss, Emanuel. 1994. *Dictionary of European Proverbs.* 3 vols. London: George Routledge.

———. 1998. *Concise Dictionary of European Proverbs.* London: George Routledge.

Walther, Hans, and Paul Gerhard Schmidt. 1963–1986. *Proverbia sententiaeque latinitatis medii aevi. Lateinische Sprichwörter und Sentenzen des Mittelalters.* 9 vols. Göttingen, Germany: Vandenhoeck & Ruprecht.

Wander, Karl Friedrich Wilhelm. 1867–1880 (1964). *Deutsches Sprichwörter-Lexikon.* 5 vols. Leipzig, Germany: F.A. Brockhaus; repr. Wiesbaden, Germany: Wissenschaftliche Buchgesellschaft.

Ward, Caroline. 1842. *National Proverbs in the Principle Languages of Europe.* London: Parker.

Yoo, Young H. 1972. *Wisdom of the Far East. A Dictionary of Proverbs, Maxims, and Famous Classical Phrases of the Chinese, Japanese, and Korean.* Washington, D.C.: Far Eastern Research & Publications Center.

Yurtbasi, Metin. 1996. *Turkish Proverbs and Their Equivalents in Fifteen Languages.* Istanbul: Serkon Etiket.

BILINGUAL PROVERB COLLECTIONS

Abrishami, Ahmad. 1997. *A Dictionary of Persian–English Proverbs.* Tehran: Zivar.

Akiyama, Aisaburo. 1940. *Japanese Proverbs and Proverbial Sayings.* Yokohama: Yoshikawa Book Store.

Aquilina, Joseph. 1972. *A Comparative Dictionary of Maltese Proverbs.* Malta: Royal University of Malta.

Ayalti, Hanan J. 1949. *Yiddish Proverbs.* New York: Schocken Books.

Ballesteros, Octavio A. 1979. *Mexican Proverbs: The Philosophy, Wisdom and Humor of a People.* Burner, Tex.: Eakin Press.

Beckwith, Martha Warren. 1925 (1970). *Jamaica Proverbs.* Poughkeepsie, N.Y.: Vassar College; repr. New York: Negro University Press.

Brezin-Rossignol, Monique. 1997. *Dictionnaire des proverbes français/anglais—Dictionary of Proverbs English/French.* Paris: La Maison du Dictionnaire; New York: Hippocrene Books.

Buchanan, Daniel Crump. 1965. *Japanese Proverbs and Sayings.* Norman: University of Oklahoma Press.

Carr, Mark William. 1868 (1988). *A Collection of Telugu Proverbs together with Some Sanskrit Proverbs.* Madras, India: C.K.S.; repr. New Delhi: Asian Educational Services.

Chen, Berta Alicia. 1998. *Dictionary of Proverbs and Sayings English-Spanish / Spanish-English—Diccionario de proverbios y refranes inglés-español / español-inglés.* Panama: CMC Publishing.

Christaller, J.G. 1990. *Three Thousand Six Hundred Ghanian Proverbs (From the Asante and Fante Language).* Lewiston, N.Y.: Edwin Mellen Press.

Cotter, George. 1997. *Ethiopian Wisdom: Proverbs and Sayings of the Oromo People.* Pretoria, South Africa: Unisa Press.

Flonta, Teodor. 2001a. *A Dictionary of English and French Equivalent Proverbs.* Tasmania, Australia: DeProverbio.com.

———. 2001b. *A Dictionary of English and Italian Equivalent Proverbs.* Tasmania, Australia: DeProverbio.com.

———. 2001c. *A Dictionary of English and Portuguese Equivalent Proverbs.* Tasmania, Australia: DeProverbio.com.

———. 2001d. *A Dictionary of English and Romanian Equivalent Proverbs.* Tasmania, Australia: DeProverbio.com.

———. 2001e. *A Dictionary of English and Spanish Equivalent Proverbs.* Tasmania, Australia: DeProverbio.com.

Galef, David. 1987. *"Even Monkeys Fall from Trees" and Other Japanese Proverbs.* Rutland, Vt.: Charles E. Tuttle.

Hamütyinei, Mordikai A., and B. Plangger. 1974. *Tsumo-shumo: Shona Proverbial Lore and Wisdom.* Gwelo, Zimbabwe: Mambo Press.

Hankí, Joseph. 1998. *Arabic Proverbs with Side by Side English Translations.* New York: Hippocrene Books.

Jensen, Herman. 1897 (1989). *A Classified Collection of Tamil Proverbs.* Madras, India: Methodist Episcopal Publishing House; repr. New Delhi: Asian Educational Services.

Karagiorgos, Panos. 1999. *Greek and English Proverbs.* Corfu, Greece: Ionian University.

Knappert, Jan. 1997. *Swahili Proverbs.* Burlington: The University of Vermont.

Kogos, Fred. 1970. *1001 Yiddish Proverbs.* Secaucus, N.J.: Castle Books.

Kremer, Edmund P. 1955. *German Proverbs and Proverbial Phrases with Their English Counterparts.* Palo Alto, Calif.: Stanford University Press.

Kumove, Shirley. 1984 (1986). *Words Like Arrows: A Treasury of Yiddish Folk Sayings.* Toronto: University of Toronto Press; repr. New York: Warner Books.

———. 1999. *More Words, More Arrows: A Further Collection of Yiddish Folk Sayings.* Detroit, Mich.: Wayne State University Press.

Lazarus, John. 1894 (1991). *A Dictionary of Tamil Proverbs.* Madras, India: Albinion Press; repr. New Delhi: Asian Educational Services.

Ley, Gerd de. 1998. *Dictionary of 1000 Dutch Proverbs.* New York: Hippocrene Books.

Lin, Marjorie, and Leonard Schalk. 1998. *Dictionary of 1000 Chinese Proverbs.* New York: Hippocrene Books.

Lipinski, Miroslaw. 1997. *Dictionary of 1000 Polish Proverbs.* New York: Hippocrene Books.

Lubensky, Sophia. 1995. *Russian-English Dictionary of Idioms.* New York: Random House.

Manwaring, A. 1899 (1991). *Marathi Proverbs.* Oxford: Clarendon Press; repr. New Delhi: Asian Educational Services.

Margulis, Alexander, and Asya Kholodnaya. 2000. *Russian-English Dictionary of Proverbs and Sayings.* Jefferson, N.C.: McFarland.

Mertvago, Peter. 1995. *The Comparative Russian-English Dictionary of Russian Proverbs and Sayings with 5543 Entries and 1900 Most Important Proverbs Highlighted.* New York: Hippocrene Books.

———. 1996a. *Dictionary of 1000 French Proverbs with English Equivalents.* New York: Hippocrene Books.

———. 1996b. *Dictionary of 1000 Spanish Proverbs with English Equivalents.* New York: Hippocrene Books.

———. 1997a. *Dictionary of 1000 German Proverbs with English Equivalents.* New York: Hippocrene Books.

———. 1997b. *Dictionary of 1000 Italian Proverbs with English Equivalents.* New York: Hippocrene Books.

———. 1998. *Dictionary of 1000 Russian Proverbs with English Equivalents.* New York: Hippocrene Books.

Nyembezi, Cyril. 1963. *Zulu Proverbs.* Johannesburg: Witwatersrand University Press.

Owomoyela, Oyekan. 1988. *A Kì í: Yoruba Proscriptive and Prescriptive Proverbs.* Lanham, Md.: University Press of America.

Paczolay, Gyula. 1991. *750 magyar közmondás és szólás / 750 Hungarian Proverbs.* Veszprém, Hungary: Veszprémi Nyomda.

Percival, Rev. P. 1874 (1996). *Tamil Proverbs with Their English Translation.* Madras, India: Dinavartamani Press; repr. New Delhi: Asian Educational Services.

Rohsenow, John S. 2002. *ABC Dictionary of Chinese Proverbs.* Honolulu: University of Hawaii Press.

Sakayan, Dora. 1994. *Armenian Proverbs.* Delmar, N.Y.: Caravan Books.

Schemann, Hans, and Paul Knight. 1995. *Idiomatik Deutsch-Englisch / German-English Dictionary of Idioms.* Stuttgart: Ernst Klett.

Scheven, Albert. 1981. *Swahili Proverbs.* Washington, D.C.: University Press of America.

Smith, Arthur H. 1888 (1965). *Proverbs and Common Sayings from the Chinese.* Shanghai: American Presbyterian Mission Press; repr. New York: Paragon Books.

Sun, C.C. 1981. *As the Saying Goes: An Annotated Anthology of Chinese and Equivalent English Sayings and Expressions.* St. Lucia, Queensland: University of Queensland Press.

Taylor, Ronald, and Walter Gottschalk. 1960. *A German-English Dictionary of Idioms.* München: Max Hueber.

Watson, Llewellyn. 1991. *Jamaican Sayings: With Notes on Folklore, Aesthetics, and Social Control.* Tallahassee: Florida A & M University Press.

Whitting, C.E.J. 1940. *Hausa and Fulani Proverbs.* Lagos, Nigeria: Government Printer.

Winstedt, Richard. 1950. *Malay Proverbs.* London: John Murray.

Yurtbasi, Metin. 1993. *A Dictionary of Turkish Proverbs.* Ankara, Turkey: Turkish Daily News.

ANGLO-AMERICAN PROVERB COLLECTIONS

Aik, Kam Chuan. 1988. *Dictionary of Proverbs*. Singapore: Federal Publications.

Ammer, Christine. 1992. *Have a Nice Day—No Problem! A Dictionary of Clichés*. New York: Dutton.

————. 1997. *The American Heritage Dictionary of Idioms*. Boston: Houghton Mifflin.

Apperson, G.L. 1929 (1969, 1993). *English Proverbs and Proverbial Phrases: A Historical Dictionary*. London: J.M. Dent; repr. Detroit, Mich.: Gale Research Company; repr. again Ware, Hertfordshire: Wordsworth Editions.

Barbour, Frances M. 1974. *A Concordance to the Sayings in [Benjamin] Franklin's "Poor Richard."* Detroit, Mich.: Gale Research Company

Bartlett, John 1849 (1989). *Dictionary of Americanisms*. New York: Bartlett & Welford; repr. New York: Crescent Books.

Baz, Petros D. 1963. *A Dictionary of Proverbs*. New York: Philosophical Society.

Benham, William Gurney. 1926. *Putnam's Complete Book of Quotations, Proverbs and Household Words*. New York: G.P. Putnam's Sons.

Bertram, Anne, and Richard A. Spears. 1993. *Dictionary of Proverbs and Clichés*. Lincolnwood, Ill.: National Textbook Company.

Boatner, Maxine, John Gates, and Adam Makkai. 1975. *A Dictionary of American Idioms*. Woodbury, New York: Barron's Educational Series.

Bohn, Henry. 1855. *A Hand-Book of Proverbs Comprising an Entire Republication of Ray's Collection of English Proverbs, with His Additions from Foreign Languages*. London: H.G. Bohn.

Brewer, Ebenezer. 1870 (1970). *Dictionary of Phrase and Fable*. New York: Harper & Row; repr. ed. by Ivor H. Evans. New York: Harper & Row.

Carmichaell, James. 1957. *The James Carmichaell Collection of Proverbs in Scots*. Ed. by M.L. Anderson. Edinburgh: Edinburgh University Press.

Casselman, Bill. 1999–2002. *Canadian Sayings. Folk Sayings Used by Canadians*. 2 vols. Toronto: McArthur.

Cheales, Alan Benjamin. 1874 (1976). *Proverbial Folk-Lore*. London: Simpkin, Marshall & Company; repr. Darby, Pa.: Folcroft Library Editions.

Cheviot, Andrew. 1896 (1969). *Proverbs, Proverbial Expressions, and Popular Rhymes of Scotland*. London: Alexander Gardner; repr. Detroit, Mich.: Gale Research Company.

Chiu, Kwong Ki. 1881 (1971). *A Dictionary of English Phrases with Illustrative Sentences*. New York: A.S. Barnes; repr. Detroit, Mich.: Gale Research Company.

Costello, Robert B., and Jess Stein. 1981. *American Expressions: A Thesaurus of Effective and Colorful Speech*. New York: Sachem Publishing.

Cowie, A.P., R.M. Mackin, and I.R. McCaig. 1975–1983. *Oxford Dictionary of Current Idiomatic English*. 2 vols. Oxford: Oxford University Press.

Dent, Robert. 1981. *Shakespeare's Proverbial Language: An Index*. Berkeley: University of California Press.

————. 1984. *Proverbial Language in English Drama Exclusive of Shakespeare, 1495–1616: An Index*. Berkeley: University of California Press.

Donald, Graeme. 1994. *The Dictionary of Modern Phrase.* New York: Simon & Schuster.

Flavell, Linda, and Roger Flavell. 1992. *Dictionary of Idioms and Their Origins.* London: Kyle Cathie.

————. 1993. *Dictionary of Proverbs and Their Origins.* London: Kyle Cathie.

Funk, Charles Earle. 1948 (1972, 1985). *"A Hog on Ice" and Other Curious Expressions.* New York: Harper & Row; repr. New York: Warner Paperbacks; repr. again New York: Harper Colophon Books.

————. 1950 (1985). *Thereby Hangs a Tale: Stories of Curious Word Origins.* New York: Harper & Row; repr. New York: Perennial Library.

————. 1955 (1972, 1986). *"Heavens to Betsy!" and Other Curious Sayings.* New York: Harper & Row; repr. New York: Warner Paperbacks; repr. again New York: Harper & Row.

————. 1958 (1986). *Horsefeathers and Other Curious Words.* New York: Harper & Row; repr. New York: Perennial Library.

————. 1993. *2107 Curious Word Origins, Sayings & Expressions from "White Elephant" to "Song Dance."* New York: Galahad Books (includes the four volumes by Funk).

Gaffney, Sean, and Seamus Cashman. 1974. *Proverbs & Sayings of Ireland.* Portmarnock, County Dublin: Wolfhound Press.

Gulland, Daphne M., and David G. Hinds-Howell. 1986. *Dictionary of English Idioms.* New York: Penguin Books.

Hazlitt, W. Carew. 1869 (1969). *English Proverbs and Proverbial Phrases.* London: Reever and Turner; repr. Detroit, Mich.: Gale Research Company.

Henderson, Andrew. 1832 (1881, 1969). *Scottish Proverbs.* Edinburgh: Oliver & Boyd; repr. Glasgow: Thomas D. Morison; repr. again Detroit, Mich.: Gale Research Company.

Henderson, B.L.K. 1937. *A Dictionary of English Idioms.* 2 vols. London: James Blackwood.

Hendrickson, Robert. 1987. *Encyclopedia of Word and Phrase Origins.* New York: Facts on File.

Hislop, Alexander. 1868 (1968). *The Proverbs of Scotland with Explanatory and Illustrative Notes and a Glossary.* Edinburgh: Alexander Hislop; repr. Detroit, Mich.: Gale Research Company.

Hyamson, Albert M. 1922 (1970). *A Dictionary of English Phrases.* New York: E.P. Dutton; repr. Detroit, Mich.: Gale Research Company.

Ichikawa, Sanki et al. 1964. *Dictionary of Current English Idioms.* Tokyo: Kenkyusha.

Kelly, James. 1721 (1976). *A Complete Collection of Scotish* [sic] *Proverbs, Explained and Made Intelligible to the English Reader.* London: William and John Innys; repr. Darby, Pa.: Folcroft Library Editions.

Kin, David. 1955. *Dictionary of American Proverbs.* New York: Philosophical Library.

Kirkpatrick, E.M., and C.M. Schwarz. 1982 (1993). *Dictionary of Idioms.* Edinburgh: Chambers; repr. Ware, Hertfordshire: Wordsworth Editions.

Korach, Myron, and John B. Mordock. 2001. *Common Phrases and Where They Come From*. Guilford, Conn.: Lyons Press.

Lean, Vincent Stuckey. 1902–1904 (1969, 2000). *Lean's Collectanea: Collections of Proverbs (English and Foreign), Folklore, and Superstitions, also Compilations Towards Dictionaries of Proverbial Phrases and Words, Old and Disused*. Ed. by T.W. Williams. 4 vols. Bristol: J.W. Arrowsmith; repr. Detroit, Mich.: Gale Research Company; repr. again Bristol: Thoemmes Press.

Lighter, J.E. 1994–1997. *Historical Dictionary of American Slang*. 2 vols. New York: Random House.

Makkai, Adam. 1984. *Handbook of Commonly Used American Idioms*. Woodbury, New York: Barron's Educational Series.

Mathews, Mitford M. 1951. *A Dictionary of Americanisms on Historical Principles*. Chicago: University of Chicago Press.

Mieder, Wolfgang. 1988. *English Proverbs*. Stuttgart: Philipp Reclam.

———. 1992. *English Expressions*. Stuttgart: Philipp Reclam.

Mieder, Wolfgang, Stewart A. Kingsbury, and Kelsie B. Harder. 1992. *A Dictionary of American Proverbs*. New York: Oxford University Press.

Nares, Robert. 1905 (1966). *A Glossary of Words, Phrases, Names and Allusions in the Works of English Authors, Particularly of Shakespeare and His Contemporaries*. London: George Routledge; repr. Detroit, Mich.: Gale Research Company.

Panati, Charles. 1999. *Words to Live By: The Origins of Conventional Wisdom and Commonsense Advice*. New York: Penguin Books.

Partridge, Eric. 1937 (1970). *A Dictionary of Slang and Unconventional English*. New York: Macmillan (7th edition).

———. 1940 (1978). *A Dictionary of Clichés*. London: George Routledge (5th edition).

———. 1977. *A Dictionary of Catch Phrases*. New York: Stein and Day.

Pickering, David. 1997. *Dictionary of Proverbs*. London: Cassell.

Rees, Nigel. 1984. *Sayings of the Century: The Stories Behind the Twentieth Century's Quotable Sayings*. London: George Allen & Unwin.

———. 1987. *Why Do We Say...? Words and Sayings and Where They Come From*. Poole, England: Blandford.

———. 1990. *Dictionary of Popular Phrases*. London: Bloomsbury.

———. 1995. *Phrases & Sayings*. London: Bloomsbury.

———. 1996. *Dictionary of Clichés*. London: Cassell.

Ridout, Ronald, and Clifford Whiting. 1969. *English Proverbs Explained*. London: Pan Books.

Rogers, James. 1985. *The Dictionary of Clichés*. New York: Facts on File.

Simpson, John A. 1982 (1998). *The Concise Oxford Dictionary of Proverbs*. Oxford: Oxford University Press (3rd edition with Jennifer Speake).

Skeat, Walter. 1910 (1974). *Early English Proverbs: Chiefly of the Thirteenth and Fourteenth Centuries*. Oxford: Clarendon Press; repr. Darby, Pa.: Folcroft Library Editions.

Smith, Charles G. 1963. *Shakespeare's Proverb Lore*. Cambridge, Mass.: Harvard University Press.

————. 1970. *Spenser's Proverb Lore.* Cambridge, Mass.: Harvard University Press.

Smith, William George. 1935 (1970). *The Oxford Dictionary of English Proverbs.* Oxford: Oxford University Press (3rd edition by F.P. Wilson).

Spears, Richard A. 1995. *Dictionary of American English Phrases.* Lincolnwood, Ill.: National Textbook Company.

————. 1996. *Essential American Idioms.* Lincolnwood, Ill.: National Textbook Company.

Spears, Richard A., and Linda Schinke-Llano. 1987. *American Idioms Dictionary.* Lincolnwood, Ill.: National Textbook Company.

Taylor, Archer, and Bartlett Jere Whiting. 1958. *A Dictionary of American Proverbs and Proverbial Phrases, 1820–1880.* Cambridge, Mass.: Harvard University Press.

Tilley, Morris Palmer. 1950. *A Dictionary of the Proverbs in England in the Sixteenth and Seventeenth Centuries.* Ann Arbor, Mich.: University of Michigan Press.

Titelman, Gregory. 1996 *Dictionary of Popular Proverbs & Sayings.* New York: Random House.

Trusler, John. 1790 (1970). *Proverbs Exemplified, and Illustrated by Pictures from Real Life.* London: Literary Press; repr. New York: Johnson Reprint.

Urdang, Laurence, Nancy LaRoche, and Walter W. Hunsinger. 1985. *Picturesque Expressions: A Thematic Dictionary.* Detroit, Mich.: Gale Research Company.

Walter, Elizabeth et al. 1998. *Cambridge International Dictionary of [British, American, and Australian English] Idioms.* Cambridge: Cambridge University Press.

Whiting, Bartlett Jere. 1938 (1969). *Proverbs in the Earlier English Drama with Illustrations from Contemporary French Plays.* Cambridge, Mass.: Harvard University Press; repr. New York: Octagon Books.

Whiting, Bartlett Jere. 1968. *Proverbs, Sentences, and Proverbial Phrases from English Writings Mainly Before 1500.* Cambridge, Mass.: Harvard University Press.

————. 1977. *Early American Proverbs and Proverbial Phrases.* Cambridge, Mass.: Harvard University Press.

————. 1989. *Modern Proverbs and Proverbial Sayings.* Cambridge, Mass.: Harvard University Press.

Wilkinson, P.R. 1993. *Thesaurus of Traditional English Metaphors.* London: George Routledge.

Williams, Fionnuala Carson. 2000. *Irish Proverbs: Traditional Wit & Wisdom.* New York: Sterling.

Woods, Henry F. 1945. *American Sayings, Famous Phrases, Slogans, and Aphorisms.* New York: Duell, Sloan and Pearce.

REGIONAL AND THEMATIC PROVERB COLLECTIONS

Alstad, Ken. 1986. *Savvy Sayin's: Lean & Meaty One-Liners.* Tucson, Ariz.: Ken Alstad.

Arora, Shirley L. 1977. *Proverbial Comparisons and Related Expressions in Spanish, Recorded in Los Angeles, California.* Berkeley: University of California Press.

Barbour, Frances M. 1963. *Proverbs and Proverbial Phrases of Illinois*. Carbondale: Southern Illinois University Press.

Bertram, Anne, and Richard A. Spears. 1996. *Dictionary of Folksy, Regional, and Rural Sayings*. Lincolnwood, Ill.: National Textbook Company.

Blue, John. 1982. *Hoosier Tales and Proverbs*. Rensselaer, Ind.: J.S. Blue.

Brunvand, Jan Harold. 1961. *A Dictionary of English Proverbs and Proverbial Phrases from Books Published by Indiana Authors before 1890*. Bloomington: Indiana University Press.

Cassidy, Frederic G., and Joan Houston Hall. 1985–. *Dictionary of American Regional English*. 4 vols. to date. Cambridge, Mass.: Harvard University Press.

Cobos, Rubén. 1973. *Southwestern Spanish Proverbs*. Cerrillos, N. Mex.: San Marcos Press.

Corum, Ann Kondo. 1985. *Folk Wisdom from Hawaii or Don't Take Bananas on a Boat*. Honolulu, Hawaii: Bess Press.

Dunwoody, H.H.C. 1883. *Weather Proverbs*. Washington, D.C.: Government Printing Office.

Fogel, Edwin Miller. 1929 (1995, 1995). *Proverbs of the Pennsylvania Germans*. Lancaster, Pa.: Pennsylvania-German Society; repr. ed. by Wolfgang Mieder. Bern: Peter Lang; repr. ed. by C. Richard Beam. Millersville, Pa.: Center for Pennsylvania German Studies, Millersville University.

Freier, George D. 1992. *Weather Proverbs*. Tucson, Ariz.: Fisher Books.

Garriott, Edward B. 1903 (1971). *Weather Folk-Lore and Local Weather Signs*. Washington, D.C.: Government Printing Office; repr. Detroit, Mich.: Grand River Books.

Glazer, Mark. 1987. *A Dictionary of Mexican American Proverbs*. Westport, Conn.: Greenwood Press.

Hall, Joseph S. 1972. *Sayings from Old Smokey: Some Traditional Phrases, Expressions, and Sentences Heard in the Great Smokey Mountains and Nearby Areas*. Asheville, N.C.: Cataloochee Press.

Hendrickson, Robert. 1992. *Whistlin' Dixie: A Dictionary of Southern Expressions*. New York: Facts on File.

———. 1994. *Happy Trails: A Dictionary of Western Expressions*. New York: Facts on File.

———. 1996. *Yankee Talk: A Dictionary of New England Expressions*. New York: Facts on File.

———. 1997. *Mountain Range: A Dictionary of Expressions from Appalachia to the Ozarks*. New York: Facts on File.

———. 1998. *New Yawk Tawk: A Dictionary of New York City Expressions*. New York: Facts on File.

———. 2000. *The Facts on File Dictionary of American Regionalisms*. New York: Facts on File.

Hines, Donald M. 1977. *Frontier Folksay: Proverbial Lore of the Inland Pacific Northwest Frontier*. Norwood, Pa.: Norwood Editions.

Humphreys, W.J. 1934. *Weather Proverbs and Paradoxes.* Baltimore: Williams & Wilkins.

Inwards, Richard. 1898 (1994). *Weather Lore: A Collection of Proverbs, Sayings and Rules Concerning the Weather.* London: Elliot Stock; repr. London: Senate.

Judd, Henry P. 1930 (1978). *Hawaiian Proverbs and Riddles.* Honolulu, Hawaii: Bernice P. Bishop Museum; repr. Millwood, N.Y.: Kraus Reprint.

Kingsbury, Stewart A., Mildred E. Kingsbury, and Wolfgang Mieder. 1996. *Weather Wisdom: Proverbs, Superstitions, and Signs.* New York: Peter Lang.

Lee, Albert. 1976. *Weather Wisdom.* Garden City, N.Y.: Doubleday.

Liu, Paul, and Robert Vasselli. 1996. *Proverbial Twists.* Highland Park, N.J.: Johanne.

McLellan, Vern. 1996. *The Complete Book of Practical Proverbs & Wacky Wit.* Wheaton, Ill.: Tyndale House.

Mieder, Wolfgang. 1986. *"Talk Less and Say More": Vermont Proverbs.* Shelburne, Vt.: New England Press.

———. 1988. *"As Sweet as Apple Cider": Vermont Expressions.* Shelburne, Vt.: New England Press.

———. 1989. *Yankee Wisdom: New England Proverbs.* Shelburne, Vt.: New England Press.

———. 1997. *"As Strong as a Moose": New England Expressions.* Shelburne, Vt.: New England Press.

———. 1998. *Verdrehte Weisheiten: Antisprichwörter aus Literatur und Medien.* Wiesbaden, Germany: Quelle & Meyer.

———. 1999. *Phrasen verdreschen: Antiredensarten aus Literatur und Medien.* Wiesbaden, Germany: Quelle & Meyer.

———. 2003. *Wisecracks! Fractured Proverbs.* Shelburne, Vt.: New England Press.

Mieder, Wolfgang, and Anna Tóthné Litovkina. 1999. *Twisted Wisdom: Modern Anti-Proverbs.* Burlington: The University of Vermont.

Mieder, Wolfgang, and Stewart A. Kingsbury. 1994. *A Dictionary of Wellerisms.* New York: Oxford University Press.

Pukui, Mary Kawena. 1983. *Hawaiian Proverbs & Poetical Sayings.* Honolulu, Hawaii: Bishop Museum Press.

Seidl, Helmut A. 1982. *Medizinische Sprichwörter im Englischen und Deutschen. Eine diachrone Untersuchung zur vergleichenden Parömiologie.* Bern: Peter Lang.

Slung, Michele. 1985. *Momilies: As My Mother Used to Say...* New York: Ballantine Books.

———. 1986. *More Momilies: As My Mother Used to Say.* New York: Ballantine Books.

Stark, Judith. 1982. *Priceless Proverbs...from the Tongue of the Young.* Los Angeles, Calif.: Price, Stern, Sloan.

Swainson, C. 1873. (1974). *A Handbook of Weather Folk-Lore, Being a Collection of Proverbial Sayings Relating to the Weather, with Explanatory and Illustrative Notes.* London: William Blackwood; repr. Detroit, Mich.: Gale Research Company.

Taylor, Archer. 1954. *Proverbial Comparisons and Similes from California.* Berkeley: University of California Press.

Thompson, Harold W. 1940 (1979). *Body, Boots & Britches: Folktales, Ballads and Speech from Country New York*. Philadelphia: J.B. Lippincott; repr. Syracuse, N.Y.: Syracuse University Press (proverbs on pp. 481–504).

Whiting, Bartlett Jere, ed. 1952. *Games and Rhymes, Beliefs and Customs, Riddles, Proverbs, Speech, Tales and Legends*. Vol. 1 of *The Frank C. Brown Collection of North Carolina Folklore*. Ed. by Newman Ivey White. 5 vols. Durham, N.C.: Duke University Press (proverbs on pp. 329–501).

Williams, Fionnuala Carson. 2003. *Wellerisms in Ireland: Towards a Corpus from Oral and Literary Sources*. Burlington: University of Vermont.

Web Resources

While it is possible to use the Internet to locate small collections of proverbs or references to individual proverbs by way of various databases, there is but one major Web site dedicated to proverbs as such:

www.deproverbio.com

The following list includes a few additional Web sites that are of some use:

www.manythings.org/proverbs
www.creativeproverbs.com
www.afriprov.org

Glossary

As much as possible this book has been written free of theoretical jargon. Nevertheless, this short glossary is provided to assist with major terms and concepts that are not part of everyday parlance.

alliteration a sequence of words beginning with the same sound.

anthropomorphize attribute human characteristics to animals, plants, or material objects

anti-proverb an intentionally changed (twisted, parodied) proverb with a new meaning.

apocryphal of doubtful authorship or authenticity.

archetype the original pattern or form (prototype) on which something is modeled.

blason populaire French term for stereotype or slur.

bona fide Latin for true or authentic (without fraud).

cognition the act or process of knowing; perception.

collocation the usual co-occurrence of a certain sequence of words.

demography the science of social statistics; statistical research using questionnaires.

demoscopy the science of studying the views and opinions of people.

diachronic the historical analysis of changes and developments.

ellipsis the omission of parts of a sentence for poetic emphasis or word economy.

emblem an allegorical illustration, often with a motto supplemental to the visual image.

empiricism the science of studying matters by way of experiment or experience.

etiology the study of the cause or origin of something.

fixity the state of being stable or permanent.

hetero-situativity appearance or use in different contexts (also hetero-situationality).

hyperbole an emphatic exaggeration.

iconography the study of the subject matter and its meaning in the visual arts.

indirection the act of communicating figuratively or metaphorically.

intertextuality the integration of a short text (quotation) in a larger text.

introductory formula a statement that identifies and draws attention to a particular utterance.

leitmotif something that is repeated throughout a piece of music or writing.

lingua franca any language that is widely used as a means of communication among speakers of other languages, for example, Latin in the Middle Ages or English today.

loan translation the direct translation of a word or expression and its acceptance from one language into another.

mentality the shared worldview of a group of people.

metaphor a figurative expression in which something is described in terms usually associated with something else.

misericord a wooden carving in the choir stalls in medieval churches depicting religious or secular themes.

modus operandi Latin for mode (way) of operating or working.

paradigmatic a set of forms (patterns), all of which contain a particular element; also the contrasting relationship between words (signs) of sentences.

paremia   the Greek word for the Latin *proverbium* (proverb).

paremiography   the collecting of proverbs and their arrangement into collections or dictionaries.

paremiology the study of proverbs.

phraseography the collecting of fixed phrases and their arrangement into collections or dictionaries.

phraseological unit any fixed and repeated phrase.

phraseologism any fixed and repeated phrase.

phraseology the study of fixed phrases (proverbs, proverbial expressions, proverbial comparisons, twin formulas, idioms, quotations, clichés, etc.).

poly-functionality having many (multiple) functions.

polyglot multilingual, knowing or containing many languages.

poly-semanticity having many (multiple) meanings.

pragmatics the branch of linguistics dealing with the factors influencing a person's choice of language (words, expressions, dialect, etc.).

proverbiality having the necessary characteristics of a proverb, that is, traditionality, currency, and numerous structural and poetic markers.

semantics the study of meaning of words, expressions, and so on.

semiotics the study of signs and symbols as found in human communication.

sign a feature of language or behavior that conveys meaning as used conventionally in a linguistic and social system.

simple forms old (oral), (near) universal, short, structured, and repeated text-types, for example, myths, legends, folktales, jokes, proverbs, riddles, chants, charms, blessings, curses, oaths, insults, toasts, tongue-twisters, greetings, ballads, counting-out rhymes, and so on.

speech play any intentional humorous, ironical, or satirical manipulation of language.

synchronic the study of language at a particular point in time.

syntagmatic the linear relationship of various words (signs) in a sentence.

terminus a quo Latin for the end from which, beginning, starting point.

tour de force French for a particularly adroit stylistic technique.

traditionality having achieved the status of being known and used over a period of time, usually in variants and different contexts.

ubiquity the state or capacity of being everywhere, omnipresence.

wisdom literature the early, even preliterate, didactic literature that is part of the moral instruction of the world's religions.

worldview the view and understanding of one's surroundings, the shared mentality of a group of people.

Index

Names of scholars cited in parentheses within the text, in the bibliographies of the four chapters, and the major bibliography at the end of the book are not listed in the name index. The subject index contains major areas of research, concepts, genres, terms, themes, and topics. The proverbs in the proverb index are listed by their key words.

Names

Subjects

Proverbs

About the Author

WOLFGANG MIEDER is Professor of German and Folklore at the University of Vermont. His many books include *A Dictionary of American Proverbs* (1992), *Proverbs Are Never out of Season* (1993), *The Proverbial Winston S. Churchill* (Greenwood, 1995), *The Politics of Proverbs* (1997), and numerous others. He is also the editor of *Proverbium: Yearbook of International Proverb Scholarship.*